Redefining the Color Line

New Perspectives on the History of the South

Florida A&M University, Tallahassee
Florida Atlantic University, Boca Raton
Florida Gulf Coast University, Ft. Myers
Florida International University, Miami
Florida State University, Tallahassee
University of Central Florida, Orlando
University of Florida, Gainesville
University of North Florida, Jacksonville
University of South Florida, Tampa
University of West Florida, Pensacola

New Perspectives on the History of the South
Edited by John David Smith

"In the Country of the Enemy": The Civil War Reports of a Massachusetts Corporal, edited by
    William C. Harris (1999)
The Wild East: A Biography of the Great Smoky Mountains, by Margaret L. Brown (2000);
    first paperback edition, 2001
*Crime, Sexual Violence, and Clemency: Florida's Pardon Board and Penal System in the Progres-
    sive Era*, by Vivien M. L. Miller (2000)
*The New South's New Frontier: A Social History of Economic Development in Southwestern
    North Carolina*, by Stephen Wallace Taylor (2001)
Redefining the Color Line: Black Activism in Little Rock, Arkansas, 1940–1970, John A. Kirk
    (2002)

Redefining the Color Line

Black Activism in Little Rock, Arkansas, 1940–1970

John A. Kirk

Foreword,
John David Smith,
Series Editor

University Press of Florida
Gainesville · Tallahassee · Tampa · Boca Raton
Pensacola · Orlando · Miami · Jacksonville · Ft. Myers

Copyright 2002 by John A. Kirk
Printed in the United States of America on recycled acid-free paper
All rights reserved

07   06   05   04   03   02   6   5   4   3   2   1

Library of Congress Cataloging-in-Publication Data
Kirk, John A., 1970–
Redefining the color line : Black activism in Little Rock, Arkansas,
1940–1970 / John A. Kirk.
p. cm. — (New perspectives on the history of the South)
ISBN 0-8130-2496-X (cloth: alk. paper)
1. African Americans—Civil rights—Arkansas—Little Rock—History
—20th century. 2. African Americans—Segregation—Arkansas—Little
Rock—History—20th century. 3. African Americans—Arkansas—Little
Rock—Politics and government—20th century. 4. African American civil
rights workers activists—Arkansas—Little Rock—History—20th century.
5. African American political activists—Arkansas—Little Rock—History
—20th century. 6. School integration—Arkansas—Little Rock—History
—20th century. 7. Civil rights movements—Arkansas—Little Rock—
History—20th century. 8. Little Rock (Ark.)—Race relations. 9. Little
Rock (Ark.)—Politics and government—20th century. I. Title. II. Series.
F419.L7 K57 2002
323.1'196073076773'09045—dc 21   2002019472

The University Press of Florida is the scholarly publishing agency
for the State University System of Florida, comprising Florida A&M
University, Florida Atlantic University, Florida Gulf Coast University,
Florida International University, Florida State University, University
of Central Florida, University of Florida, University of North Florida,
University of South Florida, and University of West Florida.

University Press of Florida
15 Northwest 15th Street
Gainesville, FL 32611-2079
http://www.upf.com

For my mother and father

Contents

List of Figures   ix

Foreword by John David Smith   xi

Preface   xv

Abbreviations   xix

Introduction   1

1. Founding a Movement   11

2. War, Race, and Confrontation   34

3. Postwar Reform and Its Limitations   54

4. *Brown v. Board of Education*   86

5. The Little Rock School Crisis   106

6. Dismantling Jim Crow   139

7. New Challenges   163

Notes   185

Bibliography   213

Index   229

Figures

1. Dr. John Marshall Robinson 75

2. Silas Hunt arrives at the University of Arkansas 76

3. Silas Hunt, with Wiley A. Branton and William Harold Flowers 77

4. Wiley A. Branton and Daisy Bates 78

5. Gov. Orval E. Faubus and Virgil T. Blossom 78

6. Black students wait to enter Central High School 79

7. Daisy Bates and the Little Rock Nine 80

8. Trial of the first sit-in demonstrators in Little Rock 81

9. White SNCC worker Bill Hansen 82

10. A two-story SNCC Freedom School in Gould 83

11. Members of Black United Youth 84

12. Dr. Jerry D. Jewell addresses the Arkansas General Assembly 85

Foreword

Little Rock, Arkansas, holds a prominent place in the historical memory of the civil rights movement. In September 1957, Gov. Orval E. Faubus attracted national and international media attention when he secured an injunction from a state court to block the federal court-ordered desegregation of Little Rock's Central High School. In doing so, Faubus openly challenged the Supreme Court's monumental 1954 *Brown v. Board of Education* school desegregation decision.

After a federal court order set aside the injunction, Faubus brazenly called out the Arkansas National Guard to prevent nine African American students from enrolling in the school. When Faubus defied a new order from a federal court, and after angry anti-integration mobs protested on the streets of Little Rock, President Dwight D. Eisenhower reluctantly but finally acted. In a historic move, Eisenhower ordered soldiers from the 101st Airborne Division to Little Rock and nationalized the Arkansas National Guard. Under military supervision the black students peacefully integrated Central High, and the Little Rock crisis of 1957–59 became a landmark in the South's desegregation struggle.

John A. Kirk's *Redefining the Color Line: Black Activism in Little Rock, Arkansas, 1940–1970* reminds us that the pivotal 1957 Little Rock school integration crisis did not occur in a historical vacuum. His path-breaking book, in line with recent works that focus on civil rights battles at a grass-roots level, is the first to locate the unfolding events in Arkansas' capital city within the context of local black activism.

For three decades blacks in Little Rock and in black communities throughout the state campaigned for the vote, fought for equal justice, demanded equity in teachers' salaries, and battled for equal educational opportunities. Kirk credits the National Association for the Advancement of Colored People and local organizations such as the Arkansas Negro Democratic Association and the Committee on Negro Organizations with launching Little Rock and Arkansas' multilayered campaigns for enfranchisement, desegregation, racial reform, and social justice.

Drawing on many new primary sources, including a rich arsenal of oral history interviews, Kirk underscores the role of indigenous black groups in effecting racial change while emphasizing the nuances that existed among those agents of the civil rights struggle. He argues that local organizations often competed over strategies, tactics, and leadership styles. Inter- and intraorganizational battles, centered on a clash of personalities and class conflict, often "forestalled the cultivation of race-based protest and the mobilization of the large black population in the city."

Despite these conflicts, Arkansas blacks and their white allies ultimately triumphed in dismantling Jim Crow. Targeting Little Rock's business community with sit-ins and with other forms of protest, local black students, the Student Nonviolent Coordinating Committee, and the Council on Community Affairs during the early 1960s first desegregated department store lunch counters and then opened restaurants, hotels, and recreational facilities to African Americans. The more united blacks were in their protest, the more successful they were in integrating Little Rock. According to Kirk, unlike in other communities across the South, desegregation in the city came with relative ease. "At the end of 1963," he notes, "Little Rock had desegregated most of its public and some of its private facilities." Years of black activism finally had borne fruit.

Still, Kirk explains that there were limits to racial progress in 1960s Little Rock. Though Central High was integrated, relatively few blacks attended the school and those who enrolled there found themselves marginalized and generally excluded from full participation in school life. African Americans increasingly voted in elections and participated in local and state politics, yet discrimination remained rampant in such areas as jobs and housing. By the end of the decade black activists, led by the Black United Youth, employed new tactics—"mass demonstrations and threats of violence"—to pry loose concessions from whites. Fearful of black radicalism, whites gradually responded to the appeals of the more moderate black middle-class leadership, according to Kirk, "allowing them access to the apparatus which enabled blacks to move further into the mainstream of southern life."

While by the 1970s, Arkansas' black middle class had expanded dramatically and few overt vestiges of Jim Crow remained in the state, racial progress nevertheless was circumscribed. Rank-and-file blacks continued to live in seemingly endless poverty. During the 1990s, they earned on average almost 40 percent less than whites and their unemployment rate was 153 percent higher than that of whites. As blacks and whites increasingly resided in racially separate neighborhoods, their children found themselves "resegregated" in separate schools. Though black Arkansans still suffer from deep-seated racial inequities and tensions, the legacy of black activism that helped overturn de jure segregation in the 1950s and 1960s offers hope for the twenty-first century. Kirk tells this story well in his fascinating and enlightening book.

John David Smith
Series Editor

Preface

In September 1957, Little Rock, Arkansas, was the scene of a dramatic confrontation between federal and state power. The standoff brought to a head the southern campaign of massive resistance against the Supreme Court's *Brown v. Board of Education* school desegregation ruling. Although numerous studies have analyzed the Little Rock school crisis from a variety of perspectives, one striking omission in existing accounts is the role played by the local black community, which was at the very center of events. This book locates the events in Little Rock of September 1957 within an unfolding struggle for civil rights at local, state, regional, and national levels between 1940 and 1970.

In so doing, this book seeks to revise the time frame for black activism imposed by the first wave of civil rights scholarship, which focused exclusively on the role played by national civil rights organizations between 1955 and 1965, and argues that only by comprehending the groundwork laid in the 1940s and 1950s, through litigation and voter registration drives at a grassroots level, can the significance of later black protests be fully understood. In line with the findings of other state studies, this study highlights the pivotal role played by the National Association for the Advancement of Colored People (NAACP) in the black struggle for equality. Assisted by local black activists and local black activist organizations, the NAACP formed the backbone of early civil rights struggles at a local level.

The aims of this book are threefold. First, it seeks to place black activism at the very heart of the Little Rock school crisis. Second, it seeks to expand the focus of the Little Rock school crisis from exclusively national to local, state, and regional perspectives. Third, it situates the Little Rock school crisis within the context of a black struggle that unfolded over three decades.

Support from a number of academic institutions and foundations has helped make this work possible. I thank friends, colleagues, and students at the American Studies Department, University of Nottingham, and at the History Departments of the University of Newcastle upon Tyne; University of Arkansas, Little Rock (UALR); University of Arkansas, Fayetteville (UAF); University of Wales, Lampeter; and Royal Holloway, University of London. Invaluable assistance was provided by archivists at UALR and UAF Special Collections; the Arkansas History Commission; Little Rock City Hall; the State Historical Society of Wisconsin; the Manuscripts Division, Library of Congress; and the U.S. National Archives. Generous financial support, gratefully acknowledged, came from the British Academy, the University of Newcastle upon Tyne Faculty of Arts, the Pantyfedwyn Fund (University of Wales), and the University of Arkansas, Little Rock.

I particularly thank Brian Ward for his diligent supervision of my Ph.D. thesis, critical guidance in turning the thesis into a book, and good friendship throughout. I am also indebted to Richard King for his initial encouragement to undertake this project and to Tony Badger for expertly helping to lay its foundations. Many others in the British-based American studies community have lent assistance and advice at various points, including Nahfiza Ahmed, Robert Cook, Sylvia Ellis, Adam Fairclough, Maureen Hackett, John Howard, George Lewis, Peter Ling, Tim Minchin, Sharon Pointer, Fawziah Topan, Steve Tuck, Jenny Walker, Steve Walsh, Clive Webb, Emily West, and John White. I am especially grateful to Philip Lane Clark and Cynthia Clark, who first nurtured my interest in U.S. history and politics.

Two trips to the United States to conduct research for this book relied upon the goodwill of many people. On my first visit, Linda Pine, head of Special Collections at UALR, provided a great deal of assistance, from astute archival expertise to helping me find a place to live. Omar Greene and Jan Cottingham started out as landlords and ended up like family. Their presence made my yearlong stay in Little Rock all the more enjoyable. On my second visit to Arkansas, Michael Dabrishus, head of Special Collections at UAF, lent assistance in tracking down new research materials; David Chappell proved a worthy local guide; and Linda Schilcher provided subsidized accommodation and good company. I also appreciate the help of those listed in the back of this book who spent time talking with me in oral history interviews, and Stephanie Flowers, Terry Pierson, and Dale Lya Pierson, who granted me access to their family papers. In addition, I am grateful to the following people in the United States for their help and assistance: Tom Dillard, Andrea Cantrell, Willard B. Gatewood, Elizabeth Jacoway, Robert McCord, Elizabeth Payne, Bill Penix, Steven Recken, Marvin Schwartz, Pat Sullivan, Jeannie Whayne, C. Fred Williams, and Lee Williams.

Throughout, as in every other endeavor, my family—Anne E. Kirk, William J. Kirk, Alan J. Kirk, and Edyth and Frank Powers—has always been there for me. I could not have written this book without them.

Finally, my thanks and my love go to my wife, Charlene.

Abbreviations

ACCA	Associated Citizens' Councils of Arkansas
ACHR	Arkansas Council on Human Relations
ADVA	Arkansas Democratic Voters Association
AIDC	Arkansas Industrial Development Commission
AME	African Methodist Episcopal
ANDA	Arkansas Negro Democratic Association
ASC	Arkansas State Conference of NAACP Branches
AVP	Arkansas Voter Project
BAD	Black Americans for Democracy
BUY	Black United Youth
CAP	Community Action Program
CCA	Community Action Agency
CCC	Capital Citizens' Council
CCIA	Crittenden County Improvement Association
CLOB	Council for the Liberation of Blacks
CNO	Committee on Negro Organizations
COCA	Council on Community Affairs
COMBAT	Community Organization Methods Build Absolute Teamwork
CORE	Congress of Racial Equality
CROSS	Committee to Retain Our Segregated Schools
CTA	Classroom Teachers Association
DNC	Downtown Negotiating Committee

DPA	Democratic Party of Arkansas
DSC	Democratic State Committee
EECL	East End Civic League
EOA	Economic Opportunity Act
FBI	Federal Bureau of Investigation
FEPC	Fair Employment Practices Committee
FRCC	Freedom Ride Coordinating Committee
HCC	Hoxie Citizens' Committee
ICC	Interstate Commerce Commission
IRS	Internal Revenue Service
LDF	NAACP Legal Defense and Educational Fund (Inc. Fund)
LRCS	Little Rock Council on Schools
LRHA	Little Rock Housing Authority
LRPA	Little Rock Police Association
LRPSC	Little Rock Private School Corporation
NAACP	National Association for the Advancement of Colored People
NCC	Negro Citizens' Committee
NYA	National Youth Administration
OEO	Office of Economic Opportunity
PCDC	Pulaski County Democratic Committee
SCLC	Southern Christian Leadership Conference
SNCC	Student Nonviolent Coordinating Committee
SRC	Southern Regional Council
STOP	Stop This Outrageous Purge
VEP	Voter Education Project
VGGA	Veterans Good Government Association
WEC	Women's Emergency Committee
WPA	Works Progress Administration

Introduction

On September 2, 1957, Gov. Orval E. Faubus called out the Arkansas National Guard to prevent the implementation of a court-ordered desegregation plan at Central High School in Little Rock. In defying the local courts and, ultimately, the Supreme Court's *Brown v. Board of Education* school desegregation decision, Faubus directly challenged the authority of the federal government as had no other elected southern politician since the Civil War. Over the following weeks, frantic negotiations took place between the White House and the governor's mansion that finally led to the withdrawal of National Guard troops. However, when nine black students attempted to attend classes on September 23, an unruly white mob caused so much disruption that school officials withdrew the black students for their own safety. The scenes of violence finally prompted President Dwight D. Eisenhower to intervene in the crisis by sending federal troops to secure the safe passage of the black students into Central High. On September 25, the nine black students finally completed their first day of classes under armed guard.

The 1957 Little Rock school crisis is a familiar landmark in twentieth-century United States history. By adopting a new analytical framework, this book seeks to provide a fresh perspective on those events. The first and most important aim of this study is to highlight the role played by black activists in the struggle to desegregate Central High. For more than four decades, numerous firsthand accounts have provided us with a variety of white perspectives on the school crisis. These include the viewpoints of President Dwight D. Eisenhower, Congressman Brooks L. Hays, Gov. Orval E. Faubus, Superintendent of Schools Virgil T. Blossom, Mayor Woodrow Mann of Little Rock, *Arkansas Gazette* executive editor Harry S. Ashmore, segregationist politician Dale Alford, and schoolteacher Elizabeth Huckaby. Secondary works by movement scholars have focused on Governor Faubus, massive resistance and the White Citizens' Councils, local white clergymen, local white businessmen, local white judges, local white women, and the interaction of national and local political and legal issues.[1]

There are no scholarly works and only two firsthand accounts to help us understand the role played by blacks in the Little Rock school crisis. For many years, the only black account of the school crisis was the memoir of Daisy Lee Bates, head of the NAACP in the state. Emerging more than thirty years later, the second work to provide a black view of events was written by Melba Pattillo Beals, one of the nine students who integrated Central High. Although it provides an interesting personal insight, Beals's memoir does little to broaden the scope of Bates's account.[2] The paucity of black perspectives obscures the fact that the Little Rock school crisis was, after all, about civil rights—specifically, about the right of blacks to have the same access to educational opportunities as whites. To comprehend the full significance of the Little Rock school crisis, an understanding of what those events meant to the local black community is needed.

A second aim of this book is to view the Little Rock school crisis from a local rather than a national perspective. By focusing on the national ramifications of events in September 1957, existing works offer little insight about how the school crisis fitted into a much larger struggle over racial issues in both city and state. This focus mirrors trends in the literature of the civil rights movement. A first wave of scholars writing in the 1950s, 1960s, and 1970s also tended to focus on the civil rights movement from an exclusively national perspective.[3] Historian Adam Fairclough has characterized this early work as belonging to the "Montgomery-to-Selma" narrative of the movement.[4] The narrative focuses on events in the national media spotlight from 1955 to 1965, concentrating in particular on the nonviolent direct-action protests of Martin Luther King Jr. and the Southern Christian Leadership Conference (SCLC). Consequently, we have a distorted vision of how those privileged events fitted into a wider context of black activism in America.

Only when a second wave of scholarship in the 1980s and 1990s shifted its focus from a national to a local perspective did the shortcomings of earlier works become fully apparent. Focusing, as William H. Chafe describes, "from the point of view of people in local communities, where the struggle for civil rights was a continuing reality, year in and year out" a raft of local and state studies has provided a new conceptual framework for the history of the civil rights movement. In particular, these studies have acknowledged that the local and state concerns of blacks, interacting with regional and national factors, were crucial in determining the rate and trajectory of racial change in the South.[5]

A third aim of this book is to locate the Little Rock school crisis within the context of a black struggle that spanned three decades. In so doing, it contends that the traditional chronology ascribed by historians to the black struggle for civil rights needs revising. Critically, the national narrative of the civil rights movement, unfolding between 1955 and 1965, fails to grasp the importance of black activism during the 1940s and early 1950s, which laid the foundations for later protests. Although less media-friendly than mass demonstrations in the streets, local litigation that chipped away at segregation in higher education, wage discrimination, and impediments to voting rights, together with early black voter registration drives in southern communities, played a vital role in blacks' attempts to stake a claim for freedom and equality.

By looking at the earlier decades of the black struggle, new perspectives on indigenous black movements emerge. This book confirms the findings of other studies in Mississippi, Louisiana, and North Carolina about the NAACP's pivotal role in the development of state and local black activism during the 1940s and 1950s.[6] It thereby offers another corrective to the Montgomery-to-Selma school of civil rights history that has sidelined discussion of the NAACP. The national-based narrative tends to concentrate on the role played by groups, such as the Student Nonviolent Coordinating Committee (SNCC), the Congress of Racial Equality (CORE), and the SCLC, who loomed large in the later mass protests.

In contrast to these organizations' operations, the NAACP's legalistic tactics were by the 1960s considered slow moving and overly bureaucratic by many activists. The NAACP was also short on the youthful dynamism of other organizations and lacked a charismatic leader at its helm. Therefore, by focusing on the 1960s, historians have tended to neglect the important pre-1954 victories and achievements of the NAACP and its legal wing, the NAACP Legal Defense and Educational Fund (LDF). Viewed from state and local levels in earlier decades, the successful litigation sponsored by the NAACP and the LDF clearly had a profound impact on blacks in local communities. Successful lawsuits offered evidence that local black initiatives could force concessions from whites, they provided tangible community gains, and they blazed a trail for local people to organize and push for their legal rights.

This book also seeks to give due attention to the black grassroots organizations that provided the local grounding for the later successes of national civil rights organizations. For example, in the late 1920s, Little Rock physician Dr. John Marshall Robinson founded the Arkansas Negro Democratic Association (ANDA), made up of prominent black businessmen and professionals, as a vehicle to campaign for black voting rights. In the 1960s, the Council on Community Affairs (COCA) emerged from the black professional community to seek the desegregation of downtown facilities. Outside the state capital, the most important indigenous movement to emerge was the Committee on Negro Organizations (CNO) in the 1940s, fronted by black attorney William Harold Flowers. All of these local organizations played a vital role in laying the foundations for black activism in Arkansas upon which national organizations later built.

Focusing intently on black activism in Little Rock, this study provides an instructive model for racial change in an Upper South city that felt the conflicting pressures of racial conservatism and racial progressivism particularly keenly. Little Rock lay at the geographical center of Arkansas, a state that in 1940 had 482,578 blacks, accounting for 24.8 percent of the total population. Arkansas ranked eighth in the nation in terms of its percentage of black population and twelfth in terms of its total black population. Little Rock's 22,103 blacks composed 25.1 percent of the city's population.[7]

Yet, drawing a diagonal line from the northeast to the southwest corner of Arkansas identified two very different regions in terms of racial composition.[8] The southeast half of the state was an area very much allied to the Lower South. From the 1830s onward, the cotton plantations of east Arkansas began a mass importation of black slave labor. After the Civil War and well into the twentieth century, a modified plantation system persisted under which many blacks remained tied to the land as sharecroppers and tenant farmers.[9] In 1940, the thirty-five counties of southeast Arkansas contained over 90 percent of the total black population in the state. Blacks accounted for 41.8 percent of the population in the region.[10]

East Arkansas shared much of the same racial history as the neighboring Mississippi Delta. White oppression, lynching, and sporadic outbreaks of extreme mass violence characterized race relations in the region.[11] Efforts by landless blacks to organize a strike in 1891 under the banner of the Cotton Pickers League was, according to historian William F. Holmes, "ruthlessly and totally suppressed" by whites.[12] In 1919, when black sharecroppers attempted to form a union in Elaine, a race riot ensued that cost the lives of possibly hundreds of black men, women, and children.[13] In 1935, an attempt by black and white sharecroppers to form a biracial Southern Tenant Farmers Union provoked such a violent response that the union moved its headquarters from east Arkansas to Memphis, Tennessee. When the leader of the American Socialist Party, Norman Thomas, tried to address sharecroppers in support of the union in Birdsong, Arkansas, a white plantation owner brushed him aside, declaring "There ain't going to be no speaking here. We are citizens of this county and we run it to suit ourselves. We don't need no Gawd-damn Yankee Bastard to tell us what to do with our Niggers." From a safer haven in the North, Thomas reported to the nation that there was "a reign of terror in the cotton country of eastern Arkansas. . . . The plantation system involves the most stark serfdom and exploitation that is left in the modern world."[14]

Northwest Arkansas was in many ways very different from the southeast. A region of rolling hills and mountains, it appeared at first glance to have more in common with the West or Midwest than with the South. Indeed, many of the counties in the northwest corner of the state opposed the South's secession from the United States in 1861, and some even sided with the Union rather than the Confederacy during the Civil War.[15] Since the plantation system had not extended into the area, few blacks lived there. The economy of the region, such as it was, revolved mainly around small dairy, poultry, and cattle farming, and fruit and berry cultivating.[16] In 1940, out of the forty counties in the region, sixteen contained fewer than one hundred blacks and seven contained no blacks at all. In total, these counties accounted for only 3.9 percent of the total black population in the state.[17]

The paucity of the black population notwithstanding, this region had its own particular racial practices, mixing latent racist sentiment with mountain folk's distrust of strangers.[18] Residents made sure blacks felt unwelcome, posting signs at entry points to villages and towns declaring

"Don't Let the Sun Set on You Here, Nigger." Only the larger towns of Eureka Springs, Fayetteville, and Bentonville allowed black travelers to stay overnight.[19]

Despite the apparent difference, the inherent conservatism of southeast and northwest Arkansas did form a common bond between the two halves of the state and produced a statewide politics remarkably bereft of controversial issues. In his 1948 study of politics in the South, V. O. Key found that Arkansas lacked the sectional politics of Alabama, the machine politics of Virginia, and the strong political coalitions of Georgia and Tennessee. Neither did it possess the "inexorable law that drives many of its political leaders to cap their careers by hysteria on the race question" found in South Carolina. In Arkansas, Key stated, there was a "multiplicity of transient and personal factions" and a politics "almost devoid of an issue other than that of the moment." Elections consisted of "a system of alliances built up in each campaign by a particular candidate." Arkansas, Key concluded, was "pure one-party politics," which allowed a large degree of factionalism and fluidity within the boundaries of the all-encompassing Democratic Party of Arkansas (DPA). Arkansas was overwhelmingly Democratic and conservative, and outside of those two givens, said Key, "genuinely important issues are not raised."[20]

"In no other Southern city," wrote Little Rock's *Arkansas Gazette* executive editor, Harry S. Ashmore, "is the upland and lowland culture so directly joined."[21] However, Little Rock's development helped transform the city from a convenient center for government and business administration servicing rural Arkansas to the state's leading urban community, imbuing the place with its own distinctive character. When Little Rock became Arkansas' state capital in 1821, it was just a frontier settlement with barely 1,500 residents. Significant population growth came only during and after the Civil War, when victorious Republican forces used the city as base for the Reconstruction government. Consequently, Little Rock's population grew from 3,727 in 1860 to 12,000 in 1870. The expansion of railroads in Arkansas more than doubled that number during the following decade to 25,874. The next major thrust of expansion came during and after the First World War. Much of this growth was due to successful efforts of local white businessmen in lobbying the federal government to open the Camp Pike army base near the city. Another boost to expansion was North Little Rock, just across the Arkansas River, which incorporated as a separate city in 1917. However, Little Rock's boom suffered a temporary setback in the 1930s with the onset of the Great Depression. By 1940, the city's population stood at 88,039, while North Little Rock's population stood at 21,137.[22]

From its earliest days, Little Rock developed a reputation for having a more progressive racial climate than the surrounding rural areas. The scarcity of labor in the city during the pre–Civil War period meant that skilled slaves were in demand and that they had some leeway in negotiating better terms of employment and more social freedom.[23] After the Civil War, many of these skilled blacks, along with other skilled and educated blacks from rural Arkansas and other states, enjoyed prominent positions as educators, businessmen, and politicians in the Republican Reconstruction government.[24] Even when segregation and disfranchisement curtailed black social and political freedom in the post-Reconstruction era, black businesses and institutions continued to flourish.[25] The influence of Little Rock's white business leaders helped insulate the city from much of the racial hostility found in rural areas. As in other southern urban centers, Little Rock businessmen looked to project a progressive and civilized image to attract the northern capital, investment, and goodwill upon which the city's prosperity depended.[26]

The Second World War was a watershed in Arkansas history, marking a decisive shift in the relationship between urban and rural sections of the state. The war accelerated the trends of collectivization and mechanization already set in motion on east Arkansas plantations by the New Deal in the 1930s. As state historian David M. Tucker explains, "Each tractor replaced nine men and mules. Each mechanical cotton picker did the work of a hundred field hands."[27] The consequence was rural depopulation, a growth in urban populations, and emigration on a massive scale. Between 1940 and 1960, two-thirds of farmers in Arkansas left the land. A total of 850,000 people left Arkansas altogether, representing 44 percent of the state's population. Blacks left at a much higher rate than whites, seeking employment in major cities of the Midwest, such as Chicago, Detroit, and Saint Louis.[28] Between 1940 and 1970, Arkansas' white population, because of the high birth rate, did actually manage to grow slightly, by 7 percent, while Arkansas' black population declined by 27 percent, from a 25 percent to a 19 percent share of the state's population.[29]

Meanwhile, Little Rock experienced a wartime boom. "For the first time in the history of the city," observed Harvard-educated poet and Little Rock native John Gould Fletcher, "Little Rock became an overcrowded urban center, surrounded by major industries."[30] The reopening of Camp Pike as Camp Robinson boosted the city's economy. A large munitions factory opened in Pine Bluff, forty-five miles southeast of Little Rock. A shell-case loading plant opened in Jacksonville, sixteen miles north of Little Rock. In total, five air bases, a prisoner-of-war camp, two Japanese-American relocation centers, half a dozen new munitions factories, and two massive aluminum processing plants, all funded by the federal government, came to the state.[31] Fletcher concluded that for the first time, the Second World War made Arkansans truly "conscious of the importance of industry."[32] Those leaving the land, black and white, sought new opportunities in rapidly expanding urban areas. Between 1940 and 1970, as the number of blacks in Arkansas declined overall, the black population in Little Rock steadily grew by more than 10,000. The white population also grew by almost 35,000, although at a proportionately slower rate, meaning that the black share of the city's population increased from about one-quarter to one-third.[33]

The Second World War was a catalyst for the transition of the state from an Old South–style plantation economy, dominated by a conservative rural elite, to a New South–style industrial and manufacturing economy, led by more progressive urban businessmen.[34] This transition saw the sharecropping and tenant farming areas of eastern Arkansas transformed into large-scale agribusiness. Crops such as soybeans and rice became more important than cotton. Agriculture employed only 7 percent of the state population, while manufacturing jobs grew to employ 24 percent of the workforce. In the 1960s, Arkansas saw the biggest rise in manufacturing employment in the South. Industry continued to grow, with textiles, apparel, shoes, wood products, paper, chemicals, metals, and machinery diversifying the economy. Arkansas became the fourth largest lumber producer and the largest processor of bauxite in the United States.[35]

Yet, the shift from farm to city, agriculture to manufacturing and industry, and planter to progressive businessman, was a long, protracted process. Indeed, as historian Raymond Arsenault points out, the process was already underway by the turn of the century, as planters began to move to towns and cities and urban businessmen made the first tentative attempts to promote industrialization. These developments already had defined a "cultural split between town and country" producing a "fundamental difference in lifestyle" and creating "two separate worlds."[36] Although the Second World War intensified the pace of change, the sheer scale of the transformation took decades to complete. Thus, although Arkansas' rural population declined from 77.8 percent in 1940, it was still 50 percent in

1970, the second highest percentage of rural dwellers in the United States. In almost every census table comparing poverty and deprivation Arkansas remained in forty-ninth position, just above Mississippi. Even in 1970, one observer noted that "a deep streak of traditional Southern conservatism, strongly rural in flavor, remains in Arkansas."[37]

Race relations were at the heart of the modernizing process in Arkansas. Rural whites moving to the city to become urban blue-collar workers faced massive upheavals in their daily lives. For them, clinging to white supremacy provided a degree of order and stability in a rapidly changing environment and a safeguard from black competition for jobs. Rural folkways and patterns of living died hard, even in the city.[38] Meanwhile, white businessmen in Little Rock and other urban areas grappled with the economic necessity of racial progress. Increasingly, it became difficult to reconcile conflicting rural and urban values. Complicating matters was the fact that many white urban businessmen were deeply ambivalent about racial change, which stopped them from taking a more proactive stance on the race issue.[39]

As resistance and ambivalence to black advancement predominated among the state's white population, black activists played a pivotal role in the struggle for racial change. The economic and demographic upheavals of the 1940s raised the capacity of blacks to launch their own challenge to white supremacy. Although there were fewer blacks in Arkansas because of population shifts, those that remained were concentrated in growing villages, towns, and cities. This created a potentially more effective base from which to mobilize the black population in the pursuit of freedom and equality. It also lowered the ability of whites to forcibly attack and intimidate those who sought to take a stand for better treatment. Thus, black activists, particularly in larger urban areas such as Little Rock, were in a better position to exert further pressure on white leaders for civil rights. Drawing upon the support of national black organizations, such as the NAACP, and a federal government increasingly sympathetic to the struggle for civil rights, local black activists took the lead in forging a new era of race relations in Arkansas.

To recap, this book charts new territory in the study of the Little Rock school crisis at a number of levels. First, it places black activism at the very center of events. Second, it locates black activism in Little Rock within local, state, and regional contexts, as well as in national. Third, it expands the traditional chronology of the Little Rock school crisis to encompass a black struggle that unfolded over three decades. In providing this new analytical framework, the book illuminates the crucial role played by the NAACP, local black activists, and local black activist organizations in the civil rights struggle. It also charts the intricate process of racial change in an Upper South city that felt the conflicting pressures of racial conservatism and racial progressivism particularly keenly. The study therefore offers a new reading of the Little Rock school crisis that forces a reevaluation both of the events of September 1957 and of the traditional framework for understanding the black struggle for civil rights in the United States.

Founding a Movement   1

In 1940, Little Rock's black population stood at 22,098, accounting for 25.1 percent of the city's 88,039 residents. Downtown, West Ninth Street was the major hub of black economic, social, political, civic, and cultural life for both the city and the state. West Ninth Street housed black businesses, Masonic temples, fraternities, professional associations, the local branches of the NAACP and Urban League, and the headquarters of the state's black Republican and Democratic groups. Black revelers on Friday and Saturday nights frequented West Ninth Street's movie theater, bars, and dance halls, leading one observer to label it "Little Rock's Harlem."[1]

Outside of West Ninth Street, Little Rock was an important center for black education. Three black denominational colleges provided limited access to higher education. Philander Smith College, supported by the Methodist Episcopalian Church, was the largest and most prosperous black college in Little Rock. Located at Eleventh and Izard Streets, Philander Smith was founded in 1877 as Walden Seminary and changed its name in 1883 to honor the husband of a wealthy patron, Adeline Smith of Oak Park, Illinois. The college had an enrollment of 320 undergraduate students, about one-third of them from other states. Little Rock blacks accounted for the largest number of home-state students. Out of twenty-three staff members, eleven had master's degrees and all the others had done some form of graduate work. M. Lafayette Harris, president of the college, was reputed to be the only black doctor of philosophy in the state.

Philander Smith was a member of the Association of American Colleges, the National Council of Church-Related Colleges, and the Methodist Educational Association. The University of Arkansas and the state departments of education in all southern states, as well as Indiana, Kansas, Missouri, and Illinois, accredited the college's courses.[2]

Arkansas Baptist College, founded in 1884, was located between Sixteenth and Seventeenth Streets in Little Rock. Supported by the Consolidated Baptist Convention of Arkansas, the college had an enrollment of 206 students, 75 in the junior college and 131 in the high school department. Most of the students came from rural areas. The junior college students attended Arkansas Baptist because of its low tuition and flexible payment plans, while the high school students attended Arkansas Baptist because there was no high school for them in their communities. The college had nineteen staff members. Although Arkansas Baptist College was once one of the most powerful black colleges in the state, the depression had severely weakened its finances and educational standing.[3]

Black Little Rock clergyman J. P. Howard founded Shorter College, supported by the African Methodist Episcopalian Church, in 1885. Located at Sixth and Locust Streets in North Little Rock, the college initially educated laymen and ministers for work in the AME church as well as black schoolteachers. After the college suffered financial irregularities and scandals in the 1930s, a new president, G. A. Gregg, tried to improve its status as a business and educational institution. Nevertheless, Shorter had an enrollment of only 33 students in the college and 77 in the high school department.[4]

The only other black college of note in Arkansas was the state-funded Arkansas Agricultural, Mechanical, and Normal College (AM&N), a land-grant institution located in the town of Pine Bluff. Founded in 1875 as Branch Normal College, with Joseph Carter Corbin as its principal, the college initially taught only seven students in a ten-by-twelve-foot rented frame building. In 1882, the college moved into a two-story brick building, awarding ten bachelor of arts degrees before it became a junior college from 1894 to 1929. In 1929, the college was renamed Arkansas AM&N, and four years later, it began to award baccalaureate degrees again. In the late 1930s, with help from two white northern philanthropic foundations, the Rosenwald Fund and the General Education Board, the college embarked on an expansion program, which doubled the size of the campus by the late 1960s. In 1940, Arkansas AM&N had an enrollment of approximately 500 students.[5]

There were eight black public schools in Little Rock, with an enrollment of 4,324 students. By far the most important was Paul Laurence Dunbar High School. When it was built in 1930, Dunbar High was reputedly the best-equipped black school in the United States. A smaller version of the white Little Rock High School (later renamed Central), which had been built in 1927, Dunbar High was constructed in part with funds from the Rosenwald Fund and the General Education Board. The impressive brick structure boasted thirty-four classrooms; physics, chemistry and biology laboratories; shops for carpentry, woodwork, plumbing, electricity, automobile mechanics, bricklaying, and printing; an auditorium; and a large library. Students could take classes in English, mathematics, social sciences, science, Latin, French, and American history, government, and economics. The school building also housed Dunbar Junior College, which acted mainly as a center for training black teachers. Dunbar High had an enrollment of 1,607 students, and Dunbar Junior College had an enrollment of 142 students. As the only accredited secondary school for blacks in Arkansas, it saw a great deal of competition for admissions.[6]

Little Rock had a rich variety of black religious institutions, to the extent that one black observer called the city "overchurched." There were more than one hundred black churches, representing fourteen different denominations. These ranged from congregations worshipping in older, well-established churches, to those worshipping in tents, front rooms, and rented houses and stores. Three churches formed the most important foundations for black religious life in the city. Little Rock's oldest black church, First Baptist, founded in 1845, was located at Seventh and Gaines Streets. Wesley Chapel Methodist Episcopal Church, founded in 1854, had moved sites several times, but in 1940 was located on the Philander Smith College campus. Bethel African Methodist Episcopal Church, founded in 1862, was located at Ninth and Broadway Streets.[7]

Three weekly black-owned papers provided the community with news of the city, the state, the South, and the nation. The *Twin City Press* was an eight–page paper with a circulation of around three thousand. The *Arkansas Survey Journal* was a four–page paper with a circulation of around four thousand. Publication of the *Southern Mediator Journal*, the city's newest black paper, began in the late 1930s. Two religious newspapers supplemented these publications. The *Southern Christian Recorder*, published by the African Methodist Episcopal Church, moved to Little Rock from Nashville, Tennessee, in 1932, after fifty-five years in print. The Consolidated Baptist Convention published the *Arkansas Vanguard*. In practice, there was a quick turnover in the commercial black press, with newspapers frequently changing management and titles.[8]

In spite of the relative benefits and opportunities that a more urbane setting offered, black life in Little Rock, as in other parts of the state, unfolded within a context of firmly established second-class citizenship. Racial segregation, political disfranchisement, and pervasive discrimination profoundly shaped black circumstances and opportunities. However, they did so in different ways, since important class divisions determined their impact within the black community. "The Little Rock Negro has his social strata," noted black journalist Samuel S. Taylor in 1939. "At the top stand the old and established families, and at the bottom stand the denizens of the slums, and there is little in common between them." Taylor warned that those who did not "have an instinctive or comprehensive grasp of the intra-racial distinctions and ratings [among Negroes]" could not "administer the affairs of Negroes in Little Rock (or elsewhere) without friction."[9]

Although Taylor's description was imprecise because it failed to take into account the more subtle economic and social differences within the black community, it did recognize the existence of significant class cleavages. At the top of the black class structure in the city was Little Rock's black elite, comprising a small group of families, referred to by some blacks as the "First Families of Arkansas," or FFAs for short.[10] In fact, the black elite originated from two distinct groups. The first group came from former slaves who had enjoyed what one termed "peculiar privileges" in Little Rock before the Civil War. Due to the shortage of skilled workers in the early years of the city's development, some black house servants and black artisans were able to "hire out" their labor to whites and sometimes "lived out" in their own quarters. These slaves formed the basis of an early black leadership class, which acted as a liaison with prominent, paternalistic whites, "obtaining, protecting and extending customs, privileges or knowledge on which a relatively free [black] social life was based." Black families such as the Rectors, Richmonds, Andrewses, Winfreys, and Sanderses formed the nucleus of this group and became leading ministers, educators, politicians, and entrepreneurs in Little Rock after the Civil War.[11]

The second group came from blacks who arrived in Little Rock during the Civil War and Reconstruction. This group included figures such as Mifflin Wistar Gibbs, a native of Philadelphia, who was a politician, businessman, and banker. According to historian Willard B. Gatewood, Gibbs was "prominently identified with every political, social, and economic enterprise of any consequence undertaken by blacks in the city." John E. Bush, a former slave from Tennessee, was a founding member of the Grand Masonic Templars of America, a black fraternal and business organization. Isaac Gillam, another former slave from Tennessee, was a blacksmith and dealer in horses. Gillam's children, including a son who graduated from Yale, became teachers and administrators in Little Rock's black public schools and private colleges. Jefferson Gatherford Ish and his wife, Marietta Kidd Ish, were both college graduates and taught in Little Rock's public schools. The Ish children, including two sons who attended Harvard and Yale, became educators and physicians in Little Rock.[12]

Although the onset of segregation and disfranchisement in the late nineteenth and early twentieth centuries circumscribed the freedoms and privileges of the black elite, they remained influential in Little Rock's black community. Marriages within and between the two established groups of families defined their status and perpetuated their influence. Members of the black elite lived in comfortable residences, often in racially mixed neighborhoods, traveled extensively, and entertained regularly. They mixed at musical and literary clubs, they were associated with Philander Smith and Arkansas Baptist Colleges, and they attended the more prestigious churches in the city. Through continuing close associations with influential whites and by occupying positions of responsibility in important black institutions and enterprises, the sons and daughters of the black elite played a prominent role in black community affairs.[13]

The black elite formed part of Little Rock's black professional and business class, which accounted for only 3 percent of the black population. Half of those in professions consisted of teachers in black schools. Although educators held prestigious positions in the black community, even they suffered from discrimination. Teachers' salaries in Arkansas were among the lowest in the United States, and black educators received even less than their white counterparts. Black principals of high schools received annual salaries of $1,340 compared to $2,099 for their white counterparts. Black teachers received an average annual salary of $724 compared to the $1,216 paid annually to white teachers.[14]

Ministers formed the next largest group of black professionals. Their salary and influence varied widely, depending upon the size of their congregations. A handful of doctors, pharmacists, dentists, lawyers, and journalists made up the rest of the black professional class in the city. The potential for expansion in their numbers was severely limited, since only whites could attend the Arkansas colleges that offered appropriate professional training to qualify for such occupations. Those seeking to enter professions other than teaching faced the prospect of funding their own out-of-state education, an endeavor well beyond the means of the vast majority of blacks in the city.[15]

Black businesses accounted for slightly more black employment than did professional occupations. However, in the 1940s predominate black businesses were restaurants, barbershops, beauty parlors, grocery stores, and sundry other small-scale operations. Many of the larger enterprises had vanished during the depression. The lack of capital and credit available to black entrepreneurs, their lack of business training and experience, and the limited market they serviced meant that black businesses remained by nature restricted operations. Opportunities for the expansion of black businesses therefore remained limited.[16]

Just below the black professional and business class in Little Rock's black hierarchy was a small band of skilled and semiskilled black workers. These workers found employment as automobile mechanics, railroad workers, brick and stone masons, carpenters, electrical workers, plasterers, plumbers, and painters. Such positions conferred their own status and opportunities. Often, these workers benefited from higher rates of unionization in a city where black union activity was negligible. Many belonged to integrated unions, and although there were numerous complaints about their treatment by white union members, the unions did offer a potential channel for upholding black workers' rights. Some employers offered significant private facilities for skilled black workers. The 530 black employees of the Missouri Pacific Railroad Company, for example, had access to private hospital facilities and the use of Booster Park in North Little Rock for recreation. Higher wages meant these workers could afford better housing than much of the unskilled black population.[17]

At the very bottom of the black class structure was the vast majority of Little Rock blacks, who found employment in low-paid occupations with little prospect of advancement. Black men worked menial jobs as domestic servants, janitors, caretakers, laborers, waiters, bellboys, shoeshines, street cleaners, and garbage collectors. Black women, who made up almost half the black workforce in the city, as in other southern cities found employment mostly as domestic servants. Black children shined shoes; cut grass; drove trucks; delivered groceries and milk; sold ice cream, confections, newspapers, and magazines on the streets; and acted as porters in barbershops to supplement family income. Unions showed little interest in organizing for the low-paid menial jobs in which most blacks were employed. The only notable exception was black laundresses, who constituted 80 percent of workers in that occupation.[18]

Many black families who worked in poorly paid jobs lived in housing described by one report as representing "the lowest extremes of poverty, primitiveness and squalor." The most common type of housing was the double shotgun: two side-by-side, narrow apartments, each consisting of two to three rooms arranged front to back, straight through without hallways. Families of up to eight and ten members were living in these dwellings, the problems of overcrowding compounded by poor sanitary conditions and the absence of all but the most basic facilities. Even in the city, some families had no running water, relying instead upon a shared outside hydrant, which often froze during the winter months. Unlike some other southern cities, Little Rock had no laws to prohibit blacks and whites living in the same area, and racially mixed neighborhoods did exist. Nevertheless, due to economic constraints, the location of black institutions, and the practicality of seeking security in numbers, there were easily discernible black districts just off West Ninth Street and toward the east part of the city.[19]

The black poor suffered disproportionately from higher rates of adult mortality, infant mortality, disease, and crime in Little Rock. Yet, though blacks had far higher rates of death and disease, they had proportionately fewer hospitals than did whites. Only the United Friends Hospital in Little Rock and the Southern Hospital in North Little Rock exclusively treated blacks, and both offered just basic outpatient treatment. Five white hospitals accepted a limited number of black patients, allocating 111 beds total for that purpose. The Thomas C. McRae Memorial Sanatorium accommodated two hundred black tuberculosis victims. Tuberculosis was rife in the black community. In 1925, Little Rock was among ten cities in the United States where the disease was the leading cause of death.[20]

The city provided blacks with few facilities to escape the squalid conditions in which most of them lived. Except for Fair Park, blacks had only limited use of recreational areas. The privately owned Crump Park at Thirty-third and State Streets hosted black baseball games. Black boxing and tennis matches took place on a vacant lot at Twenty-eighth and Spring Streets. A ten-acre tract on the outskirts of Little Rock provided a place for Sunday school and church picnics. The city had appropriated funds to create a black park in 1936, but little came of the project. Black schools that could afford it sponsored sporting events, plays, bands, and musical groups. Outside of these activities, the main center for black entertainment was West Ninth Street, with its bars, dance halls, and the white-owned Gem Movie Theatre. Dances took place at the Masonic Temple and Dreamland Hall, with "the slums having them one night, the bon tons the next, and the schools the next."[21]

Crime rates were reportedly higher among blacks than whites. The most common crimes committed by black men were "gambling, drunkenness, illicit liquor traffic, assault, burglary, petit larceny, and carrying concealed weapons." Arrests of black women included charges of "gambling, drunkenness, liquor law violations, and prostitution." Many of the crimes were symptomatic of the conditions under which most blacks in the city lived. There was a great deal of concern in the black and white communities that an exclusively white police force showed minimal interest in prosecuting white-on-black and black-on-black crimes. This situation only contributed to further lawlessness, since black perpetrators of crime within the black community knew they could escape arrest and victims of black crime in both the black and white community were more inclined to take the law into their own hands.[22]

Educational opportunities offered some hope of escape from these conditions, although, except for the highly competitive Dunbar High, black schools were generally in poor shape. Black schools were proportioned significantly less of the education budget than were white schools, with $39.59 a year spent per black student compared to $66.56 per white student. Even Dunbar High had its problems. As the flagship of black secondary education in the state, the school often took more black students than it could reasonably handle. Black teachers regularly instructed classes of forty to fifty pupils. This made it difficult to offer adequate attention and instruction to individual students. All of the black city schools lacked playground space, athletic equipment, and gymnasiums. Any extracurricular activities depended upon self-financing fund-raising drives within the black community.[23]

In many cases, blacks relied heavily upon white charity for help in alleviating the conditions they encountered. Two important organizations in channeling this help were the Little Rock Urban League and the Phyllis Wheatley Club. Both organizations had an interracial board of directors and received funds from the Community Chest. Like other southern cities, Little Rock had a few whites who were prepared to work for black improvement, albeit strictly within the bounds of segregation. The Little

Rock Urban League, founded in 1937, was an affiliate of the New York–based National Urban League, founded in 1910. Like the national organization, the local branch worked to better living conditions and employment opportunities for blacks. Little Rock's Phyllis Wheatley Club, founded in 1919, served as a segregated branch of the YWCA. The Phyllis Wheatley Club worked to improve social, cultural, and recreational activities. Other charitable organizations providing help to blacks included the Red Cross, Goodwill Industries, Parent Teacher Associations, Legal Aid Bureau, Visiting Nurse Association, Pulaski County Tuberculosis Association, and the Goodfellows.[24]

Although blacks in Little Rock encountered numerous problems because of wide-ranging discrimination, no formal protest agenda or concerted effort for redress had emerged from the city. This was largely because many members of the city's black elite, who were influential in shaping community affairs, leaned toward the Booker T. Washington philosophy of "accommodation." Washington was the leading national black spokesperson from the 1890s until his death in 1915, and his views continued to have strong influence in the black community. As the principal of Tuskegee Institute in Alabama, Washington extolled the value of education and hard work as the primary means for racial uplift over social and political protest. Washington's philosophy of accommodation therefore stressed economic advancement within the boundaries of segregation instead of head-on confrontation with whites.[25]

In part, Washington's accommodationist stance was a pragmatic response to white oppression and the limited opportunities blacks faced in the Jim Crow South. However, it also reflected the fact that the segregated order worked to the advantage of the black elite. Segregation provided black businesses and black professionals with an exclusive black clientele for their services. Thus, many were reluctant to push for social equality. Moreover, black leaders relied on their position as race spokespersons to gain status and prestige within the white community. Working to destroy segregation for the black elite ultimately meant undermining the black leader's financial position, by abolishing their protected market, and community standing, by alienating influential whites.[26]

The personal stakes of Little Rock's black elite in the segregated order forestalled the cultivation of race-based protest and the mobilization of the large black population in the city. It also meant that there was no nurturing environment for national civil rights organizations, such as the NAACP, that could potentially provide a catalyst for grassroots black activism. The New York–based NAACP, founded in 1909 by a group of black activists and white liberals, opposed Booker T. Washington's accommodationist stance. W. E. B. Du Bois, a founding member of the NAACP and editor of the organization's newspaper, *The Crisis*, was Washington's chief black critic. Instead of accommodation, the NAACP advocated a more forthright protest against segregation, first by lobbying for antilynching legislation, then later by encouraging voter registration and by pursuing civil rights in the courts.[27]

One of the most celebrated cases of the NAACP's early history occurred in Arkansas in 1919. The case involved the defense of twelve black prisoners handed the death penalty for their alleged role in a race riot at Elaine, Arkansas. During a lengthy and expensive five years of litigation, the NAACP finally won a reprieve for the convicted men. In a landmark victory for the organization, the court overruled the men's sentences on the grounds of improper influence by a hostile courtroom.[28]

In spite of the victory, the NAACP was unsuccessful at winning widespread support in Arkansas. The indifference of the existing black leadership to its activities stymied the progress of the local NAACP branch at Little Rock. The Little Rock NAACP, founded in 1918, failed to make any headway in building support in the city, let alone in the surrounding rural areas.[29] Beyond the efforts of a few dedicated black female secretaries, most notably Carrie Sheppherdson, who won the Madam C. J. Walker Gold Medal in 1925 for her outstanding fund-raising drive, there was very little interest in NAACP activities.[30] As local branch secretary Mrs. H. L. Porter complained in 1933, "the lawyers, Doctors, preachers and businessmen . . . are just a bunch of egoistic discussers and not much on actual doings [*sic*]."[31]

Instead of enlisting the help of outside organizations such as the NAACP, Little Rock's black leaders proudly boasted that they could best handle racial matters at a local level. This was highlighted by the example of the Grand Mosaic Templars of America, a Masonic fraternity-cum-insurance-agency and one of the most successful black business concerns in Little Rock. Established in 1882 by John E. Bush and Chester Keats, the Templars at the height of their success in 1924 boasted a membership of 108,000 people in twenty-four states and combined assets of $280,000. The Templars' offices, in an ornate four-story building downtown, offered a central meeting place for the black professional, civic, religious, fraternal, and political groups in the city. The NAACP occupied only one room there among the many other groups trying to advance the cause of blacks. The Templars provided insurance for blacks, bolstered the local and regional black economy, and housed local black organizations. In so doing, the Templars considered its efforts to further the cause of the race better than those of the NAACP, based far away in New York.[32]

One important area in which some black leaders had managed to exercise influence with the white community was in politics. However, black political participation remained strictly a pursuit of the privileged few, who primarily represented their own interests rather than those of the black masses. During Reconstruction, well-to-do blacks occupied a number of important positions in local, county, and state government in Arkansas. Although their influence declined toward the end of the nineteenth century, due to the reemergence of the DPA as the main force in state politics, the struggle for a black political voice continued.[33]

Scipio Africanus Jones was at the forefront of the black political struggle during the early twentieth century. Born a slave in Tulip, southwest Arkansas, Jones worked as a field hand after emancipation, moving to Little Rock in 1881. After gaining an education at Philander Smith and then Shorter College, he became a self-taught lawyer, opening a practice in 1889. Jones was a talented attorney and became counsel to many of the black fraternal and Masonic groups in the city, as well as an early advocate for civil rights in the courtroom. Jones's most notorious case came in 1919 when, employed by the NAACP, he successfully managed to win a custodial rather than a death sentence for the twelve black prisoners convicted after the Elaine Race Riot.[34]

These exploits undoubtedly helped Jones in his successful political career, which most notably included taking on the "lily-whites" in the Republican ranks who tried to prevent black participation in the party after the end of Reconstruction. Jones and his followers won the long, bitter, and hard-fought battle in 1928. That year, Jones gained election as a delegate to the Republican National Convention, forcing Arkansas Republicans to acknowledge and accept the legitimacy of black participation in the state organization.[35] By the time Jones had successfully established a black voice in the Republican Party, however, the resurgence of the DPA meant that the struggle of black Republicans counted for little.[36]

A dramatic incident—the lynching of John Carter in May 1927—saw a shift in the direction of black political activism in Little Rock. Accused of attacking two white women on the outskirts of the city, Carter was hunted down by a white mob and summarily executed. The mob strapped Carter's body, riddled with more than two hundred bullets, to the front of a car and drove into Little Rock, where they dragged his body around the city for several hours. The lynching party finally ended its procession on West Ninth Street. There, whites made a makeshift funeral pyre from pews torn from the Bethel AME Church and set it on fire, throwing Carter's body into the flames. The mob, which at one point swelled to more than one thousand individuals, dispersed only when Gov. John E. Martineau sent in National Guardsmen to quell the disturbance.[37]

Although barbaric forms of asserting white supremacy, such as lynching, existed in the hinterlands of Arkansas, displays of such racial violence in Little Rock were rare. This was due to the size of the black community lending some protection and to the influence of the city's white business leaders.[38] The desire to repair the harm many businessmen believed the lynching of Carter had caused the city was apparent in their swift and outright condemnation. At a meeting the day after the lynching, they roundly denounced the "cravenly and criminal act," promising "any amount of money necessary" to bring the perpetrators to light. Meanwhile, the *Arkansas Gazette* lamented that the incident would paint an "unjust" picture of the city, ignoring the "thousands of law-abiding men and women" who distanced themselves from such acts. With suitable protestations of remorse on the front pages of the city's newspapers and a full investigation underway, the grand jury subsequently met only briefly before deciding there was not enough evidence to bring convictions.[39]

As the black community took stock of events in the aftermath of the Carter lynching, some decided to leave the city altogether.[40] Others decided to stay and take a stand. Most notably, black physician Dr. John Marshall Robinson founded ANDA to fight for black political rights.[41] Robinson, born in Pickens, Mississippi, in 1879, attended Rust College in his home state before graduating from Meharry Medical College in Nashville, Tennessee, in 1904. He opened a medical practice at Seventh and Main Streets in Little Rock in 1906 and was a founding member of the Little Rock NAACP. As a relatively late arrival to the city, Robinson did not share the mainly Republican loyalties of the established black elite. Indeed, his mobilization of black Democrats offered a new direction in black leadership.[42]

ANDA's first action was to sue white Democrats for the right to vote in the party's primary elections. Since the DPA dominated virtually every political office in Arkansas at the time, the primary elections were the true source of political power in the state. General elections provided for little more than a ratification of a Democratic nominee. DPA regulations forbade black participation in the party's primary elections, thereby denying blacks any meaningful say in state politics.[43]

ANDA's attack on the white primary built upon regional developments in black activism initiated by black Democrats in Texas, who with the aid of the NAACP won an important ruling before the Supreme Court in *Nixon v. Herndon* (1927). In *Nixon*, the Court ruled that state laws preventing black suffrage in Democratic Party primaries were unconstitutional. This victory, however, proved only partial, since the Court did not rule on the constitutional rights of black voters but only on the use of state laws to prevent black voting. This left the way open for state Democratic parties, as private organizations, to introduce rules preventing black suffrage in party primaries. Since the white primary system in Arkansas was identical to that used in Texas, ANDA sought to clarify and extend the *Nixon* ruling. What ANDA specifically wanted was a court decision that would rule out the use of exclusively white party primaries.[44]

Unlike blacks in Texas, however, black Arkansans found it difficult to enlist the support of the NAACP in their struggle. Requests for help met with a cool response.[45] NAACP executive secretary Walter White in a memo to NAACP president Arthur Spingarn about the ANDA lawsuit declared, "[A] reason to feel we should not give much, if anything towards this case . . . [is that] we have never been able to get any considerable support from the state." White concluded, in a pragmatic manner, that "we send say fifty or one hundred dollars as a contribution [so if] it turns out to be the one on which we get the definitive decision, we will at least have given something."[46]

On November 27, 1928, Judge Richard M. Mann of the Pulaski County Second Division Circuit Court, sitting in the absence of Chancellor Frank H. Dodge in the Pulaski County Chancery Court, upheld an application by Robinson and others for an injunction against the DPA to prevent it from barring black voters from its party primaries. Meanwhile, Judge Mann ordered the separation of black and white ballots in primary elections pending an appeal.[47] On August 30, 1929, Chancellor Dodge, having returned to court, again revoked black voting rights. ANDA then took the case to the Arkansas Supreme Court and the U.S. Supreme Court, which both failed to overturn the decision.[48]

During the 1930s and 1940s, a significant shift took place in the balance between local support and outside help in the struggle for civil rights. The depression years crippled many black businesses in Little Rock and other parts of the state. Successful enterprises, such as the Mosaic Templars, which had survived a worsening racial climate, now went into terminal decline. At the same time, a new agenda for black advancement was emerging that went beyond the capacity of existing black leaders to handle. The majority of blacks in the state suffered far more at the hands of the depression than did the black elite. Increasingly, many blacks looked to the federal government for help. In return, the government offered the New Deal, which brought the potential for change, renewing optimism and raising hopes throughout the state's black population.[49]

While the New Deal's impact on black lives was ultimately limited and its positive aspects very often undermined by segregation and discrimination, it did provide some hope for blacks. The New Deal brought construction of more black facilities, such as schools and hospitals, in the 1930s than ever before. It provided more jobs, more training, and greater access to adult education, offering the black population a small glimpse of the federal government's potential to make a difference in their daily lives. Demographic shifts helped consolidate black aspirations: the movement of blacks from rural areas to villages, towns, and cities offered a growing base for collective action.[50]

The Second World War was a further catalyst for change. Wartime army bases that located in the South helped the region's ailing economy, which President Franklin D. Roosevelt recognized as the nation's "number one economic problem," investing twelve billion dollars to combat the problem. Encroaching industrialization went hand in hand with increased black urbanization. Blacks pushed hard to win their share of wartime prosperity not only in the South but nationwide. The threat of a mass march on Washington by black labor leader A. Philip Randolph led President Roosevelt to form the Fair Employment Practices Committee (FEPC) to monitor racial discrimination in employment. Even with its shortcomings, the FEPC contributed to a tripling in the federal employment of blacks. Hundreds of thousands of blacks enlisted to help fight in the war for democracy. They did so with the firm intention of winning support for what the black press termed the "double V"—victory for democracy and equality at home as well as abroad.[51]

Black activists in Arkansas sought to capitalize on the promise of change brought about by the New Deal and the looming prospect of the United States entry into the Second World War. Yet there was a lack of enthusiasm among the state's established black leadership for a mass mobilization of the black population. The entrenched conservative elite in Little Rock still wielded considerable influence and still dominated organizational activities. Compounding these problems was the NAACP's continued lack of interest in the state, which denied Arkansas blacks a possible antidote to the stagnation of local black leadership. By 1940, only six local NAACP branches existed in Arkansas.[52]

The implementation of an activist agenda was something young lawyer William Harold Flowers sought to address. Flowers, born in Stamps, southwest Arkansas, in 1911, was the son of an insurance salesman and a schoolteacher. The Flowers family was part of a small black elite in Stamps and lived in an integrated neighborhood. Yet rather than sharing the complacency of other well-to-do blacks, Flowers, because of his early experiences, formed a more militant attitude toward civil rights. Enamored by childhood trips to the courthouse with his father, Flowers finally determined to pursue a legal career after a harrowing and graphic introduction to another side of southern justice. At the age of sixteen, on a visit to Little Rock, he witnessed the burning of John Carter on West Ninth Street. It was then, Flowers recalled in later years, he was "truly converted to be a lawyer."[53]

Flowers attended Lincoln High School in East Saint Louis, Illinois, for two years before completing his education at Philander Smith College in Little Rock. Flowers then worked his way through law school, taking classes part time at the Robert H. Terrell School of Law in Washington, D.C., a night school founded by black lawyer George A. Parker in 1931. After graduation from law school, Flowers returned to Arkansas and set up practice in Pine Bluff in 1938.[54] Young, eager, and idealistic and with firsthand experience of southern injustice, Flowers, from his first days in Pine Bluff, used his legal talents to try to secure civil rights. Initially, Flowers looked to the NAACP to help in this ambitious task. In October 1938, Flowers wrote to NAACP executive secretary Walter White, informing him that Arkansas badly needed organization and leadership and that he wanted to try to provide it but needed financial assistance to do so. As a novice lawyer just starting to build his business, Flowers explained he could not afford to take time away from his livelihood without recompense.[55]

Despite these pleadings, no help from the NAACP's national office in New York was forthcoming. Letters arrived from special counsel to the NAACP Charles Houston and his aspiring protégé, assistant special counsel to the NAACP Thurgood Marshall, both offering sympathy but little help.[56] Although Houston and Marshall initially stalled, Flowers's call for black lawyers to take a more active role in the struggle for civil rights was in line with developments taking place in the NAACP's national office in the late 1930s. Under pressure from the Internal Revenue Service (IRS), which denied the NAACP tax-exempt status because of its lobbying activities, the NAACP in 1939 created the NAACP Legal Defense and Educational Fund, Incorporated, known later as the LDF or "Inc. Fund." The LDF dealt with legal and educational matters only, thus ensuring its tax-exempt status. Although the NAACP and the LDF remained closely intertwined, with overlapping board membership, the creation of the LDF signaled the beginning of an increasing emphasis on litigation by black activists in the NAACP's national office during the 1940s. In particular, it provided Thurgood Marshall, who became director-counsel of the LDF and special counsel to the NAACP, and other talented black lawyers with a platform to pursue civil rights through the courts.[57]

By the time the NAACP had rebuffed all his requests for assistance, Flowers decided he could wait no longer for them to act. On March 10, 1940, at a meeting in Stamps, Flowers officially launched the CNO to take on the task of mobilizing the state's black population.[58] Flowers was determined to create a "single organization sufficient to serve the social, civic, political and economic needs of the people." Such an organization would stand up for the rights of Negroes to have a say in government, fight "un-American activities . . . enslaving the Negro people," and devise a "system of protest" to remove them.[59]

From the outset, the CNO sought to build what sociologist Aldon D. Morris refers to as an "organization of organizations." This is an organization that seeks to coordinate the activities of various other organizations and draws upon their collective strength to achieve a unified purpose and goal. Under this umbrella organization, Morris asserts, "activists prepare communities for collective action and actually initiate struggles . . . to bring about social change." Moreover, he says, "[t]hese struggles often pursue limited goals perceived as attainable and positive steps toward realizing ultimate goals." Later black activist efforts in other localities often adopted this mobilization strategy. Examples include the Montgomery Improvement Association, founded in Montgomery, Alabama, in 1955, the Inter-Civic Council, founded in Tallahassee, Florida, in 1956, and the Alabama Christian Movement for Human Rights, founded in Birmingham in 1956. The emergence of the CNO in 1940 suggests that such direct-action protest organizations existed long before they captured national attention and met with greater success later in the civil rights struggle.[60]

The cornerstone of the CNO's program was to encourage black participation in the political process. This was by no means a new idea, as the efforts of Scipio Jones and black Republicans and Robinson and black Democrats testified. Indeed, Flowers and the CNO were part of a long tradition of black political activity in Arkansas. However, in direct contrast to all previous attempts to secure black political participation, Flowers had a much broader vision of what the vote could achieve. Older black political leaders had always viewed politics as a way of articulating the grievances of a small, well-educated black elite. Flowers envisaged it as a vehicle for advancing the black community as a whole.[61]

Flowers, although a staunch Republican, insisted that efforts to mobilize the black population in Arkansas would be nonpartisan. Moving beyond the confines of white-dominated party politics, Flowers proposed the creation of a race-based political organization that would represent all black interests in the state and tackle the common problems they encountered. Half a generation younger than the established black leadership in the state, this band of professionals for the first time recognized the potential for issuing a wholesale challenge to racial discrimination. By using the ballot box and the courts and by harnessing the support of all black Arkansans, the younger leaders believed they could bring about the kinds of benefits that would improve the position of the race.[62]

The first step toward the type of black political participation Flowers and the CNO envisaged was payment of the state poll tax. Unlike other southern states, which used a variety of legal and extralegal measures to prevent blacks from voting in general elections, Arkansas required only the payment of a one-dollar poll tax, which qualified a person to vote irrespective of color. Whites allowed blacks to vote at general elections because the all-white DPA primaries effectively prevented blacks from having any influence on state politics. Flowers and the CNO were convinced that if blacks began to purchase poll-tax receipts and cast their vote at elections, it would prove a vital first step in raising black political consciousness to challenge the all-white DPA primaries.[63]

The goal of mass political mobilization called for coordination and organization. Hence, the CNO's first objective was to "seek the endorsement of Negro church, civic, fraternal and social organizations."[64] Only by bringing about unity and direction of purpose and by exerting power through an expansive statewide representative body could the task of raising black political consciousness be effectively completed. Flowers believed he was well suited to such a task. His father was not only a businessman but also a leading Mason. His mother was a schoolteacher. He was a lawyer. The Flowers family, which was well respected and well known in black Arkansas, had strong links to the church. Flowers possessed firsthand knowledge of these different organizational power structures within Arkansas' black community and had direct contact with them. Flowers therefore understood exactly which channels he needed to work through for the campaign to be effective.[65]

After the initial meeting at Stamps that launched the CNO, Flowers set off on a speaking tour to secure support from grassroots organizations across the state. On April 7, 1940, under the sponsorship of the Hope Interdenominational Ministerial Alliance in south Arkansas, three hundred blacks turned out to hear the CNO program explained. At Postelle in east Arkansas on April 14, six hundred people listened to a meeting held under the auspices of the local branch of the NAACP. On April 16, the Negro Business Club of Morrillton sponsored a meeting in central Arkansas, which was attended by more than two hundred citizens. On May 5, the Lewisville Negro Taxpayers Association in south Arkansas acted as host. There, more than two hundred fifty persons pledged their support to the program. Other meetings followed throughout the state.[66]

The series of meetings culminated in the First Conference on Negro Organization, September 27, 1940, at Lakeview Junior High School, in Phillips County, east Arkansas (near Elaine, site of the 1919 race riot). In his opening address, Flowers told the crowd they had been brought together to "devise a program of action" to combat discrimination against Negroes "merely because of the color of their skin." Flowers claimed that "[f]or six months we have obtained the endorsement of twenty-one organizations, with a numerical strength of approximately ten thousand Negro citizens." Further, Flowers outlined the achievements of the CNO to date. There had been thirty-five investigations over charges of color discrimination in public-works employment. This had led to the lifting of a ban that previously prevented blacks from participating in opportunities provided by the National Youth Administration (NYA). The state had employed its first black census enumerator. Sixteen mass meetings had taken place, with a total attendance of more than four thousand people. For the first time, blacks were beginning to show their collective disdain of the segregated system, and the white power structure in the state was responding, albeit on a small scale, by acquiescing to some black demands.[67]

After the successful three-day conference at Lakeview, Flowers kept up the pressure for a concerted challenge to whites. On January 1, 1941, Flowers spoke to the White County chapter of the Lincoln Emancipation League, urging its members to help build an organization that would be "truly representative of the people." Moving on to the Salem Baptist Church, in Lee County, east Arkansas, Flowers expounded the NAACP's message that "a voteless people is a hopeless people." Explicitly drawing upon the fight against racism in Europe, Flowers declared that "the success of our effort to make democracy a way of life for the peoples of the world must begin at home, not after a while, but now." Flowers focused blame for the lack of black activism in the state on the complacency of existing black leaders, particularly lambasting "the pussyfooting educators on the public payroll, who are only submissive to those responsible for their jobs."[68]

Flowers continued to stump the state, making speeches throughout the year in an effort to mobilize support. The next step, converting organizational strength and enthusiasm into direct gains, came with the poll-tax drives in September 1941. Under the direction of the CNO, a physician from the town of Hope, Roscoe C. Lewis, ran a poll-tax purchasing campaign in southern Arkansas, while an undertaker from Morrillton, W. L. Jarrett, supervised in the north.[69]

"Drive to Increase Race Votes Is Successful" proclaimed the headlines in the *Arkansas State Press* (hereafter, *State Press*), the Little Rock–based black newspaper, at the end of the CNO's campaign. The *State Press* anticipated a record turnout of black voters.[70] Emboldened by this expectation, Flowers and the CNO began to test the impact the upsurge of interest in black voting rights would have. Before the election, in line with the NAACP's fight to pressure state boards of education to provide equal facilities for black graduate students, the CNO petitioned Gov. Homer M. Adkins to lend assistance to Arkansas' black graduates. "We direct your attention to the growing unrest on the part of the Negro race," Flowers wrote to Adkins. "They no longer are willing to remain on their knees begging for the rights, privileges and immunities of Negro citizenship."[71] Adkins passed the letter on to the Arkansas Department of Education, which fervently resisted the idea of spending money on education for blacks. Instead, it suggested using the latest increase in funds at Arkansas AM&N, the state's only publicly funded black higher education institution, to pay for out-of-state scholarships. With the implementation of this plan left to college trustees, the situation remained deadlocked.[72]

Flowers was dissatisfied with the way Adkins and the Arkansas Department of Education feigned action while in fact doing nothing to address the situation. He called together influential Negro educators from across the state for a conference with Commissioner for Education Ralph B. Jones. After the meeting, the state made fourteen one hundred dollar awards to blacks wishing to pursue an out-of-state education. The scholarships still enabled the state to dodge the issue of properly providing for black graduate students within Arkansas. However, the action did offer the beginning of a solution and paved the way for Flowers to later successfully press for an end to segregated black graduate facilities.[73]

Two years after the launch of the CNO, the organization could claim a number of concrete achievements, each more probing of the policy of segregation and discrimination than the last. Significantly, the first big breakthrough for civil rights in Arkansas came in the same year the *State Press* printed Flowers's photograph with the caption "HE FOUNDED A MOVEMENT."[74] In March 1942, a member of the Little Rock Classroom Teachers Association (CTA), Sue Cowan Morris, sued for the right of black teachers to receive the same salary as white teachers in the city's school system. The case proved to be the first successful attempt by blacks in Arkansas to win equal rights through the courts.[75]

The court victory had a long-term impact on the struggle for civil rights in Arkansas. The teachers' salary suit was not only a breakthrough for black Arkansans but also proved an important national triumph for the NAACP.[76] The local effort attracted the help of Thurgood Marshall, whose presence in Little Rock helped in turn to garner support there for the organization. NAACP local branch secretary Mrs. H. L. Porter reported a surge of new members. Marshall "sure did shoot them some straight dope as to their part and membership to be played in the NAACP cause," Porter declared, adding, "Then and there at that meeting we collected $68.50 in membership."[77] In response to this rising local interest, the NAACP's national office began to take more of an interest in the state. In 1945 an Arkansas State Conference of NAACP Branches (ASC) was established, with Flowers appointed as its chief recruitment officer.[78]

As the NAACP grew in Arkansas, the groundwork laid by Flowers and the CNO remained apparent. The state organization created the infrastructure, provided the leaders, and ensured the successes that were to follow for the national organization. The year before the ASC came into existence, the *Smith v. Allwright* (1944) ruling by the U.S. Supreme Court outlawed the all-white Democratic Party primaries.[79] The work of Flowers and the CNO assured that when blacks could finally reap the benefits of the vote, their numbers began to make an immediate impact. In 1940, black voter registration stood at only 1.5 percent. By 1947, that number had increased to 17.3 percent. Through poll-tax drives, voter education rallies, and the general raising of political awareness, the activities of Flowers and the CNO meant that black political organization predated national rulings.[80]

Other local political groups who worked alongside the NAACP in the unfolding civil rights struggle emerged in the 1940s. These groups dedicated themselves to mobilizing the black vote and using it as a tool to elicit concessions from the white power structure. In Little Rock, black soldiers returning from the Second World War formed the Veterans Good Government Association (VGGA) under the charge of Charles Bussey, who, like Flowers, hailed from Stamps. In 1947, Bussey successfully ran for "bronze mayor" in an annual election that was usually a formality, a ratification of an unofficial mayor for blacks who was handpicked by whites. Bussey and the VGGA upset the usual smooth operation of the election by persuading blacks to vote for him instead of the white-supported candidate, a result that clearly upset whites—they canceled the usual celebration banquet after his victory.[81] Bussey also had a hand in helping to form the East End Civic League (EECL), which represented a depressed black area in Little Rock. The EECL, run by Jeffrey Hawkins, helped pressure white politicians to improve the street lighting, roads, and pavements in the community.[82] These groups built upon the interest in black activism awakened by Flowers and the CNO. In so doing, they became part of the wider struggle to translate a raised black political consciousness throughout the state into various forms of political activism, assisting blacks to secure material improvements in their everyday lives.[83]

In the state courts, Flowers continued to blaze a trail for civil rights. Of the many cases Flowers fought in an effort to win equal treatment for blacks, the *Wilkerson* case in 1946 had the most profound impact. In the case, two black men stood accused of killing two white men, an act that usually brought an automatic death sentence. However, in this instance, Flowers managed to get the men's sentences commuted to jail terms. At the same trial, Flowers successfully demanded that some black jurors should sit in judgment on the case, the first time this had happened in the state since Reconstruction. Flowers was the only black lawyer practicing in the state to represent his clients without the counsel of a white lawyer, thereby contravening Arkansas' established courtroom etiquette and making his exploits even more remarkable. As a courtroom pioneer, Flowers was a role model other emerging civil rights lawyers aspired to emulate. One of his admirers was Wiley A. Branton, who later became a distinguished national figure in the civil rights struggle. Branton recalled that Flowers's courtroom battles had "a major impact on the view of black people . . . that maybe there is justice after all."[84]

Branton was one of a number of young lawyers in the 1950s to benefit directly from Flowers's struggle to improve black educational opportunities. In 1948, Flowers handled the admission of Silas Hunt to the University of Arkansas Law School. Flowers's demands, coupled with national rulings gained by LDF lawyers, finally persuaded white authorities to desegregate without going to court. When Hunt enrolled in February 1948, he became the first black student to attend classes with whites at a southern university since Reconstruction. More black students, including Branton, soon followed his example.[85]

In the field of black secondary education, Flowers played an important role in the attempt to get school boards to desegregate state facilities. In 1949, Flowers filed one of the earliest suits for school desegregation, against the DeWitt school board in east Arkansas. Significantly, DeWitt was one of the areas that witnessed the most intense pressure to desegregate schools after the Supreme Court's *Brown v. Board of Education* decision. Flowers thus directly helped lay the foundations for the statewide attack on desegregation through the courts upon which later black activists successfully built.[86]

The campaigns run by Flowers and the CNO in the early 1940s were, within the context of the times, a resounding success. Working with limited resources, Flowers and the CNO managed to provide the leadership, organization, and direction to channel the rising aspirations of the state's black population into political action, which began to yield concrete rewards. Yet Flowers and other CNO members realized their efforts could not succeed without the help and support of other black groups at local, state, and national levels. Flowers and the CNO saw themselves as catalysts for change, primarily encouraging others to lend support in the struggle for civil rights in Arkansas.

A major obstacle to effective statewide mobilization of the black population, as Flowers and the CNO continually emphasized, was the conservatism and complacency of established black leaders and organizations in

Little Rock. However, only by enlisting the help of blacks in Arkansas' capital city, the most important hub of black organizational activity, could blacks throughout the state begin to attract the vital outside help required from organizations such as the NAACP. Therefore, one direct consequence of the success of Flowers and the CNO was the increasing pressure on Little Rock's black leadership to take a more active and forthright stand in the emerging struggle for civil rights.

War, Race, and Confrontation | 2

Throughout the Second World War, blacks in Little Rock responded to the newly emerging activist agenda forged by Flowers and the CNO with an increasingly militant pursuit of civil rights. Three important episodes of black protest highlighted the changes taking place. First was the ongoing effort of Robinson and ANDA to stake a place for blacks in the DPA primaries. Second was a salary equalization suit from Little Rock teachers, who, critically, were more successful in winning outside help from the NAACP for their cause than Robinson and ANDA. Third was the campaign by the *State Press* to convict a white city policeman of murdering a black soldier on West Ninth Street and to win appointment of black police officers in Little Rock. Not only did the campaign draw national support to take on white authorities, but for the first time it managed to unite blacks in Little Rock and across the state in protest.

After its defeat in the 1928 lawsuit, ANDA lay dormant for more than a decade. Only with the new interest in voting rights stimulated by Flowers and the CNO did the organization make a comeback. In December 1940, Robinson petitioned the new Democratic State Committee (DSC) to modify its rules to allow blacks to vote in the DPA primaries. Robinson, while seeking the right to vote, still assured whites that ANDA did not seek mass voting by blacks. DSC chair Robert Knox referred the matter to a subcommittee, which decided to shelve the matter indefinitely. Without the strength of numbers to back its demands, ANDA could do little to protest the decision. Whereas Flowers and the CNO could draw upon a grassroots statewide network of members and organizations for support, the limited scope of action, aims, and backing for ANDA precluded such bold measures. Consequently, it took another two years for the next black voting rights campaign to emerge in Little Rock.[1]

The issue of black voting rights only resurfaced because of developments at a national level, when *United States v. Classic* (1941) came before the Supreme Court. The case, which concerned fraud in the Louisiana primary elections, did not deal directly with racial issues, but it did involve the legal question of the constitutional status of primary elections. When the Court handed down its decision, it ruled that discriminatory practices in primary elections "may . . . operate to deprive the voter of his constitutional right of choice." The Court therefore concluded, "the authority of Congress . . . includes the authority to regulate primary elections."[2]

The *Classic* decision appeared to undermine claims by Democrats across the South that their own rules should govern primary elections. Certainly, the director-counsel of the LDF, Thurgood Marshall, regarded the decision as "striking and far reaching" in terms of future possible attacks on the white primary system in the South.[3] A letter from ANDA to U.S. Attorney General Francis Biddle asked for his support in allowing black Arkansans their legitimate voting rights as inferred in the court ruling. Robinson informed Biddle that the DPA had ignored a petition to secure such rights.[4] Meanwhile, white Democrats in Arkansas insisted they would still bar blacks from voting in primary elections.[5]

The reply to Robinson from the attorney general's office insisted that "the denial of the right to Negro voters to participate in the primary elections has been the subject of a series of conferences within this department." Encouraged by the news, Robinson informed ANDA supporters that he expected no trouble at the polls from whites in the forthcoming primary elections. ANDA secretary J. H. McConico declared that ANDA was "not asking pity or any special favors, we are simply seeking to exercise those rights and privileges guaranteed to free men in a free country."[6] The decisive test for the *Classic* ruling came at the Little Rock DPA primaries the following Tuesday. Election officials turned away the first black voter, a Baptist minister, from the polling booth. They even refused the minister's request to see a blank ballot. Similar events occurred throughout the city, with an estimated seventy-five to one hundred blacks being denied the right to vote.[7]

After the election, Robinson filed a report of events to Marshall. In a mood of resignation, Robinson wrote, "They [white Democrats] made their decisions and made it stick. We'll just have to let things cool off for a while until everybody gets level headed again." However, indicative of the influence that support from outside organizations could have on sustaining local black protest, discussions with the NAACP's national office brought a more emboldened statement from ANDA. Robinson declared that if Democrats did not allow blacks to vote in the following Tuesday's second primary, ANDA would appeal to the federal courts for relief. At the same time, Robinson sought to maintain good relations with the DPA. In a letter to DPA state secretary Harry Combs, Robinson stated, "We hope you understand that this will be a friendly suit, with no financial or penal objectives." Combs bluntly replied, "The same rule that applies to the first primary applies to the second primary."[8]

As the position of stalemate continued at the local level, it took another Supreme Court ruling three years later to stimulate further action. Soon after the *Classic* ruling, Marshall launched a case in Texas, attempting to get the courts to apply the new precedent in party primaries to black voting rights. The *Smith v. Allwright* (1944) case, similar to litigation existing in several other states, finally came down decisively for black voting rights. It declared that the all-white Democratic Party primaries were indeed unconstitutional.[9] Secretary of the Pulaski County Democratic Committee (PCDC) June Wooten conceded that the *Smith v. Allwright* ruling meant blacks would be able to vote in federal elections. However, Wooten did not completely admit defeat. He still believed white Democrats could deny blacks the vote in state elections. Even in the federal elections, at which blacks were able to vote, Wooten believed that some semblance of segregation could continue by providing separate ballot boxes for black and white voters.[10]

Some encouragement for Robinson and ANDA came when U.S. Assistant Attorney General Cleveland Holland put forward a more liberal interpretation of the Supreme Court's ruling. Holland emphasized the "state and national" clause of the written judgment, which, he said, meant that blacks "may be able to vote for state and local offices" as well as in federal elections.[11] With this backing from the federal government, ANDA held another meeting, at Dunbar High School, to discuss plans for voting in the DPA primaries that summer. In a letter of invitation to the meeting, Robinson expressed confidence that finally ANDA had "a definite understanding with the majority group."[12] Such optimism was borne out by the announcement on May 17, 1944, that the DSC would meet in the morning at the Hotel Marion in Little Rock to amend party rules, allowing full participation by blacks in DPA primaries.[13]

However, in a letter to the meeting, Governor Adkins informed the DSC that the proposal to remove black voting restrictions "does not coincide with my views in any respect." Furthermore, Adkins urged the DSC not to act, "as it is entirely a matter for the convention and legislature to settle."[14] In the meantime, Adkins pressed for the initiation of further steps to prevent blacks from voting. Seeking to circumvent the *Smith v. Allwright* decision, in June 1944, just before the summer primaries, Adkins advocated barring black voters on another basis than "that of race or color." What he had in mind, he revealed, was a loyalty clause, refusing blacks the vote because they had been loyal to and had participated in the Republican Party. DSC chair Joe C. Barrett suggested the introduction of further membership qualifications, along with procedural mechanisms, to prevent blacks from voting.[15]

The Democratic State Convention ratified new measures to prevent the casting of black ballots the following month.[16] Shortly afterward, when Robinson announced ANDA's support of Governor Adkins for the forthcoming election, Adkins replied curtly that the endorsement was "neither wished or solicited by me." Adkins went on to declare that "the Democratic Party in Arkansas is the white man's party and will be kept so. . . . If I cannot be nominated by the white voters of Arkansas I do not want the office."[17] While the DPA waited for the state to sanction its new party rules, it allowed blacks to vote in the Little Rock city primaries. This right was short-lived. In January 1945, the Arkansas General Assembly passed the Trussell Bill, which ratified changes to DPA membership rules, and the Moore Bill, which initiated a complex segregated "double primary" system to disfranchise black voters. The double primary system provided for city and statewide primaries that excluded blacks and federal primaries at which blacks could vote, but only at segregated ballot boxes.[18]

Shortly after the public renouncement of Robinson's support, white Democrats contrived a direct personal smear against him to discredit black Democrats. In September 1944, Arkansas Secretary of State C. G. Hall claimed Robinson was not eligible to vote because of a conviction for manslaughter in 1911. The conviction came after an entangled love affair with a woman, which led Robinson to shoot and fatally wound another man. Robinson served two years in the penitentiary for the crime before receiving parole without pardon. Hall asserted that Robinson's lack of a pardon meant that he could not qualify as a registered voter.[19] The blatant attempt to intimidate Robinson worked. In exchange for his citizenship rights restored, Robinson offered not only to resign as the president of ANDA but to "permanently cease and terminate all my activities, political or otherwise" linked to the organization.[20] Adkins issued a pardon only after the elections had passed and he had been reelected as governor. The DPA's harassment of the ANDA leader was successful in ensuring that no more attempts to assert black voting rights were forthcoming from the organization.[21]

The teachers' salary equalization suit filed by the Little Rock CTA in 1942 proved more effective than ANDA's attempts to take on the white power structure. Largely this was because the CTA proved more successful in securing the necessary resources and experience of the NAACP's national office, which could sustain and nurture their local efforts.[22]

In the mid-1930s, special counsel to the NAACP Charles Houston recommended a two-pronged attack on segregation in education, by pursuing teachers' salary cases and attempting to gain admission for blacks into university and professional graduate programs. The teachers' salary cases were especially appealing, because the pay disparity between black and white teachers was in most cases blatantly apparent. Establishing the fact that discrimination existed was therefore relatively easy. Teachers also offered a large potential pool of plaintiffs. Gains made in teachers' salary suits, Houston argued, would bring more money into the black community. Thus, the cases would help bolster black businesses and potentially bring greater support from influential local black leaders for the organization's activities.[23]

From the teachers' point of view, salary suits offered the immediate gain of higher wages plus the incentives of legal and financial assistance from the NAACP to help strengthen their cause. With a high degree of self-interest, there was a greater likelihood of escaping the debilitating rivalries in the black community. The teachers' salary suits were also less threatening than other forms of litigation. They made no challenge to the ethos of separate but equal and to some extent upheld the principal by simply asking for its application. The suits theoretically caused less strife to defendants, who were more likely to concede to equalization than desegregation, and appealed to teachers, who were less likely to support more militant and controversial forms of action.[24]

The first successes in the teachers' salary cases came through the efforts of Marshall, who quickly became the champion of the cause. In his home state of Maryland, Marshall won the first out-of-court settlement to equalize black teachers' salaries in 1937 and the first successful court ruling in favor of equalization in November 1939. Building upon these victories, Marshall looked to pursue similar suits across the South. However, although there were inquiries from teachers' groups in Florida, Alabama, Kentucky, and Louisiana, no significant breakthroughs came. In some places, teachers withdrew from cases because their jobs were under threat. In others, school boards managed to string out cases in the courts, disheartening and intimidating the teachers through delay tactics. Another ploy used by school boards was to offer out-of-court settlements on condition that teachers first drop the salary suits, which then left the teachers in a legal limbo.[25]

The NAACP also encountered problems when working with local black communities. Lawyers who were willing to handle litigation were difficult to find, and even when local lawyers agreed to help, communications with them could break down and jeopardize the cases. Since the NAACP legally could not openly solicit teachers' cases, it was dependent upon plaintiffs' coming forward. A decision to take on a local white school board required considerable courage, exposed the plaintiff to recriminations, and, because cases were often very lengthy, required considerable perseverance. In spite of these drawbacks, the NAACP continued with its campaign and was rewarded with a victory in 1940 when an appeals court upheld the case of Melvin O. Alston, president of the Norfolk Teachers' Association in Virginia, for equal pay.[26]

The ruling represented the first teachers' salary suit success in the South and had a direct bearing on the decision by Little Rock teachers to take similar action. The CTA watched teachers' salary cases develop from Maryland to Virginia with a keen interest. After the court ruled in favor of Alston, the CTA organized a Salary Adjustment Committee (SAC) to launch its own suit.[27] In February 1941, secretary of SAC Solar M. Caretners wrote to Alston at Norfolk, Virginia, and to NAACP executive secretary Walter White in New York. Caretners asked for advice about "the method of procedure and techniques of bringing about equal salaries for teachers" that would pave the way for such a suit in Little Rock.[28]

Following recommendations from Alston and White, SAC conducted research to ascertain the exact disparities that existed between black and white teachers' salaries in Little Rock. On average, SAC discovered, white teachers received an annual salary of $1,216, while black teachers received $724, for the same work in the same school system.[29] In light of these figures, the teachers drew up a petition for the equalization of salaries and presented it to Little Rock Superintendent of Schools Russell T. Schobee. He in turn passed the matter on to the Little Rock school board. The school board chose to shelve the subject indefinitely. Over the summer, the school board actually increased the pay disparity between black and white teachers. Enraged by this action, the teachers began to contribute to a fund for a salary suit and retained local black lawyers Scipio Jones, J. R. Booker, and Myles B. Hibbler in preparation for the case.[30]

The determination of the CTA to press ahead with the case took director-counsel of the LDF Marshall by surprise. Ignoring his advice to wait until the teachers received their salary schedules for the 1942–43 academic year, an adamant CTA insisted it was ready to go to court immediately. Since the teachers' salary suit offered an ideal opportunity to advance the NAACP's national agenda and appeared to garner enthusiastic support in Little Rock, the LDF agreed to lend its support. Marshall arrived in Little Rock in February 1942 to assist local attorneys.[31]

The day before the trial, Marshall attended a meeting of the CTA and watched its members adopt a final resolution to proceed with the action. Marshall noted with interest that the teachers insisted upon voting individually and performing a roll call of votes to ensure complete unanimity. All of the teachers present voted to press ahead with their demands. "Boy," Marshall wrote to assistant executive secretary of the NAACP Roy Wilkins, suitably impressed, "these Southern Teachers have acquired new backbones." Marshall also noted in his letter that all members of the CTA had pledged themselves as NAACP members, "and not just for one dollar memberships either."[32]

In consultation with its attorneys, the CTA chose Sue Cowan Morris as standard-bearer for the lawsuit. Morris was born and reared in the small town of Eudora in south Arkansas, where both her parents were schoolteachers. With a keen understanding of the value of a good education, Morris's parents made the necessary financial sacrifices to send their daughter to the best southern black schools available. Morris first attended a private school at Clinton, Mississippi, before moving to Spelman College in Atlanta. She finally completed her schooling in Alabama at Tougaloo High School and Talladega College. In 1940, Morris became head of the English department at Dunbar High. During the summer of 1941, she attended a graduate program at the University of Chicago, where she made straight A's in methods of teaching english. This outstanding educational career made Morris an ideal candidate to front the CTA's salary case.[33]

On February 28, 1942, Judge Thomas C. Trimble heard the CTA lawsuit, filed against the Little Rock school board and superintendent of schools, in the federal district court at Little Rock. In his opening statement, Jones argued that the disparity in pay between black and white teachers was a violation of the Fourteenth Amendment, which guaranteed equal treatment under the law.[34] Attorneys for the school board disagreed. They claimed no racial discrimination existed in the policy of teachers' pay. Rather, the criteria the school board used to determine salaries was based solely upon the "special training, ability, character, experiences, duties, services and accomplishments" of teachers. By implying that black teachers were inferior to white teachers for reasons that had nothing to do with race, the attorneys dodged the issue of discrimination and justified the present situation of inequality. Trimble upheld the school board attorney's argument by refusing to rule on Fourteenth Amendment rights. Moreover, he dismissed the case altogether on the technicality that the CTA was an unincorporated organization, which could not sue in a federal court. Trimble did not kill the suit completely, however, because he agreed to hear the plea of Morris as an individual plaintiff.[35]

At the subsequent trial, held between September 28 and October 2, 1943, Marshall continued to argue that inequalities in salary violated Morris's Fourteenth Amendment rights. Principal of Dunbar High, John Lewis, testified that in his opinion Morris "ought to be a Group 1 [highly rated] teacher." Indeed, this was Lewis's recommendation to the principal of white Garland High, Charles R. Hamilton, who was in charge of setting the salary ratings for Dunbar High teachers. In court, Hamilton admitted he based his judgments on salary ratings on only three or four visits to Dunbar High every year. In support of Lewis's testimony, Morris told the court about her educational background and her qualifications.[36]

Though the plaintiff gained the early upper hand, when the school board put its case, Marshall's anxiety about the board's having hired "top flight lawyers . . . determined to fight this out" proved well justified. The school board attorneys continued to hammer the argument that their clients judged teachers not by the color of their skin but on a merit system. The attorneys then produced what Marshall referred to as their "trump card"—a merit ratings sheet for 1941. The ratings aimed to show that most black teachers in the Little Rock schools system were, as Marshall put it, "lousy."[37] Next, the school board attorneys bolstered their argument by calling Annie Giffey to the stand. Giffey, the white supervisor of primary teachers in Little Rock, was a well-known and well-respected woman who had thirty-one years of teaching experience. Giffey testified that "regardless of college degrees and teaching experience no white teacher in Little Rock is inferior to the best Negro teacher." From finely argued points of law to blatant racism, the school board attorneys covered all the ground they thought might sway the court. The hearing, which Marshall referred to as "the hardest so far," did not leave him optimistic about the eventual outcome of the suit.[38]

While Trimble deliberated over his ruling, black educators in Little Rock found that the school board was prepared to take the fight beyond the courtroom. At the end of the 1942–43 academic year, the school board fired Morris. After spending a brief time teaching at Arkansas AM&N, Morris moved back to Little Rock to work in a munitions factory. Ten years later the school board rehired Morris but only after insisting upon and receiving an apology from her for suing them in 1942.[39] The principal of Dunbar High, who testified in the teachers' salary case, left his position at the end of the 1942–43 academic year. In his letter of resignation to the superintendent of schools, Lewis stated that it was the "definite dissatisfaction" shown by the school board over his part in the teachers' salary suit that had forced him to leave his post. Shortly afterward, John Gibson, head of the CTA, abdicated his position.[40]

When Trimble finally announced his verdict, it was in favor of the school board. The decision pandered to both the legal and the racist arguments put forward by attorneys.

Trimble rebutted the legal argument of Marshall and the CTA lawyers by ruling that Fourteenth Amendment rights were not relevant in the case. Rather, Trimble stated, the defendants had a right to "fix the salary of each individual teacher according to their real worth and value to the system as teachers." Moreover, the school board was not bound to "adhere to some arbitrary standard of college degree, years of experience, or some other mechanical method in determining salaries."[41]

Trimble's decision clearly reflected his own racial beliefs. The judge praised the "sincerity, frankness" and "fair-mindedness" displayed by the superintendent of schools and the demeanor of all the white teachers who had testified in the case. Trimble described them as "men and women of the highest caliber, civic minded [and] desiring to serve the community." Although they had nothing whatsoever to do with the legal case argued in court, Trimble upheld the tactics used by the Little Rock school board against those who had sought to challenge the racial status quo. Trimble asserted that the board was well within its rights to "refuse or fail to execute a new contract at the expiration of the old . . . whatever their reason for doing so."[42]

Nevertheless, Morris, on behalf of the CTA membership, continued to fight the case to a successful conclusion in the Eighth Circuit Appeals Court at Saint Louis. One significant advantage black Arkansans had in appealing lower court decisions was the fact that, through a quirk of political geography, Arkansas was the only southern state in the Eighth Circuit Federal Court District. The other states in the district were all in the North or the Midwest. Judges sitting in the appeals court therefore tended to be less steeped in southern racial mores, and there was a greater likelihood of an impartial ruling.[43] On June 19, 1945, appellant judges John B. Sanborn Jr., Joseph W. Woodrough, and Seth Thomas ruled that "very substantial inequalities have existed between the salaries paid to white teachers [and black teachers] and that such inequalities have continued over a period of years." The crucial question in the case, the justices decided, was whether there existed a "policy or custom of paying negro teachers less for comparable service than was paid to white teachers solely on the basis of color." In direct contrast to the ruling of Judge Trimble at Little Rock, the appeals court ruled that such discrimination did exist.[44]

Although the teachers' salary case proved local blacks could take on figures of white authority in the courts and win, it also illustrated the potential pitfalls of litigation. The case cost the jobs of plaintiff Sue Morris, principal of Dunbar High John Lewis, and head of the CTA John Gibson. Moreover, the white school board successfully demonstrated that it still could exercise control over black teachers' pay. By the time the appeals court handed down its decision, the school board had already instituted a new rating system that largely preserved existing inequalities.[45] This again made it necessary for black teachers to seek redress through the courts in later years.[46] The teachers' salary suit also highlighted the limitations of civil rights campaigns organized around the self-interests of the black elite. Although the case fostered some amount of community pride by attacking discrimination, the vast majority of the black population was neither involved in nor directly affected by the teachers' salary suit. Consequently, there was no widespread impetus or backing for further action.

In direct contrast to the efforts of ANDA and the CTA, a third instance of black activism in Little Rock during the early 1940s did generate widespread interest and action in the black community. The murder of Sergeant Thomas P. Foster by a white city policeman was part of a nationwide upswing in racial conflict during the Second World War. More than 80 per cent of black soldiers trained at army bases in the South. Many of these came from the North and were unaccustomed to southern racial practices. Consequently, racial tensions heightened, particularly in large urban areas close to those bases. The sight of black troops in uniform in towns and cities, often in large numbers and sometimes armed, was an affront to southerners who believed blacks should be deferential and "know their place." Both on army bases and off, Jim Crow laws were stringently enforced and small-scale scuffles over minor infringements could quickly develop into full-scale riots.[47]

Racial conflict between black soldiers and white military and civilian policemen who enforced Jim Crow policies was a particular source of concern. In 1941, there were reports of fighting between black soldiers and white police at army bases across the South, from Camp Davis, North Carolina, to Camp Wallace, Texas. During 1942, interracial violence escalated. Early that year, an attempt by a white military policeman to arrest a drunken black soldier in Alexandria, Louisiana, sparked a race riot that resulted in the deaths of twenty-eight blacks and nearly three thousand arrests. Throughout the year, a wave of race riots spread across the nation, from Fort Dix, New Jersey, to Vallejo, California.[48]

Arkansas had already experienced racial conflict over black troops before the killing of Foster. In August 1941, the all-black Ninety-fourth Engineers Regiment, composed mostly of men from Chicago and Detroit, went to Louisiana on maneuvers. Many of the soldiers experienced southern racism on the journey from their base in Fort Custer, Michigan, for the first time. At Murfeesboro, Tennessee, the highway patrol harassed the troops. While the unit was stationed at the newly opened army base at Camp Robinson, near Little Rock, a fight between a black sergeant and a white city policeman received a good deal of publicity. A few days' later, three hundred black soldiers from the Ninety-Fourth Engineers went into the small town of Gurdon, Arkansas, on day passes. Local whites instantly demanded their removal. The soldiers were incensed when their white commanding officers ordered them to leave, which they did, hurling abuse at passersby and blocking traffic in town to show their displeasure.[49]

The following night, state policemen arrived at the army camp of the black soldiers, warning them to leave the area quickly to avoid further trouble. As the soldiers moved out the next day, state policemen accosted them, because of complaints about an unruly black "mob" in the vicinity. The policemen began pushing the black soldiers off the road, demanding that the white commanding officers "get them black bastards off the concrete." The regiment retreated into the woods. That night, sixty blacks went AWOL and fled the South. Six of these black soldiers subsequently faced charges of desertion, and five cases went to trial, though there were no convictions. None of the white state policemen, who had broken the law by invading a military camp, faced charges.[50]

The incident at Gurdon and the conflict that had already occurred at Little Rock provided a backdrop to the arrival of the Ninety-Second Engineers, a new black regiment, at Camp Robinson later that year. Ongoing tensions between black soldiers and local whites finally came to a head on March 22, 1942. The episode began with the arrest of Private Albert Glover by two white military policemen for being drunk and disorderly. Glover was in the black downtown area of West Ninth Street on a weekend pass from the army base. Intoxicated, Glover became obstreperous and resisted the efforts of the two military policemen to take him back to the army base. Two nearby city policemen, Abner J. Hay and George Henson, decided to intervene. The two policemen rushed to the scene and beat Glover over the head repeatedly with their nightsticks, causing a head wound that began to bleed profusely. The military policemen took Glover to a first-aid station located on the eight hundred block of West Ninth Street.[51]

The scuffle between Glover and the policemen in the busy downtown area drew a mainly black crowd of about four hundred people. Henson stood outside the first-aid station, his gun drawn and trained on the crowd.[52] Inside, Glover remained uncooperative, refused to submit to treatment, and insisted he would not leave the downtown area until he found "the boy [he] came into town with." The military police then dragged him outside to a truck that stood waiting to take him back to the army base.[53]

Just as Glover exited from the building, Foster, a twenty-five-year-old black North Carolinian, also of the Ninety-Second Engineers and on a pass from Camp Robinson, saw the commotion outside the first-aid station. Foster pushed through the crowd and demanded to know why the two white military policemen were handling the case in such a manner. The black sergeant protested in particular at the involvement of the two city police officers. Foster explained he had direct orders from his superiors to investigate and take charge of any incidents occurring in town involving the men of the Ninety-Second Engineers. One of the military policemen told Foster that if he did not like the way they were dealing with Glover, he could investigate it later. In an attempt to calm rising tempers, the other military policeman offered to take Foster to speak with a superior. Foster stood his ground and insisted upon an immediate justification for the heavy-handed treatment of Glover. At that point, the military policemen placed Foster under arrest and attempted to remove him from the scene by force. Each grabbed an arm, and they dragged Foster down West Ninth Street. Enraged at this treatment, Foster broke loose, whereupon the two military policemen grabbed him again, and a fight ensued.[54]

The crowd that had formed outside the first-aid station followed the struggle between Foster and the military policemen down West Ninth Street. Some demanded Foster's release. When that failed, they attempted to free the sergeant themselves. In the ensuing melee, one of the military policemen lost his nightstick and drew a pistol. When Foster saw the gun, he grabbed hold of its cylinder, attempting to divert its aim. The other military policeman then hit him over the head with his nightstick to make him release his grasp. During the scuffle, the pistol went off, and city policeman Hay fired his gun in the air to clear the crowd. Foster pulled clear of the policemen and stumbled across the road. A section of the crowd followed and found Foster backed into an alcove. Hay offered to grab Foster and put him in the army truck for transportation back to Camp Robinson if the two military policemen would clear a path through the crowd. They agreed to the plan.[55]

However, when the military policemen parted the crowd, instead of apprehending Foster, Hay dived on top of him, and another fight ensued. When it appeared Foster was getting the better of Hay, the other policemen weighed in with their nightsticks, hitting Foster over the head repeatedly until, dazed and semiconscious, he let go of Hay.[56]

Hay immediately stood up and emptied his gun into Foster's prostrate body, hitting him with four shots, three in the stomach, one in the arm, with a fifth bullet going astray.[57] Further incensing black onlookers, Hay then calmly filled and lighted his pipe and blew smoke over the dying soldier's body as they waited for an ambulance to arrive.[58] At the hospital, doctors operated on Foster, but he died a few hours later.[59] While Foster received treatment, city policemen flooded into the black downtown area of West Ninth Street to quell what the *Arkansas Gazette* termed the "riot" that followed. Officials at Camp Robinson took immediate steps to diffuse the situation by sending a convoy of army trucks into town to round up all black soldiers in Little Rock and return them to camp.[60]

The following day, investigations of the incident began. In Little Rock, chief of police J. A. Pitcock and deputy coroner Dr. C. C. Reed Jr. took charge of the proceedings. At Camp Robinson, a board of inquiry was set up to determine whether Foster had died in the line of duty.[61] While military investigations continued, the city investigation within three days ruled that the shooting of Foster by Hay was a "justifiable homicide." Reed declared that statements given by the military police corroborated Hay's testimony "in every detail" in insisting that Foster had grabbed Hay's nightstick and was about to attack when the policeman shot in self-defense. For his part, Pitcock considered banning the sale of alcohol on Saturday and Sunday nights in some black areas of town, but beyond that he took no further action.[62]

As far as the white authorities in Little Rock were concerned, the matter ended there. The reaction from the black community was not so casual. In particular, black anger was inflamed and sustained by *State Press* reports of the incident.

The owners of the *State Press* were Lucious Christopher ("L.C.") Bates and his wife, Daisy. Bates was born to Rev. Morris and Lula Bates in Liberty, Mississippi, in 1901, and was reared in Indianola, Mississippi. Because of his father's good community standing, Bates was allowed to attend an all-white grammar school in Indianola, although he could not officially enroll at the school because of the state's segregation laws. From an early age, he worked in a local print shop, and he decided he would become a journalist. After finishing high school, he studied journalism at Alcorn A&M College in Mississippi and then at Wilberforce University in Ohio. Impatient to embark upon his chosen career, he left Wilberforce before graduating and joined the staff of the *Kansas City Call* in Missouri, where he worked under Roy Wilkins, who later became executive secretary of the NAACP. After moving to publish his own paper in Pueblo, Colorado, Bates subsequently worked on black newspapers in California and in Memphis, Tennessee. He lost his job during the depression and turned to selling insurance. It was through selling an insurance policy to her foster father that Bates met his future wife, Daisy Lee Gatson.[63]

Daisy Gatson was born in 1914 and reared in the small sawmill town of Huttig in southwest Arkansas. The discrimination she experienced while growing up in Huttig made her determined to take a stand for civil rights. In particular, the knowledge that her mother had been raped and killed by a group of local white men when Daisy was still an infant embittered her against southern white supremacy. Raised by foster parents in Huttig, Daisy rebelled against whites and blacks in the community, the former for perpetrating discrimination and the latter for appearing to accept it. On his deathbed, Daisy's foster father implored her to work positively for civil rights. "Hate can destroy you," he warned. "Don't hate white people just because they are white. If you hate, make it count for something. Hate the humiliations we are living under in the South. Hate the discrimination that eats away at the soul of every black man and woman . . . and then try to do something about it, or your hate won't spell a thing."[64]

Shortly after the Bateses moved to Little Rock in 1939, L. C. tried to convince Daisy that they should set up a newspaper as a vehicle for their commitment to black activism and civil rights. At first she objected, fearing the venture would bankrupt them both. Ultimately, their conviction that "a newspaper was needed to carry on the fight for Negro rights" in the city persuaded them.[65]

As in other cities during the Second World War, the dissenting voice of a militant black newspaper played a significant role in shaping black activism in Little Rock.[66] The Bateses purchased the *Twin City Press* in 1941, renamed it the *Arkansas State Press*, and published the first of its weekly issues on May 9, 1941. The newspaper's motto, "This Paper Stands For Honesty, Justice and Fair Play. And It Stands Behind What It Stands For," declared its intent for uncompromising journalism. The *State Press* offered a varied diet of local, regional, and national news, focusing particularly on civil rights issues in front-page headlines and editorials. At its peak in 1952, the newspaper had a circulation of twenty-two thousand, with approximately one thousand of its readers living outside of Arkansas. The *State Press* had offices in several Arkansas cities and a distribution network in a number of counties, making it the largest and most influential black newspaper in the state. Bates believed that a significant number of whites bought the newspaper to keep in touch with black community affairs.[67] The Bateses were good friends of Flowers, who connected the couple to black activist efforts statewide. The *State Press* helped disseminate the program of the CNO in Little Rock, carrying news of and lending support to its campaigns across the state. In turn, Flowers wrote for the *State Press* and regarded the Bateses' home as a welcome stopover whenever he visited Little Rock.[68]

The *State Press* encountered some competition from the more conservative *Southern Mediator Journal*, founded by black publisher and editor

C. H. Jones in the late 1930s. With the motto "We Lift As We Serve," the *Southern Mediator Journal*, like the *State Press*, published local, regional, and national news, but it presented an accommodationist perspective. As a much smaller operation, the *Southern Mediator Journal*'s influence did not extend much outside of Little Rock.[69]

The *State Press* reported the shooting of Foster as one of the "most bestial murders in the annals of Little Rock tragedies" and gave the story extensive front-page coverage.[70] Unhappy with the investigation of the white city authorities, the newspaper pressured local black leaders to form a committee to further examine the case.[71] The findings of the black investigation committee, which included respected members of Little Rock's black elite, were unequivocal on the matter. The committee declared that Hay clearly exceeded his authority and used unnecessary force. Directly contradicting the white investigation, the committee claimed that "white and colored" witnesses had confirmed that Hay was not under threat from Foster when he shot the soldier. Rather, Hay had "deliberately stood over Sgt. Foster while he lay helpless on the ground . . . and pumped five bullets into [him]."[72]

The dogged reporting of the *State Press*, together with the formation of a Negro Citizens' Committee (NCC), meant that interest in the Foster case grew in the city and the state. The NCC planned to deliver its findings at a public meeting on Sunday, March 29, at the First Baptist Church in Little Rock. A large crowd gathered for the meeting, with blacks from across the state turning up to hear the evidence. Secretary of the NCC, J. H. McConico, read the principal findings. First, the NCC found that Foster was unarmed and prostrate on the ground when Hay shot him and that "regardless of what had transpired previously, the shooting was unjustifiable." Second, the NCC declared that the white military police stood "idly by" and did not offer proper protection to prevent the shooting of the soldier. Third, the NCC contended no rioting took place in the aftermath of the shooting, as had been reported in the white newspapers. Furthermore, the crowd had not attempted to interfere with civil or military officers but rather "under the influence of mass psychology [the crowd] attempted to push up as close to the center of excitement as possible."[73]

The meeting ended with a resolution to send the report of the NCC, along with a petition for a more thorough investigation of events, to the mayor of Little Rock, the Little Rock prosecuting attorney, and the U.S. district attorney. Copies of the affidavits and petitions went to President

Franklin D. Roosevelt, U.S. Secretary of War Henry L. Stimson, and the commanding general at Camp Robinson, Brig. Gen. Francis B. Mallon.[74] In response to the letter sent to Little Rock prosecuting attorney Sam Robinson, the NCC received a reply promising a thorough investigation of Foster's death. In spite of this, no fewer than four subsequent reports returned the same verdict of justifiable homicide. Continued pressure from the *State Press* and the NAACP's national office, together with the national news coverage the case began to attract, finally helped bring federal intervention.[75] Federal officials previously had dismissed such incidents as local concerns. However, earlier in 1942, the Japanese had used the lynching of Cleo Wright in Missouri as a propaganda tool to embarrass the United States about its human rights record. Consequently, the federal government's policy of noninvolvement in racial issue cases began to change.[76]

Inspector General of the War Department Virgil L. Peterson reviewed the Camp Robinson investigation and found significant conflict between its findings and those of city officials. Although the Camp Robinson report stated Foster's death was a result of "misconduct," since he "unlawfully resisted arrest," it also criticized the military policemen's handling of the situation with Private Glover. More important, the Camp Robinson report found fault with the actions of Hay: "[P]oliceman Hay was too hasty in opening fire [and] his further action of firing three more shots into the body of Sergeant Foster and then lighting his pipe nearly caused a riot and are major factors in the present state of tension existing between the two races in this area at the present time."[77] Peterson's office was informally advised that the Civil Rights Section of the Criminal Division at the Department of Justice was interested in the case because the circumstances surrounding the shooting seemed to be "far from justifiable." The crux of the matter, Peterson believed, was the "necessity that soldiers, white or colored, be afforded protection when on a pass in a civilian community."[78]

In late 1942, the case against Hay finally came before the federal grand jury of the Eastern Arkansas Division in Little Rock. U.S. Attorney General Francis Biddle sent a special assistant, Frank Patton, to present the case. On the opening day of the proceedings, blacks packed the courtroom. From the outset, however, it was apparent that even in a federal court white intimidation played a role in the case. Judge Trimble advised the twenty-three jurors, which included three token blacks, to use "common sense" in returning a verdict. Trimble pointed out that they should indict Hay only if it "would . . . serve some useful purpose."[79]

After hearing testimony from twenty-five of the forty-three witnesses called, including ten blacks, it took just two days for the jury to reach its verdict not to indict Hay, by a vote of nineteen to four, even though the shooting of Foster by Hay, the grand jury reported, had been "investigated, considered, and ignored." Testimony from white witnesses indicating Hay had fired at Foster only when under attack partly helped secure the police officer's release.[80] Of more influence in the case, the attorney general's office concluded, was the "strong racial sentiment" involved, together with the cunning ploy of the defense attorney in announcing that Hay had enrolled in the army. The racial element involved and the sense of not serving "some useful purpose" by indicting a white soldier were the two key factors that the attorney general's office believed had allowed Hay to escape conviction.[81] The verdict of the grand jury left Little Rock's black citizens far from satisfied. Outrage in the black community led to a *State Press* crusade to highlight the mistreatment of both black soldiers and civilians by white city policemen. The Bateses called for black police officers to be instated to patrol black areas. The campaign proved so venomous that white city businessmen, fearful of a negative effect on the city's image, attempted to put the paper out of circulation by withholding advertising revenue. When that failed, they offered a direct bribe to editor L. C. Bates to let up on the criticism. The Bateses weathered the boycott, refused the bribe, and continued to campaign for black police officers.[82]

Wary of the sentiments expressed by the black population, white city newspapers began to join in the debate about the Foster killing. The *Arkansas Democrat* claimed the issue was not about police brutality but that the incident was being used as part of a "nation-wide campaign by the black press and the [NAACP] to use the war to undermine white supremacy on the home front."[83] Contrary to these claims of sedition, the army backed the demands made by the *State Press*. When a new detachment of black troops arrived at Camp Robinson in August 1942, their white commanding officer Major Richard Donovan also pressed for changes. Donavan suggested to local white businessmen that white city police officers "make less use of the night-stick technique of reasoning with black soldiers." Donavan also advocated the hiring of black police officers to patrol black areas to prevent a repeat of the tragedy that befell Foster.[84]

Donovan's remarks, the campaign by the *State Press*, and pressure exerted by the white business community finally led to the appointment of Little Rock's first black police officers. Even then, the appointments did not come without substantial opposition from the Little Rock Police Association (LRPA). In an effort to guard white supremacy on the force, the LRPA complained that black officers would not police black areas strictly enough, which would lead to further lawlessness. The Little Rock City Council chose to ignore the objections. Eventually, eight black policemen were hired to patrol black areas, albeit with only limited powers of arrest.[85]

The episodes of black protest during the Second World War demonstrated that although there was evidence of increasing racial consciousness in the black community, there remained a great deal of opposition to alterations in the racial order in the white community. Whites proved more than capable of thwarting embryonic black protest through a variety of mechanisms. Informal pressures and implicit threats of retribution effectively prevented the mobilization of the black community in the first place. If black protest did occur, white power could be deployed at a number of levels to halt it, as the threats to Robinson and the firing of Morris and other school teachers demonstrated. Even if black protest did manage to overcome these obstacles, it met with racism in the courts. Local and state judges in the South shared the racial outlook of the rest of southern society. Few were willing to rule in favor of civil rights. Only by taking complaints to higher federal courts did black activists stand a chance of a fair hearing. Still there were no guarantees of success, as any decisions were still subject to local white discretion when and if they were implemented.

During the postwar period, white reactions to black activism began to change. Efforts by local blacks coincided with a rising tide of black militancy nationwide. Notably, the growing numbers of black voters in the North, who had escaped southern disfranchisement, were beginning to make an impact on national politics. In 1947, responding to shifts in the electorate, President Harry S. Truman appointed a Committee on Civil Rights to investigate racial discrimination and charged its members with finding ways to address the issue. Later that year, the committee produced a report, *To Secure These Rights*. The report proposed civil rights measures including legislation to end lynching, to remove obstacles to black voting, and to end segregation in areas such as interstate transport.[86] A year later, according to sociologist Jack Bloom, "treatment of blacks emerged as a central issue for the first time ever in a presidential election."[87] The Supreme Court also responded to a changing racial climate. Throughout the early 1940s, the Court had taken an increasingly emboldened stance against black disfranchisement in the South, culminating in the landmark *Smith v. Allwright* decision. In the late 1940s, the Court began to extend its rulings against white supremacy to higher education.[88]

Whites across the South grew wary of shifting national sentiments concerning civil rights. With the federal government less likely to tolerate civil rights violations or support overt racism, white Arkansans found they had to rethink the nature of the racial order within the state. The tension between rising black activism coupled with federal pressure and whites' desire to maintain the status quo helped usher in a new era in race relations.

Postwar Reform and Its Limitations | 3

The election of Sidney Sanders McMath as governor in 1948 indicated Arkansas might respond to a changing social and racial climate voluntarily, without the need for federal government intervention. McMath was part of a southern movement that pressed for regional reform based on a platform pledging better public health, education, and welfare. This so-called "G.I. Revolt" (McMath was a former marine, and many of the other new southern politicians were also ex-servicemen) promoted economic growth and industrialization as a cure for southern financial and social ills. The GI politicians also recognized that to make a start on tackling poverty and social deprivation in the South inevitably meant including blacks in the program of reform. Blacks took heart from this, with even the normally skeptical *State Press* declaring that in the 1948 elections "FOR THE FIRST TIME IN OUR LIVES we felt we were voting for SOMETHING."[1]

President-elect Harry S. Truman hailed McMath as "governor of one of the most progressive states in the Union." Truman added, "Arkansas stands on the threshold of a great opportunity. It can go forward with progress under . . . enlightened leadership." Yet, the election of McMath proved a false dawn. Two successive administrations failed to live up to the high expectations of change the 1948 election promised. Across the South, the drive for economic and social progress crumbled due to a conservative retrenchment and allegations of corruption that haunted many of the GI state governments. Instead, it would take growing federal pressure, coupled with the efforts of black activists, to transform race relations in Arkansas in the late 1940s and early 1950s.[2]

The first indication of racial change in Arkansas came in 1948 when the University of Arkansas Law School admitted a black graduate student. This resulted from demands issued by black Arkansans and a series of federal court decisions in the area of black graduate education won by NAACP lawyers. The first success for the NAACP was in *Missouri ex rel. Gaines v. Canada* (1938). In that case, the Supreme Court ruled that states could not furnish black graduates with out-of-state scholarships to avoid the issue of a failure to provide black graduate facilities. However, the Court still left open the possibility of maintaining segregation in higher education by providing separate state graduate schools for blacks. This was upheld in *Sipuel v. Board of Regents* (1948), when the University of Oklahoma opted to furnish separate law school facilities for Ada Lois Sipuel, the one black student in the state who applied for admission.[3]

Applications from other prospective black graduate students in Oklahoma subsequently highlighted the impracticality of maintaining separate graduate schools for blacks. Faced with the impossible economic burden of providing separate but equal facilities in a number of academic disciplines, the University of Oklahoma reluctantly allowed blacks into formerly all-white graduate schools. In an effort to discourage such applications, the university made life as unpleasant as possible for black students. It implemented demeaning segregated arrangements, such as forcing black students to sit partitioned from whites by a screen in classrooms, providing segregated library facilities, and limiting the use of the refectory to inconvenient hours. When LDF lawyers challenged this segregated regime in *McLaurin v. Oklahoma State Regents* (1950), the Supreme Court upheld the contention that the segregated arrangements did not provide a truly equal education. The day afterward, in *Sweatt v. Painter*, the Court declared that a separate law school provided for black graduates in Texas was not equal to that of whites in terms of facilities and staff. By implication, the Court indicated, unless graduate facilities were identical for whites and blacks—a situation southern states clearly could not financially afford and were unwilling to provide—they were unconstitutional. Although the Court drew back from explicitly declaring an end to segregation, its rulings, by denouncing every conceivable alternative, rendered segregated graduate education legally indefensible.[4]

It was against the backdrop of increasing pressure by LDF lawyers on southern universities that the University of Arkansas first addressed the issue of racial inequality. In 1941, Scipio Jones wrote to dean of the law school J. S. Waterman on behalf of Prentice Hilburn. Hilburn, Jones informed Waterman, wished to pursue graduate study in law. Jones suggested the best way to handle the matter would be for the law school at Fayetteville to pay out-of-state tuition fees. This would allow Hilburn to continue his studies elsewhere and was in line with the established policy of some other southern states.[5]

Using the *Gaines* ruling for negotiation, Jones hoped to establish a precedent for out-of-state scholarships in Arkansas as a preferable compromise to further legal challenges. Unmoved by the appeal, Waterman insisted that there were no state laws that required the university to fund the education of black graduates. This unsatisfactory reply prompted Jones to set up a meeting with university officials at which he reminded them of the implications of the *Gaines* decision should they fail to meet his relatively modest request. Persuaded by his reasoning, the university agreed to pay a onetime sum of $134.50 toward Hilburn's tuition.[6] Shortly afterward, Flowers managed to win additional out-of-state scholarships for black graduates, and the arrangement became the established norm in Arkansas.[7]

Out-of-state scholarships managed to stave off further attempts to press for improved black educational opportunities in Arkansas until 1946. That year, a black student from Little Rock, Clifford Davis, applied for admission to the law school with the help and counsel of Flowers. The new dean of the law school, Robert A. Leflar, considered Davis's request seriously in the light of contemporary Court rulings. Leflar drafted five possible responses to prospective black applicants. First, he considered allowing black students to enter the university in principle and then contriving a disqualification other than race to deny them admission. The drawback to this approach was that it threatened to bring the university into disrepute and could not guard against further legal action by black applicants. Second, he considered the option of increasing the amount of money awarded to black out-of-state scholarship students to make the option look more attractive. This, however, depended upon the cooperation of those students and again did not prevent the possibility of further legal action. Third, he considered promoting the idea of a regional graduate school for blacks to comply with the *Gaines* decision. The expense of this, together with its dubious constitutionality, led Leflar to reject that option. Fourth, he considered taking a confrontational approach, point-blank refusing admission to black students. To pursue this course of action would involve taking a risk on litigation developing and then dealing with consequences as they arose. Again, this had the disadvantage of making the university a center of unwanted attention. The fifth option Leflar considered was to allow blacks to enroll at the university under a segregated regime similar to that of the neighboring University of Oklahoma.[8]

Leflar presented his findings first to the chair of the board of trustees of the university, Herbert L. Thomas, who agreed to discuss the matter with other board members at the next meeting. Once raised, the issue came as no great shock. In fact, the board had discussed informally for a number of years the possibility of such an application's arising.[9] The cases before the courts in the neighboring states of Oklahoma and Missouri had helped intensify the debate.[10] In June 1946, the board of trustees agreed they would hand Leflar, one of the nation's leading authorities on constitutional issues, discretionary powers to act as he saw fit.[11]

Leflar immediately began to try to win backing for his proposal to admit black students while preserving the ethos of segregation. In April 1947, he addressed the Arkansas Bar Association in Hot Springs, with Gov. Benjamin Laney in attendance. Laney was an important figure in winning widespread approval for the plan, but also a staunch segregationist. When President Truman's Committee on Civil Rights produced *To Secure These Rights* later that year, Laney roundly denounced its proposals for racial justice as "[d]istasteful, unthinkable, and ridiculous." He vowed to oppose them, "even to extreme measures." In 1948, Laney emerged as a leader of the Dixiecrat revolt, as states' rights Democrats sought to oppose the reelection of Truman and a Democratic Party that supported civil rights pledges.[12]

In presenting his findings to the bar association, Leflar drew particular attention to the cost of establishing a separate law school for blacks. He estimated that it would initially cost $100,000 to build such a school, with $20,000 needed every year for maintenance. Under his plan, Leflar pointed out, the costs incurred by the state would be only $3,000 to $5,000 per year to hire an extra lecturer. Laney remained unconvinced. Nevertheless, afterward, the governor told Leflar in private that he respected his judgment enough to leave the matter in his hands and promised not to interfere.[13]

Meanwhile, Clifford Davis continued in his attempts to gain admission to the law school. On August 25, 1946, he wrote to Leflar, inquiring about the status of his application. Leflar, stalling, advised Davis that his application was still incomplete and that in view of the large veteran enrollment for the year he might not make the university's quota for entry. However, Leflar assured Davis that the university was working on a plan to enable blacks to attend graduate classes in the not-too-distant future. After several more exchanges, Leflar revealed his plan to admit black students on a segregated basis. Leflar told Davis that if he wanted to enroll for the forthcoming February semester, he would have to pay an advance fee of $70 by December 15, 1947. The deadline passed without any more letters, or payment of fees, from Davis.[14]

Events came to a head at the beginning of 1948, just before the start of the February semester. At the Conference on Graduate and Professional Educational Opportunities for the Negro in Arkansas held at Arkansas AM&N on January 30, Governor Laney extolled the idea of a regional graduate school for southern blacks. However, as Laney spoke, it became clear many of his audience were unenthusiastic about the plan. Toward the end of the meeting, an undergraduate student at Arkansas AM&N, Wiley A. Branton, announced that he intended to apply for admission to the University of Arkansas in business administration the following week. Branton made it clear that if university officials refused to enroll him, he fully intended to pursue the matter through the courts. Flustered, Laney promptly ended the meeting.[15]

The application of Branton complicated matters for the university. The board of trustees had already agreed not to admit black undergraduate students if similar courses were available for them at Arkansas AM&N. Lewis Webster Jones, president of the University of Arkansas, and Thomas, chair of the board of trustees, therefore agreed not to grant Branton admission, but to admit Davis if he could prove he met the required academic standards. The two university officials accordingly instructed law school personnel to make the necessary arrangements for the admission of a black graduate student. Thomas then began to call board members at their homes to ask for support. Most, in light of the recent discussions, readily agreed. The final decision came, Thomas remembered in later years, only with the realization that "segregation laws existing in Arkansas never could survive a high Federal Court case."[16]

No significant opposition to the decision emerged in the state from either white politicians or the white population at large. Undoubtedly, this in part reflected the fact that the university was located in one of northwest Arkansas' more tolerant cities, far removed from the Delta, where race relations were particularly fraught with tension. Nevertheless, there was also a clear recognition that outside of massive expense to the state or the risk of losing a court case, which might lead to wholesale integration, there was really only one option. Even Governor Laney acknowledged that the university had acted correctly under the circumstances. Yet Laney was quick to add that the "improvement of Negro educational facilities is the prime objective of efforts to enroll Negroes in established white schools. . . . Abolishing racial segregation won't work in this country, and those people who have it in their minds had better get it out."[17]

One important source of support for the university was the *Arkansas Gazette*. The newspaper was a venerable Arkansas institution, published since 1819 and based in Little Rock since the founding of the city in 1821. For much of the twentieth century the *Arkansas Gazette* was under ownership of one family. From 1902 until his death at the age of one hundred in 1972, J. N. Heiskell was president and editor of the newspaper. Under Heiskell, the *Arkansas Gazette* developed a reputation for freethinking and generally rose above the petty factionalism of Arkansas politics, becoming Arkansas' leading white newspaper. The *Arkansas Gazette* often took a moderate stance on controversial issues and sought to temper the rural conservatism that dominated much of Arkansas.[18]

The reputation for moderation and reason in the *Arkansas Gazette* grew during the postwar era, in no small part owing to the arrival of executive editor Harry S. Ashmore. Born in Greenville, South Carolina, in 1916, Ashmore began his career in journalism at the *Greenville Piedmont* and the *Greenville News* before he moved to the North Carolina *Charlotte News* in 1939. In 1941, he won a Nieman Fellowship to Harvard. Ashmore enlisted in the army in 1942, taking part in European campaigns and rising to the rank of lieutenant colonel. Upon his return, Ashmore rejoined the *Charlotte News*, where he became associate editor and then, in 1947, editor. In line with the sentiments of many other returning GIs, Ashmore's editorials urged the building of a more progressive South. Thus, Ashmore campaigned for two-party politics, racial and religious tolerance, the right of blacks to vote, and higher pay for teachers. In April 1947, Ashmore addressed the American Society of Newspaper Editors in Little Rock, impressing J. N. Heiskell, who recruited him as executive editor of the *Arkansas Gazette* and put him in charge of editorials. At the *Arkansas Gazette*, Ashmore continued to write editorials promoting southern progress, enhancing the reputation of the newspaper as a significant force for modernization.[19]

As in many other cities at the time, the *Arkansas Gazette* was competing with another newspaper, the *Arkansas Democrat*. After changing ownership and names several times during Reconstruction, the *Arkansas Democrat* began continuous publication in 1878. Between 1926 and 1968 the *Arkansas Democrat* came under the control of one man, K. August Engel, president and general manager. The *Arkansas Democrat*, published in the afternoon, tended to be more conservative than the morning *Arkansas Gazette*. The *Arkansas Democrat* also, according to its critics at the *Arkansas Gazette*, tended to pander to popular sentiment rather than challenge prevailing public opinion. Ashmore claimed that since Engel began his journalistic career as a bookkeeper, he "had never been known to take a position on any issue that threatened his balance sheet."[20]

On Monday morning, February 2, 1948, the first day of enrollment for spring term, Lewis Webster Jones learned that Branton and another black student, Silas Hunt, were on their way to Fayetteville.[21] Hunt replaced Davis, who decided at the last minute not to apply for admission.[22]

Wiley A. Branton, born in Pine Bluff, Arkansas, in 1923, belonged to one of the city's prominent black families. Branton's father, Leo, owned a taxicab company in Pine Bluff, which operated from the same Masonic building in which Flowers printed the *CNO Spectator*.[23] Branton's great-grandfather was Choctaw Chief Greenwood Leflore. This fact contributed to his light-colored complexion, which fooled many people into thinking he was "white."[24] After briefly working in his father's taxicab business, Branton enrolled at Arkansas AM&N in 1941. In 1943, Branton entered the army, where he served as a battalion construction foreman in Saipan and Okinawa during the Second World War. Upon his return, Branton took over his father's business while continuing his education at Arkansas AM&N.[25]

Hunt, born in Ashdown, southwest Arkansas, in 1922, came from a more modest family background; his parents lived mostly on relief during the 1930s. After moving to Oklahoma briefly, the family settled in Texarkana, in southwest Arkansas, in 1936, where Silas attended Washington High School. He graduated as class salutatorian in 1941 and enrolled at Arkansas AM&N, where he worked a number of jobs during his first year to pay his way, including construction work at Pine Bluff Arsenal. Hunt's excellent academic record during his first year earned him financial aid for the rest of his undergraduate career. Like Branton, Hunt suffered an interruption in his education during the Second World War when he was drafted into the army and served with the construction engineers in Europe. Seriously wounded at the Battle of the Bulge, Hunt, after recovering from his injuries, returned to Arkansas AM&N, where he graduated in 1947.[26]

Branton and Hunt had been friends since enrolling together at Arkansas AM&N in 1941. When they returned from the Second World War, they were increasingly dissatisfied at their ongoing second-class treatment in Pine Bluff and often discussed how they could take a stand to promote civil rights in Arkansas. One major influence was their former classmate, Ada Lois Sipuel, who took on authorities at the University of Oklahoma by applying to study at its segregated law school. Branton and Hunt attempted to follow Sipuel's lead, but their applications to study at the University of Arkansas failed to meet with success. Hunt had his bags packed to study law at the University of Indiana when he heard that university officials in Arkansas were willing to consider black applicants.[27]

Hunt and Branton arrived at Fayetteville, accompanied by Flowers and Geleve Grice, a black photographer from Arkansas AM&N. Hunt's grades were checked, and he was allowed to enroll for classes. University officials refused to enroll Branton as an undergraduate student. University president Jones met with the delegation briefly and discussed the segregated arrangements under which Hunt would study. Chiefly, this would involve attending classes in the basement of the law building, using the library only through a white intermediary, and eating alone, since he would not be able to use the university cafeteria.[28]

Despite the segregated regimen envisioned by university authorities, Hunt's stay at Fayetteville turned out to be far less lonely than expected. Some white students chose to attend Hunt's lectures in the basement of the law building because they believed they received better instruction in the smaller classes. A small but significant number of white students did offer more genuine support in a variety of ways, from eating lunch with Hunt in his segregated classroom to going to his home for study sessions. Unfortunately, Hunt's admission to the University of Arkansas had a tragic ending. A recurrence of medical problems related to his wartime service forced Hunt to withdraw from studies before completing his first semester. Hunt died just three months later at a Veterans Hospital in Springfield, Missouri.[29]

Hunt's admission to the law school in February 1948 opened an important path. The next black student to study law at Fayetteville, Jackie Shropshire, enrolled the following autumn and became the first black student to graduate from the University of Arkansas in 1951. An increased enrollment of graduates in 1949 meant that more white students studied with Shropshire in his basement classroom. To counteract this creeping integration, university authorities built a wooden railing to fence Shropshire off from the rest of the class. A few days later, at the insistence of white students, the railing was removed. Other black graduates followed Hunt and Shropshire through the law school during the next few years, including Branton, Christopher Mercer, George Haley, and George Howard Jr. Each of these new entrants played an important role in the development of black activism in Arkansas. In particular, they provided the NAACP with able black lawyers at a grassroots level who could pursue the cause of civil rights through the courts.[30]

The admission of black students to the law school at Fayetteville also paved the way for the admission of blacks to the medical school at Little Rock. In the spring of 1948, Jones received an urgent call from the dean of the medical school, Henry Chenault. A black applicant, Elizabeth Mae Irby, wished to enroll. Jones, this time without hesitation, told Chenault to proceed according to the already established policy and to admit Irby to the medical school. Irby enrolled without incident the following autumn semester. As happened with the law school, Irby's admission brought more successful applicants to study at the University of Arkansas Medical School. Again, this helped produce qualified, professional people who would have a significant impact on the future development of black activism.[31]

The admission of the first black postgraduate students in 1948 was the beginning of a long process of desegregation at the University of Arkansas. After the Supreme Court's school desegregation ruling in *Brown*, the university began to admit black undergraduate students. In 1955, Billy Rose Whitfield, Maxine Sutton, and Marjorie Wilkins were the first black undergraduates to enroll in the university's nursing program. In 1963, black undergraduate George Whitfield, brother of Billy Rose Whitfield, successfully sued the university for the integration of campus dormitories. In 1966, black students formed Black Americans for Democracy to promote a better black social life on campus and to fight lingering vestiges of racial discrimination. In 1969, the university hired its first black academic, Gordon D. Morgan, as associate professor in the sociology department. The same year, the university launched a black studies program. In the 1970s, black athletes played on all of the university's sports teams. By then, Morgan claimed, "blacks were given most of the reasonable concessions they requested."[32]

While the desegregation of the state law and medical schools constituted encouraging signs of racial progress, those developments were the exception in 1948. Moreover, they occurred only in direct response to threats from federal courts to uphold civil rights in the specific area of higher education. In most communities across the state, the segregated order remained wholly intact. One clear exception to this was Little Rock, the only city to follow the lead of the university authorities in addressing racial issues by instigating a subtle and complex rearrangement of segregation in a number of areas.

The first sign of change in Little Rock came with the tentative experiment of desegregating the public library. At first, a few blacks sat out of sight at the back of the building. Gradually, over a number of years, blacks were permitted more extensive use of facilities. Blacks also gained admission to a selected few of the city's public parks. However, this was only by prearrangement, in small numbers, and with restrictions, such as prohibited use of the swimming pools or the golf course. The Little Rock Zoo began to admit blacks, but only on Thursdays and with use of the amusement park and picnic areas discouraged. Pfeiffer, a downtown department store, built a segregated lunch counter to cater to black customers who previously had been refused service altogether. Other establishments removed the "white" and "colored" signs from drinking fountains but still stringently enforced segregated rest rooms. Downtown hotels began to allow groups such as the Urban League to hold interracial meetings at their facilities but still seated blacks and whites at different tables for lunch. By the early 1950s, hotels were accepting group bookings of visiting black sports teams while still prohibiting black individuals from renting a room. The *Arkansas Gazette* and *Arkansas Democrat* changed their policy of denying courtesy titles of "Mr." and "Mrs." to blacks, dropping "Mr." except for members of the clergy (black and white) and applying "Mrs." equally. The first press pictures of blacks in white newspapers began to appear. The *Arkansas Democrat* even hired Ozell Sutton, the first black reporter to work for a white newspaper, to write a weekly column about news in the black community.[33]

The easing of certain racial restrictions was in reality little more than tokenism. All the measures essentially preserved the ethos of social separation between the races within what the white community deemed to be the acceptable boundaries of Jim Crow. The fundamental goal of the changes was to enable whites to retain control over the segregated system by self-regulating reforms rather than risk being forced to change more radically by federal order. Nevertheless, within such a hitherto rigid structure of racial segregation, these developments were significant. As federal rulings began to undermine segregation, whites in the capital city became increasingly worried about the possibility of racial change in their locality. Many were aware the black community had already demonstrated that it was able and prepared to take its grievances to the courts.[34]

The fear of enforced change to the racial order was compounded by changes taking place within the black community during the postwar era, which led to new leaders and organizations coming to prominence in the city. A growing dissatisfaction with established leaders in Little Rock's black community led to its own "G.I. Revolt." In the vanguard of the movement was Charles Bussey, who led a band of ex-servicemen to form the VGGA, a direct response, he said, to "the way we were being treated by the elders of the city of Little Rock—black and white."[35] Bussey helped form another group, the EECL, led by Jeffrey Hawkins, to represent the interests of the run-down east end of the city, where a large number of blacks lived. I. S. McClinton, another member of the new cadre of emerging black politicos, challenged Robinson's claim to speak for black Democrats in the city. McClinton attempted to usurp Robinson's authority by forming his own Young Negro Democrats organization, which later became the Arkansas Democratic Voters Association (ADVA). Rev. W. H. Bass also emerged as a community spokesperson through his affiliation with the Little Rock Urban League branch.[36]

These aspiring community leaders issued a direct challenge to the way the established black elite addressed racial issues. Typically new arrivals to the city from rural areas and predominantly drawn from working-class backgrounds, they looked to build upon an enlivened constituency of support for civil rights. Perceiving the change in sympathy for their struggle at the national level and drawing upon the support of growing numbers of registered black voters, they began to issue demands for change.[37]

Yet, not everyone in the black community saw these postwar developments as beneficial. The *State Press* remained skeptical about the possibility of meaningful change. The Bateses complained that some blacks posing as leaders were interested in self-aggrandizement rather than in advancing the cause of the race as a whole.[38] At best, the *State Press* claimed, they still settled for reform rather than exerting pressure to end the existing system of racial discrimination altogether.[39] The *State Press* echoed the increasingly belligerent line of the NAACP that nothing short of a complete end to segregation would suffice. Often, *State Press* editorials went so far as to suggest that the new aspiring black leaders were re-tarding the black community's progress. By still settling for second best, they were to blame in part for the absence of black "parks, playgrounds, enough Negro police, employment . . . and other lacks."[40]

No single episode illustrated the complexities and subtleties of race relations in Little Rock during the postwar era more vividly than did the struggle to establish a park for blacks. The fight actually began at a meet-ing of the Little Rock City Council Finance and Parks Committee on November 22, 1934. On that date, the committee authorized Mayor Horace A. Knowlton to begin negotiations to acquire a 497–acre tract of land located six miles south of the city to develop as a park for blacks.[41] The city decided it would offer the park as "sop" to appease the black population since it was planning to build a costly segregated auditorium, for which it needed black taxpayer's dollars. At the same time, the city authorities hoped to show good faith in keeping the promises of the sepa-rate but equal doctrine that obliged the city to provide such facilities. A delegation of handpicked black leaders enthusiastically endorsed the idea.[42]

Over the next few years, the commitment to develop the park waned. After defaulting on several payments for the land, the city council allo-cated $15,000 for improvements. The money was part of a package of bond issues, which also included $468,000 for building a segregated mu-nicipal auditorium and $25,000 for a whites-only city library.[43] For the next few years, little of the promised $15,000 actually was made available. The city council simply continued to ignore protestations from the black community.[44] Further demands for the development of park facilities within the city limits, on a plot of land donated by Philander Smith Col-lege, brought stirrings of activity on the out-of-city site.[45] The Works Progress Administration (WPA) began building a log pavilion, twelve bar-becue pits, a baseball diamond, picnic grounds, tables, benches, footpaths, a lake, and a swimming pool.[46] Just over a year later, with little of the work completed, the city council debated whether to abandon the site.[47]

In the postwar years, as black protest intensified, the absence of a city park for blacks became even more contentious, especially when the *State Press* took up the cause. In 1945, columnist A. M. Judge wrote, "Every so often somebody out of nowhere comes up with a lot of 'Negro park' bunk and keeps the newspapers full of hot air for a few weeks, and then the whole thing dies down to where it started." Why, Judge demanded, was the city straining to "build and keep up another park" when it owned several perfectly good parks already? The city, he surmised, had "no business trying to support a dual system for segregational purposes" that it could not afford. Judge declared that "if our Negro 'leaders' had the bone transferred from their heads to their backs, we would have recreational facilities damn quick or [Little Rock] would tell the world just why Negroes are being taxed for recreation and not permitted to enjoy it."[48]

The *State Press* protested that the development of the remote Gillam Park site simply was the cheapest financial option, not one in the best interests of the black community. "Let the county or state develop [Gillam Park] for county or state purposes," L. C. Bates editorialized. "Let the Negro have a park in the city [limits]."[49] When the city council declared it would go ahead with the Gillam Park project regardless, Bates fumed: "White people will go to no end to prove they are right when they know they are wrong. Look at all the money being spent . . . on the so-called Gillam Park for Negroes. . . . If and when Gillam Park is developed we still ain't got a damn thing."[50]

Despite the rhetoric of good intentions from the city council, no further development occurred at Gillam Park.[51] It took the efforts of two emerging black politicos, Bass and McClinton, to challenge this state of inactivity. They demanded a bond issue of $359,000 to pay for the development of Gillam Park. If the city refused, the two threatened court action.[52] "Anybody who knows how things have been going in recent years in the matter of Negro civil rights should be sufficiently warned by that knowledge," cautioned the *Arkansas Gazette*. "[I]t would be a reproach to Little Rock for the Negro Park matter to reach that stage. It is enough reproach for Little Rock that after 15 years groping and fumbling the city has not yet met the need for Negro recreational facilities."[53]

When city council members finally met to decide the matter, they agreed to endorse the bond proposal, even though, as the *Arkansas Gazette* reported, it was "apparent several Aldermen doubt[ed] the large issue w[ould] be approved by the voters."[54] To most on the city council, the eventual outcome of the proposal was not the issue. Allowing the bond to go to the voters would at least show some token effort to meet black demands and forestall the threat of court action, no matter how unlikely the possibility of its success.[55]

The idea of a bond issue met with a mixed reaction in Little Rock. The *State Press* vehemently opposed the idea of developing Gillam Park, complaining about the distance of the site from the city center. The *Arkansas*

Democrat also ran a campaign of opposition, arguing the project would cost too much. Meanwhile, the *Arkansas Gazette* continued to support the plan, making a plea to its readers to "correct a glaring inequality" and reminding them of their "clear moral obligation" to do so. As a further incentive, the newspaper pointed out that if whites did not vote for improved and extended segregated facilities now, the issue of full integration might go to the courts sooner rather than later.[56]

On the morning of February 2, 1949, the population of Little Rock awoke to headlines that the electorate had voted to spend the massive sum of $359,000 to develop a park for blacks. By the narrowest of margins, 2,936 voting for the bond issue and 2,812 against, in one of the smallest turnouts in any city vote, the bond issue for the park won. Whether the bond passed because white voters had been complacent or simply ambivalent about the outcome was unclear. Readily apparent was the increasing ability of the new black politicians to rally enough black voters to make a difference in close-run city elections.[57]

The outcome of the election again divided both the black and the white communities. The most vocal in condemning the bond issue was the *State Press*, which remained unconvinced at the sincerity of the city's white population. L. C. Bates claimed that "$359,000 . . . is entirely too much money to be spent upon Negro recreation in Little Rock." He added that the issue had "made the city the acme of deception and the laughing stock of the entire South." Bates contended that it was nothing but a "smart political scheme to garner Negro votes." He also remained highly skeptical about the intention of the city council to fulfill its promise. Rather, he asserted, advances in the black community "will have to be gained through the courts or the ballots and not through BEGGING."[58]

As Bates predicted, whites were slow to use the money voted for the park. The city council first decided it should go ahead with the development of Gillam Park. Then it decided to hire an architect and an engineer to decide where to build a park in the city.[59] The council's continuing procrastination only came to an end with Congress's passage of the National Housing Act and establishment of the Slum Clearance and Blighted Area Fund in 1949. The legislation made money available to develop rundown urban areas, to transform them into industrial sites, public housing, and recreational facilities. The city promptly put up the $359,000 as matching local funds in hope of obtaining a federal grant. The federal grants could be used not only to develop a park for blacks but also to lure industries and provide improvements within white areas of the city. The decision to locate black recreational facilities at the moribund Gillam Park site virtually guaranteed the award of a federal grant.[60]

The federal money came through in early 1950. In August, the new Gillam Park swimming pool had its grand opening.[61] In his coverage of the opening ceremony, L.C. Bates acknowledged the work done by local black leaders in getting anything at all but remained unconvinced about the project. "We are a little puzzled over the dedication of a new pool exclusively for Negroes," Bates wrote. "We believe it came about twenty odd years too late for us to shout for joy. In this day and time when the entire country is planning programs to stamp out segregation, it seems a little ironical that Little Rock Negroes should be dedicating the outmoded principles [of separate but equal]."[62]

The *State Press* continued to report on developments concerning the park. In less than a year, the pool began leaking.[63] The park's popularity in the black community quickly faded, quite naturally the *State Press* pointed out, since "people do not support the things they do not want. Negroes did not want a swimming pool built out of the city in an insect infested mountain."[64] Events came to a head in July 1954 when a young black boy, Tommy Grigsby, drowned in the pool. Tommy's death was a result of an insufficient number of lifeguards at the pool, the lack of resuscitation equipment, and the remote location. The pool was so far from the nearest hospital that neither a doctor nor a rescue squad could get to the scene in time. Tommy was a member of the South End Boys Club, pointed out the *State Press*, which was located in the neighborhood where many of the city's black population had wanted the pool built in the first place. If the pool had been there, Tommy might not have died. To those looking on, Bates reported, "the whole affair was a study in second class citizenship."[65]

Significantly, it was precisely the political and legal activism advocated by the *State Press* that brought one of the most important victories for the black community during the immediate postwar period. The efforts of the Bateses and the NAACP finally led to black participation in the DPA party primaries. In May 1950, black minister Rev. J. H. Gatlin announced his intention to run for election as a city alderman in Little Rock. To win nomination for the post meant running in the local DPA primaries. The initial reaction from the secretary of the Pulaski County Democratic Committee, June Wooten, was that he saw "no way under the rules of the State Committee that a Negro would qualify for a place on the state ballot."[66] To run for office, Gatlin had to pay a filing fee to Wooten. An attempt to do so on June 3 resulted in the return of Gatlin's money. Wooten maintained Gatlin could not run for office since he was ineligible for membership in the DPA.[67] The final deadline for filing in the city race was June 24. On June 7, Gatlin sent a letter prepared by the Legal Redress Committee of the Little Rock NAACP, headed by L. C. Bates, to DSC members. In his letter, Gatlin requested a rule change that would allow his name to go on to the DPA primary election form. DPA chair Willis R. Smith subsequently called a meeting of the DSC for the following Tuesday at the Hotel Marion in Little Rock.[68]

At the meeting on June 13, committee members decided not to act and referred the matter to the Democratic State Convention, which was due to meet later that year, after the party primaries had taken place.[69] In light of the DSC's inaction, L. C. Bates indicated Gatlin was ready to go to court.[70] On June 17, local attorney J. R. Booker and LDF southwest regional attorney Ulysses Simpson Tate filed Gatlin's case with the federal district court. The attorneys also requested an injunction preventing the exclusion of Gatlin "or any other person qualified . . . on account of race, color, religion, national origin or any other unconstitutional restriction" from the Little Rock DPA city primaries.[71]

On July 5, 1950, Judge Trimble upheld the argument of the NAACP attorneys. Trimble based his decision on precedents set in recent court rulings and finally clarified the status of the primary election. The primary was, Trimble declared, "an integral part of the state election system . . . tantamount to election at the general election." Furthermore, he continued, "it is not sufficient that a citizen have a token exercise of his right and privilege [to vote]."[72] Gatlin subsequently became the first black Arkansan to stand under the DPA banner. He was defeated in the election. The court victory prompted other black candidates to file for office in other elections, most notably ANDA's Rev. Fred T. Guy, who unsuccessfully made a bid for a position on the Little Rock school board.[73]

The Democratic State Convention changed its rules to allow full black membership of the DPA later that year. Governor McMath in his closing speech declared that he was "proud, and I know you are proud . . . [that the convention] . . . has said the Negro citizen is entitled to the rights and privileges of Party membership." The only dissent came from Amis Guthridge, the one delegate to vote against allowing black membership in the party. Guthridge told the party conference, "Sid McMath is all right but is just a man of the moment. You are going to do something here today that you may regret for years to come." Guthridge resurfaced later in the mid-1950s as one of the leading figures in the Little Rock White Citizens' Council, heading opposition to the *Brown* decision.[74]

The success of the NAACP in winning black representation in the DPA primaries in Little Rock coincided with a serious bout of factionalism within the state organization. Much of the unrest revolved around a struggle between supporters of Flowers and supporters of more conservative black leaders for control of the ASC. When the NAACP decided to form the ASC in 1945, Flowers was given the job of chief organizer of branches, but the presidency was given to Rev. Marcus Taylor, an older and more conservative figure from Little Rock. The decision seemed to reflect a desire of those at the NAACP's national office in New York to impose a balance between the younger and more dynamic Flowers and the more cautious Taylor.[75]

Since a major part of Flowers's campaign with the CNO had been to challenge older leaders like Taylor to get them to accept a more militant agenda for black activism, conflict between the two soon arose. With no real communication between the two rival power bases in Little Rock and Pine Bluff, the NAACP in Arkansas quickly became divided along broadly conservative and activist lines and as a result the factions often operated as separate organizations. Jealous of the support Flowers received, Taylor began to fire accusations of financial misconduct at the younger leader. Taylor even went so far as to tell the NAACP's national office that Flowers was keeping half of the funds collected from the foundation of new branches for himself.[76] Although it was true funds were slow in making their way from Pine Bluff to New York, an investigation of Flowers gave no reason to relieve him of his duties.[77]

Despite Taylor's slighting of Flowers's administration of the NAACP, the organization grew and prospered in the following years. This was in no small measure due to the abilities of the younger leader. In fact, it quickly became apparent that far more blacks were attracted to Flowers's brand of activism, which proposed using the NAACP as an organizational tool to fight for local civil rights, than to the more conservative approach of Taylor. Nowhere was this more apparent than in Pine Bluff, where the NAACP branch became the largest in the state.[78]

In 1948, Flowers finally won the struggle with Taylor by gaining election as president of the ASC. By this time, even representatives from the NAACP's national office realized they needed his support to operate effectively in Arkansas. "I will admit that I may have underrated Pine Bluff and its leadership," wrote national membership secretary of the NAACP Lucille Black.[79] When NAACP regional secretary Donald Jones attended the annual ASC conference where Flowers was elected president in 1948, he reported that spirits were "high and militant." Jones's observations of the meeting confirmed that Flowers was the man behind the NAACP's success in the state. Pointing out what had been obvious to those already familiar with the situation in Arkansas, Jones noted, "Largely responsible for the fine NAACP consciousness in Pine Bluff and the growing consciousness in the state is Attorney Flowers whose . . . tremendous energy ha[s] made him the state's acknowledged leader."[80]

The glowing praise of Flowers's ability, together with his election as president of the ASC, encouraged others in the state who were dissatisfied with the direction of black activism in their own localities. In 1948, for example, Daisy Bates filed an application to form a Pulaski County Chapter of the NAACP.[81] By forming a countywide NAACP chapter, Bates hoped to usurp the power base of older leaders who still dominated the Little Rock NAACP. In her application for a branch charter, Bates included fifty membership subscriptions and a filing fee and nominated herself as president. The response Bates received from the NAACP's national office revealed clear limits to the autonomy the national organization was prepared to grant local activists. The NAACP's director of branches Gloster B. Current, in a short reply, pointed out that there was already a NAACP branch in Little Rock and if people were interested in helping the organization, they should join there.[82]

The increasingly heated relations between local NAACP activists in Arkansas and the national office in New York finally sparked in 1949. The question of financial improprieties again became a contentious issue when the ASC defaulted on its annual contribution to the NAACP's Southwest Regional Conference Fund. The delay in the contribution, along with previous allegations of financial irregularities by Rev. Taylor and the increasingly assertive nature of local activists, prompted the NAACP's national office to act quickly and decisively. At an emergency meeting of the ASC, Donald Jones recommended Flowers be given the opportunity to resign within fifteen days or face expulsion from the NAACP.[83]

Members of the local NAACP in Pine Bluff felt aggrieved at Jones's proposal. In particular, they claimed the NAACP's national office had not adequately taken into account the work done by Flowers in the state in the struggle for civil rights. This was, they believed, a major factor in the delay of administrative tasks. Wiley A. Branton, on behalf of the Pine Bluff NAACP branch, responded to the actions of the NAACP's national office by leading calls for the local branch to withdraw from the jurisdiction of the national office.[84] The hornet's nest stirred by the suggestion of firing Flowers took the NAACP's national office by surprise. The response to the dissent was to call upon the NAACP's acting executive secretary Roy Wilkins and former executive secretary Walter White to plead for unity. They urged the Pine Bluff NAACP branch to accept the decision of the national office. Only when Flowers resigned to keep the peace did talk of outright mutiny cease.[85]

The deep dissatisfaction of local NAACP activists at the loss of such an influential force within the state continued to smolder. Many were extremely reluctant to accept Flowers's replacement, Dr. J. A. White, who represented the old guard of black leaders, imposed by the NAACP's national office. This dissension within NAACP ranks caused much concern. President of the Texas State Conference of NAACP Branches Lulu B. White reported that "no place in the country is there so much strife and division amongst Negroes as it is in Arkansas." Furthermore, said White, "they say the work of the NAACP is in charge of a few favorites in the state, who are Lackies, what ever that is, for New York, and that New York is not worth a D——to them."[86]

The anger felt immediately after Flowers's resignation slowly abated. Nevertheless, local NAACP members made it plain they would not tolerate a conservative president of the ASC for long, no matter how much the national office tried to interfere with local matters. When Dr. White fell ill and resigned from office in 1951, W. L. Jarrett, a veteran of early CNO campaigns, acted as a temporary replacement.[87] The issue of a conservative versus an activist leadership being in charge of Arkansas' NAACP activities was finally resolved with Daisy Bates's election as president of the ASC in 1952. Reporting to the NAACP's national office after watching the proceedings, Ulysses Simpson Tate questioned Bates's ability to work with older, more established leaders in the state. Moreover, he was wary of her tendency "to go off the deep end at times" in her forceful pursuit of civil rights. But, he concluded, "[although] I am not certain that she was the proper person to be elected . . . there was no one else to be elected who offered any promise of doing anything to further the work of the NAACP in Arkansas."[88]

The admission that only an activist could advance the cause of the NAACP within the state marked a major triumph over the forces of black conservatism and was a defining moment in the development of black activism in Arkansas. Bates's election as president of the ASC was the culmination of a long struggle over the direction black leadership should move. Finally, a strong local activist had secured a position at the helm of the NAACP and at the same time was able to marry this to an important strategic base in the state capital of Little Rock. Bates was consequently in a prime position to mobilize a more effective push for civil rights, using the NAACP as a vehicle to promote a greater commitment to black activism in Little Rock and across the state.

Bates's ascent to the presidency of the ASC coincided with local and national intensification of the black struggle for equality. This new wave of black activism focused on the testing of segregation statutes in secondary schools. Several suits filed in Arkansas in the late 1940s and early 1950s, both through the offices of the NAACP and independently by W. H. Flowers, paved the way for later attacks on segregated education through the courts. Though the suits met with varying degrees of success, none of them actually won a definitive ruling against discriminatory practices. Events at a national level finally overtook the local challenge to segregation when on May 17, 1954, the Supreme Court handed down its ruling in *Brown*, which declared that segregated schools were "inherently unequal." Moreover, the Court stated that even if southern school boards provided equal facilities, the very fact of separation meant black students received an inferior education. Following to a logical conclusion the decisions in black graduate education throughout the 1940s, the Court maintained that "in the field of public education the doctrine of 'separate but equal' has no place."[89]

The *Brown* decision appeared to herald an end to the ambiguities of race relations in postwar Arkansas and, indeed, throughout the South. An exuberant Thurgood Marshall declared, "[O]nce and for all, it's decided, and completely decided."[90] Daisy Bates expressed similar sentiments, convinced that "the time for delay, evasion, or procrastination was past."[91] For black activists, the Supreme Court decision vindicated their calls not to accept half measures but to insist upon full equality. To whites, the *Brown* decision embodied the worst of their fears. In spite of their efforts to reform, many believed that the Supreme Court had now turned against them and wrested control of race relations out of their hands. The choice of reform within the boundaries of Jim Crow was no longer an option. Federal government demanded the dismantling of segregation, first in the schools and then, many feared, in all other areas of southern life. However, the Court did offer some respite by providing a one-year delay be-fore ruling on implementation guidelines for school desegregation. This gave the South a chance to come to terms with the proposed racial change and to draw up voluntary plans for compliance.[92]

Arkansans found themselves at a crossroads over race relations. They could extend changes that had already taken place in the state, or they could dig in their heels and risk conflict with federal law. To the vast ma-jority of whites, neither option held much appeal.

Fig. 1. Dr. John Marshall Robinson, president of the Arkansas Negro Democratic Association (ANDA). Courtesy of Dale Lya Pierson.

Fig. 2. Silas Hunt arrives at the University of Arkansas, February 1948. Photo by Geleve Grice, courtesy of the Special Collections Division, University of Arkansas Libraries, Fayetteville.

Fig. 3. Silas Hunt *(seated)*, accompanied by Wiley A. Branton *(left)* and William Harold Flowers, enrolls at the University of Arkansas Law School, February 1948. Photo by Geleve Grice, courtesy of the Special Collections Division, University of Arkansas Libraries, Fayetteville.

Above: Fig. 4. Wiley A. Branton *(second from left)*, Daisy Bates *(third from left)*, and two others discuss the *Aaron v. Cooper* (1956) case. Courtesy of the Special Collections Division, University of Arkansas Libraries, Fayetteville.

Left: Fig. 5. Gov. Orval E. Faubus *(left)* and Little Rock superintendent of schools Virgil T. Blossom shake hands. Photo by Larry Obsitnik, courtesy of the *Arkansas Democrat-Gazette* and Special Collections Division, University of Arkansas Libraries, Fayetteville.

Fig. 6. Black students wait to enter Central High School under the protection of federal troops. Photo by Larry Obsitnik, courtesy of the *Arkansas Democrat-Gazette* and Special Collections Division, University of Arkansas Libraries, Fayetteville.

Fig. 7. Daisy Bates and the Little Rock Nine with their Spingarn Medals at the NAACP Forty-Ninth Annual Convention at Cleveland, July 1958. The Little Rock Nine *(left to right)*: Thelma Mothershed, Elizabeth Eckford, Gloria Ray, Jefferson Thomas, Melba Pattillo, Ernest Green, Carlotta Walls, Minnijean Brown, Terrance Roberts, and *(seated)* Daisy Bates. Courtesy of the Special Collections Division, University of Arkansas Libraries, Fayetteville.

Fig. 8. State prosecutor J. Frank Holt *(left, leaning)* confers with attorneys Harold
B. Anderson *(center)* and George Howard, Jr., *(right, leaning)* at the trial of the first
sit-in demonstrators in Little Rock, 1960. Photo by Larry Obsitnik, courtesy of
the *Arkansas Democrat-Gazette* and Special Collections Division, University of
Arkansas Libraries, Fayetteville.

Fig. 9. "Black and White Together." White SNCC worker Bill Hansen leads a demonstration in Pine Bluff, ca. 1963. Arkansas State Police surveillance photograph, courtesy of the Special Collections Division, University of Arkansas Libraries, Fayetteville.

Fig. 10. A two-story SNCC Freedom School in Gould, Arkansas, 1966. There were two other freedom schools, at West Helena and Forrest City. They provided education and citizenship classes and served as a base for black community activism. Courtesy of the *Arkansas Democrat-Gazette*.

Fig. 11. Members of Black United Youth (BUY) confront city officials in Little Rock after Curtis Ingram's death at the Pulaski County Penal Farm, August 1968. Courtesy of the *Arkansas Democrat- Gazette*.

Fig. 12. Dr. Jerry D. Jewell addresses the Arkansas General Assembly. In 1972, Jewell became the first black person elected to the Arkansas Senate in the twentieth century. Photo by George C. Douthit, courtesy of the *Arkansas Democrat-Gazette* and Special Collections Division, University of Arkansas Libraries, Fayetteville.

Brown v. Board of Education   ↞4↠

As news of the Supreme Court ruling spread across the South, there were mixed reactions from politicians. On the one hand, there were calls for calm and restraint. Mississippi governor James P. Coleman appealed for "cool thinking" and moderation. Alabama governor James E. Folsom stated that "when the Supreme Court speaks, that's the law." On the other hand, there were those such as Sen. James O. Eastland of Mississippi, who labeled the *Brown* decision a "monstrous crime." Georgia governor Herman Talmadge, playing upon white's deep-seated fears of miscegenation, declared that the ultimate objective of the exercise was to admit the black man into the white women's bedroom. The southern populace as a whole appeared undecided about the ramifications of the *Brown* decision. Although obviously concerned at the turn of events, they were not altogether surprised with the ruling, given the steady attack on segregation throughout the postwar period. Previous handling of such changes meant that many whites felt confident they could find some way to mute the potential impact of the Court decision.[1]

Reactions to the *Brown* decision in Arkansas reflected the range of opinions across the South. In some northwest Arkansas school districts and in urban areas across the state, there was a general acceptance of the need to comply with the ruling. "Arkansas will obey the law," declared Gov. Francis Cherry in Little Rock, adding that the people of the state would "not approach the problem [of desegregation] with the idea of being outlaws."² The *Arkansas Gazette* echoed the call for sensible handling of a potentially explosive issue by imploring for "[w]ise leadership at the upper levels" and warning that "emotional excursions by the leaders of either race can do great harm." In sharp contrast, rumblings of dissent came from east Arkansas, where Congressman E. C. "Took" Gathings condemned both the *Brown* decision and the Supreme Court for interference in racial matters.³ Although no groundswell of opinion advocating outright violent resistance to the law emerged, there were moves by some to formulate measures that would allow a legal circumvention preventing, or at the very least delaying, the implementation of the desegregation ruling.⁴

The regional division in attitudes toward the *Brown* decision was clear in the actions of various school boards across the state. In northwest Arkansas, three school districts immediately drew up plans to desegregate, based largely on financial considerations. Just four days after the ruling, the Fayetteville school board announced it would allow the nine black students in its district to attend the local high school with five hundred whites the following academic year. Previously, the black students had been bused to segregated schools at Fort Smith and Hot Springs, a distance of 60 and 150 miles respectively, at a cost of $5,000 a year. Fayetteville's superintendent of schools Wayne White bluntly told reporters that "segregation was a luxury we could no longer afford." The school boards at Charleston and Bentonville, both in similar circumstances to Fayetteville, also voted to integrate. None of the districts encountered hostility because of their actions.⁵

Meanwhile, the one attempt to desegregate in east Arkansas aroused a storm of opposition. The incident occurred at Sheridan, a school district just a few miles outside the state capital of Little Rock, on the edge of the Delta. Like the three school districts in northwest Arkansas, Sheridan bused its small black student population to the nearest segregated schools. On May 21, the Sheridan school board voted unanimously to integrate its twenty-one black students with the six hundred whites at the local high school. As with the school boards' decisions in northwest Arkansas, Sheridan sought to alleviate the financial burden involved in maintaining segregation. The move led to an immediate protest from the white community, which forced the school board to take a second vote the following night, resulting in a unanimous recanting of the plan to desegregate. Still not satisfied, three hundred parents held a meeting a week afterward and agreed to circulate a petition calling for the resignation of the entire school board. Four school board members resigned forthwith. When the September school term began in Sheridan, black students were still bused 27 miles to a black school in an adjoining county at an estimated yearly cost of $4,000. Segregation was to stay, residents decided, whatever the cost. No other school districts in the Delta offered any immediate signs of compliance with the *Brown* decision.[6]

The pronounced differences in attitudes and approaches to school desegregation brought a deadlock over the issue at the state level. Although east Arkansas interests won concessions to prevent major headway being made toward desegregation, they proved unsuccessful at imposing their agenda for a legal circumvention of the *Brown* decision. At the state board of education meeting in September 1954, chair of the West Memphis school board, Harold Weaver, hysterically claimed that the *Brown* decision would "tear our school system all to pieces." Although members from other areas expressed sympathy with Weaver and were prepared to assist in formulating a gradualist approach to desegregation, there was little enthusiasm for a posture of defiance. To mollify east Arkansas members, they agreed school districts should wait for the Supreme Court's desegregation implementation order before taking any decisive action. Furthermore, the state board voted to ask Arkansas Attorney General Tom Gentry to file a friend-of-the-court brief with the Court, outlining the strong feelings the decision had aroused in the state. In doing so, members hoped to influence a lenient implementation plan. Gentry agreed to help. Nevertheless, he sternly warned, the *Brown* decision was "the law of the land and we are going to have to abide by it." All he could do now, he told the board, was to advise the Court on how, not whether, to desegregate.[7]

The stalemate over the *Brown* decision was also evident in the election for governor in 1954. The victorious candidate, Orval Eugene Faubus, beat incumbent Francis Cherry without taking any firm position on the race issue. Faubus was born in the Ozark Mountains of northwest Arkansas in 1910 and raised in a poor white farming family. Faubus's early political development was strongly influenced by his father, Sam, an ardent socialist. Indeed, in 1935, Sam persuaded his son to enroll at the leftist Commonwealth College in Mena, west Arkansas. However, Orval left Commonwealth after only a short stay, rejecting its idealism for hardheaded pragmatism as the road to political success. As a youth, Faubus worked variously as an itinerant farm laborer, lumberjack, rural schoolteacher, postmaster, and editor and publisher of the weekly *Madison County Record*. In 1942, Faubus entered the army and served as a commissioned officer in Europe during the Second World War. Upon his return to Arkansas, Faubus began to pursue his political ambitions in earnest. In 1949, he joined Governor McMath's administration, sitting on the state highway commission and later becoming director of highways. Hailing from northwest Arkansas, Faubus had limited experience of interaction with blacks, although he solicited the help of influential black political figures and actively sought black votes during his campaign for governor.[8]

As the son of a socialist and a former member of the liberal McMath administration, Faubus was generally inclined toward a moderate stance on the question of school desegregation. Yet, the need to court votes across Arkansas prevented him from expressing unequivocal support for compliance with the *Brown* decision. What emerged instead was an ambiguous and confusing stance that pandered to racism while leaving the way open for compliance and racial progress. Aiming to win votes in east Arkansas, Faubus proclaimed, "Arkansas is not ready for complete and sudden mixing of the races in public schools." To placate other parts of the state, he advocated tackling school desegregation at a "Local Level with state authorities standing ready to assist in every way possible." The noncommittal approach of Faubus provided an interesting political barometer on the school desegregation question. The stance appeared to demonstrate that even seasoned politicians were not yet able to detect a popular sentiment either strongly in favor of school desegregation or strongly opposed to it. Apparently, they were willing to wait for public sentiment to develop before committing to any policy.[9]

The politically ambiguous role of the school desegregation issue was equally in evidence at the Arkansas General Assembly in January 1955. Halfway through its sixty-day session, a bill aimed at circumventing the *Brown* decision was introduced in both houses by east Arkansas state senators Fletcher Long and W. E. "Buck" Fletcher and state representative Lucien C. Rodgers. The bill outlined a plan to appoint an assignment officer in each Arkansas school district who would decide which schools students should be allocated to on a variety of criteria. In essence, the move sought to preserve segregation by allowing for the assignment of blacks to black schools and whites to white schools without actually mentioning race as a factor.[10]

Opposition to the bill came from Max Howell, whose constituency covered the affluent white suburbs of Little Rock. In a delaying maneuver, Howell demanded a full reading of the bill. Next, Howell asked for the bill to be shelved. By a narrow vote, the Arkansas Senate decided to retain the bill. However, Howell won a delay in its implementation until after the Supreme Court had issued its desegregation directive. In an impassioned speech to the senate, Howell declared, "Just because some other dyed-in-the-wool southern state jumped in haste to preserve [segregation] doesn't mean that Arkansas should." The delay robbed east Arkansans of a pre-emptive strike against the Court's school desegregation order and kept hope of constructive progress on the issue alive in the state.[11]

The equivocation over the Pupil Assignment Law by the general assembly distinguished Arkansas from other southern states, where such a measure had become a common minimal defiance to *Brown*. Moreover, many southern states had proposed far more extreme measures of resistance. These variously called for using police power to stop integration, for financing litigation opposing desegregation, for investigation of pro-integration organizations, and for leasing public schools to private corporations to avoid federal orders to desegregate. By comparison, the Arkansas General Assembly appeared a model of calm and restraint.[12]

The finely balanced position of the state between compliance with and circumvention of the *Brown* decision heightened the importance of the Little Rock school board's stance on desegregation. Other communities looked to Little Rock, the largest school system in the state, located between northwest and southeast Arkansas, for guidance. As a concerned superintendent of schools from Union County in south central Arkansas put it, "I don't like to see a leading community like Little Rock take the lead too fast. . . . In the end, other communities will have to follow suit." Steps taken toward compliance in the state capital potentially weakened the east Arkansas crusade to circumvent *Brown* while any sign of wavering potentially strengthened it. Therefore, what happened in Little Rock would prove vital in influencing the statewide stance on school desegregation.[13]

Recognizing the pivotal importance of Little Rock, the local branch of the NAACP had attempted to establish negotiations with the city school board before the *Brown* decision. In the mid-1950s, the Little Rock branch had around 370 members. However, the active membership consisted of only a dozen or so people, who all sat on the Executive Committee. The Little Rock NAACP Executive Committee drew support from a number of different constituencies. There were older members, such as Rev. J. C. Crenchaw, pastor of Mount Pleasant Baptist Church. Crenchaw had been a member of the NAACP for more than forty years, becoming branch president in 1952. J. R. Booker, who had acted as a legal counsel for Sue Morris in her successful salary equalization suit, was a prominent black Republican. Alongside figures such as Crenchaw and Booker were L. C. Bates and a group of younger blacks, including reporter Ozell Sutton. There were two medical practitioners, optometrist William H. Townsend, who opened a practice in Little Rock in 1950, and dentist Garman P. Freeman, the next-door neighbor of L. C. and Daisy Bates, and two recently qualified black lawyers, Thaddeus D. Williams, a former president of the Little Rock NAACP branch, and Jackie Shropshire, the first black graduate of the University of Arkansas Law School. From the early 1950s, two white professors at Philander Smith College, Georg Iggers and Lee Lorch, also sat on the executive board.[14]

In February 1952, with NAACP support, the Little Rock Council on Schools (LRCS), an ad hoc interracial group , approached the Little Rock school board with a plan for limited integration. The proposal was to allow a limited number of black students to enroll in courses and to use facilities at Central High School that were not available at Dunbar High School. The LRCS drew support from the Little Rock NAACP, the Little Rock Urban League, and the Little Rock–based branch of the Southern Regional Council (SRC). The Atlanta-based SRC was founded in 1919 as the Commission on Interracial Cooperation and worked to promote racial justice in the South. Iggers represented the NAACP, the Rev. W. H. Bass represented the Urban League, and the Rev. Lewis Deer of the white Pulaski Heights Christian Church represented the SRC branch on the LRCS Steering Committee.[15]

The Urban League, the SRC branch, and the NAACP demonstrated three different levels of white support for civil rights in the 1950s. The Urban League, which worked to improve black life and opportunities strictly within the bounds of Jim Crow, contained the largest number of white members. The SRC branch, which reorganized in 1954 as the Arkansas Council on Human Relations (ACHR), took a more progressive stance, advocating gradual desegregation through interracial cooperation. The SRC branch traditionally had fewer members than the Urban League, although white support for the ACHR began to grow from the mid-1950s. The NAACP branch was much more black-oriented than either the Urban League or the ACHR, and it sought an immediate end to segregation by pursuing civil rights through the courts. Very few whites belonged to the NAACP. In practice, there was some overlap in membership between the three organizations, although there was far more likelihood of blacks belonging to the Urban League and ACHR than of whites belonging to the NAACP. A core handful of active members in each group understood the distinctiveness of their respective organizations and guided their activities accordingly.[16]

Both Urban League and SRC members played an important part in the proposals for limited school integration. Vital to developments, however, was Iggers, a German Jew, who had fled to America from the Nazis in 1938. During his college days in Richmond, Virginia, he became actively involved with interracial groups who were working to promote a better understanding between the races in the South. After earning a doctorate from the University of Chicago in 1950, Iggers moved to Little Rock with his wife to take a teaching post at Philander Smith College, which he held until moving to Louisiana in 1956. From his first days in Little Rock, he was an active NAACP member, winning appointments to various committees within the organization. As chair of the Education Committee, Iggers drew up the proposals for limited integration on behalf of the LRCS.[17]

Several school board members seriously considered the LRCS plan. Only the disquiet of the school superintendent Harry A. Little, a committed segregationist, cast a shadow over the proceedings. Nevertheless, the school board did agree to meet again with the LRCS.[18] Before the next meeting, however, one of the local NAACP lawyers, Thaddeus D. Williams, seeking to enhance his prestige in the black community, leaked news of developments to the press. The move backfired, because it breached the board's insistence on confidentiality, ending the prospect of further negotiations.[19]

The Little Rock school board's willingness to consider proposals for change indicated Arkansas' capital city might well lead the way to compliance with the *Brown* decision in the state. Just four days after the Court ruling, an expectant black delegation gathered in Little Rock to hear the report of new superintendent of schools Virgil T. Blossom about the board's intentions. Blossom, born and reared in Brookfield, Missouri, graduated with an education degree from Missouri Valley College, which he had attended on an athletic scholarship, in 1930. Blossom's first job was teaching and coaching athletics at a high school in Fayetteville, Arkansas. Moving in 1935 to a school in Okmulgee, Oklahoma, he returned to Fayetteville three years later as a high school principal. In 1942, as Fayetteville's superintendent of schools, he devised a system of busing black students out of the city to preserve the all-white school district. Blossom stayed in Fayetteville for eleven years before taking his new post in Little Rock in February 1953.[20]

As he started to outline the school board's plans, Blossom noticed that the "high spirits" with which the meeting began soon transformed in a "rapid [loss of] enthusiasm." Blossom told the black delegation that the school board did not intend to move ahead with desegregation immediately. Instead, the board would wait for the Supreme Court implementation order. In the meantime, Blossom indicated he would draw up plans in the event the Court forced Little Rock schools to desegregate. After Blossom finished his speech, L. C. Bates stormed out of the meeting in outright disgust at the board's unwillingness to implement a desegregation program immediately. Others stayed, but the black delegation's overall disappointment was clear. Blossom tried to reassure the delegation the school board was not proposing to "delay for delay's sake, but to do the job right."[21] Privately, Blossom told whites of his intention to devise a school desegregation plan that would provide "the least amount of integration over the longest period."[22]

Blossom's initial statement set the pattern for school desegregation in Little Rock and for other urban school districts in Arkansas over the following years. As Lower South states geared up for a campaign of "massive resistance" to oppose any integration whatsoever through legal and extralegal tactics, Little Rock promoted a campaign of "minimum compliance." In line with tactics used in other Upper South cities, minimum compliance employed gradualism and tokenism to delay and limit implementation of school desegregation as long as legally possible. The driving force behind minimum compliance was that it theoretically placated those who did not want school desegregation, by limiting integration to the bare minimum, while allowing school districts to maintain that they were in fact implementing the law. Blossom viewed such a stance as "moderate" relative to the "extremes" of significant integration and outright opposition through massive resistance. But in fact, minimum compliance was merely a diluted form of resistance, providing a subtle and insidious way of frustrating the process of school desegregation. Although massive resistance and minimum compliance first appeared quite different approaches, in the years following *Brown* those differences quickly narrowed as the two combined to undermine the process of school desegregation across the South.[23]

Unhappy with the school board's response to *Brown*, the black community, spearheaded by the Little Rock NAACP, pressed Blossom for a definite declaration of plans for desegregation. At a subsequent meeting, Blossom told local NAACP representatives that before any desegregation took place, the board intended to build two new schools. Horace Mann

High would be built in the predominantly black eastern part of the city and Hall High would be built in the affluent white western suburbs. Blossom stressed that the two new schools, though located in predominately black and predominately white residential areas, would not have set racial designations. Rather, Blossom assured local NAACP members, the school board planned to desegregate all three of the city's high schools, Horace Mann, Hall High, and Central High, through color-blind attendance zones in 1957. Elementary schools would follow sometime around 1960.[24]

The so-called "Blossom Plan" divided members of the Little Rock NAACP's executive board. L. C. Bates opposed the plan; he quite rightly believed it was "vague, indefinite, slow-moving and indicative of an intent to stall further on public school integration." Nevertheless, a clear majority supported the plan and cautioned against pushing the school board too hard. Most believed Blossom and the school board should be given a chance to prove their good intentions, that the plan was reasonable, and that it would be acceptable to the white community. The local branch therefore decided against immediate action and to await further developments.[25]

In April 1955, the Little Rock NAACP held a meeting in anticipation of the Supreme Court implementation order. The main speaker was a field worker for the LDF, Vernon McDaniels, who had spent six months in Arkansas assessing the school desegregation situation. McDaniels admitted that different communities would offer different degrees of resistance to school desegregation. Yet, he insisted, with increased efforts by blacks across the state to urge local school boards into compliance, Arkansas represented the "brightest prospect among the southern states for integration."[26]

This upbeat assessment followed the encouraging developments of the past year. A few school districts in northwest Arkansas had already moved to desegregate, whereas in many other southern states there had been no progress at all. No widespread, organized campaign of resistance to school desegregation had developed. Moreover, the legislature had delayed the one direct attempt to circumvent *Brown*. This indicated the presence of law-abiding influences in Arkansas that could stymie any protest. Although the situation concerning school desegregation remained somewhat ambiguous, there were grounds for cautious optimism that a more definite timetable for desegregation would consolidate the state's position of moderation.

Yet to those who had faith in the ability of the Supreme Court's implementation decree to clear a path for compliance, the words of the justices on May 31, 1955, came as a major blow. Instead of following up on its initial conviction, the Court equivocated. The implementation order, which became known as *Brown II*, ambiguously told school boards they must make a "prompt and reasonable start" to desegregate "with all deliberate speed." No deadline was set for when integration had to begin, and there was no indication of what constituted compliance in terms of how many students were to be integrated or at what grades. Indeed, the Court even listed "local problems" that might be given as reasonable excuses for delay. The Court also handed the task of administrating school desegregation to federal district judges and local school boards. The former had no means of enforcing their rulings, and the latter could potentially drag out the process of integration indefinitely. The overall message to the South seemed to be that it could take as long as it wanted to desegregate schools. To many southerners, this meant never.[27]

The reasons behind the Supreme Court's indecisiveness were complex. Rumors abounded that in exchange for unanimity over *Brown*, some southern justices had obtained for the South the benefit of the doubt in awarding a lenient implementation order. Lack of political backing also seems to have played a major role. President Eisenhower continually refused to strongly support the *Brown* decision in public. In private, he admitted he feared catastrophic massive resistance in the South if its racial mores were so quickly and directly threatened. Southern leaders, emboldened by the delay between the school desegregation decision and its implementation order, warned of impending violence. Playing upon the fears of massive resistance voiced by the president, the leaders warned of the need to not alienate the white population by too quickly forcing racial change. White southerners increasingly sought to demonstrate the fears articulated by their leaders. Reluctance to implement *Brown* quickly began to crystallize into direct opposition. Because of a perceived lack of support from other branches of the federal government and the public at large, as well as because of divisions in its own ranks, the Court climbed down from its original lofty position on racial change. Instead, it offered an ambiguous and confusing compromise.[28]

Brown II proved an important turning point for school desegregation in Arkansas. Whites who previously had adopted a stance of minimum compliance viewed the court implementation order as a mandate for further measures to limit the impact of *Brown*. In turn, this paved the way for a movement toward outright defiance of the law and total opposition to school desegregation. Before the Supreme Court implementation decree, the most outspoken opponents of school desegregation in Arkansas had looked to find legal means to circumvent desegregation. Encouraged by the reluctance to enforce *Brown*, an organized band of segregationists issued the first calls for resistance by any means. This hardening of sentiment in the white community in turn helped strengthen the resolve of blacks. As the earlier optimism that whites would implement *Brown* vanished, the NAACP increasingly became the leading force in the black community.

The belief that *Brown II* meant school boards could take as long as they liked to desegregate was evident in the actions of Blossom, who announced plans to modify his original desegregation proposals. The most important development was the introduction of a transfer system that would allow students to move out of their assigned attendance zones. Under the original Blossom Plan, attendance zones clearly were being gerrymandered to ensure a majority black Horace Mann High and a majority white Hall High. The assignment of many black students who lived closer to Central High to Horace Mann confirmed the intentions of the school board to pursue a policy of minimum compliance and limit desegregation as much as possible.[29]

Even so, the original plan involved integrating several hundred black pupils. The new plan, however, allowed whites to opt out of attending Horace Mann without giving blacks the right to choose to attend Hall High, and it further limited integration at Central High. To encourage the shift of white pupils from Horace Mann, the school board assigned it an all-black teaching staff. The board then declared Horace Mann would open as a segregated black school in February 1956, a move that would establish a clear precedent for black attendance the year before the school was due to desegregate.[30]

The modified Blossom Plan incensed members of the Little Rock NAACP's executive board, even those who had been willing to accept Blossom's original proposal for school desegregation.[31] Adding insult to injury, Blossom did not even bother to consult the NAACP about the changes. When local NAACP representatives met with the school board to request immediate integration of the city's schools, the school board rejected the proposal outright.[32] Little Rock's policy had a domino effect in the three other large municipal school districts in the state. Fort Smith, North Little Rock, and Hot Springs all delayed school desegregation until the state capital made the first move.[33]

That *Brown II* not only encouraged backpedaling but also helped create an active movement of opposition and resistance to school desegregation was first in evidence at Hoxie, a small town in northeast Arkansas. With a population of just over a thousand, Hoxie was close enough to the Arkansas Delta to have a split school term to allow for the cotton harvest. Yet it was atypical in that, with only fourteen black families living there, it did not reflect the density of the black population in other areas of the Delta.[34] On June 25, 1955, the school board at Hoxie voted, largely for financial reasons, to desegregate.[35] On July 11, the first day of integrated classes, a small group of disgruntled local men gathered outside the school to witness proceedings. Some parents voiced their misgivings, with one, Mrs. John Cole, worriedly telling reporters her eight-year-old daughter Peggy "feared Negroes." Despite the apprehension surrounding integration, the consensus in the town was "[W]e have to obey the law." Although there was some tension in classes at first, teachers soon made black students feel welcome, and normal school life quickly resumed. At noon recess, black and white boys tried out for the school baseball team together, and photographers even caught the fearful Peggy playing and walking arm in arm with black female students.[36]

Ironically, the very success of school desegregation at Hoxie made it the rallying point for massive resistance forces in the state. Journalists and photographers were present to document the experience for *Life*, producing an article with numerous pictures showing the mixing of black and white students.[37] Whereas other school boards were generally at pains to avoid the glare of publicity, desegregation at Hoxie became a national story. With the help and encouragement of segregationists in other states, particularly neighboring Mississippi, local whites held a meeting to discuss the situation. There, they elected Herbert Brewer, a local soybean farmer and part-time auctioneer, as chair of a new prosegregation group.[38] Brewer and the Hoxie Citizens' Committee (HCC) picketed and petitioned the Hoxie school board to try to persuade its members to reverse their decision to desegregate. The board held firm in its conviction and rebuffed the demands of segregationists. However, to provide a cooling-off period, the board closed the school two weeks before the scheduled end of term.[39]

The concession to close the schools early proved unfortunate, since it encouraged more disruption from segregationists. The gathering storm also helped draw support from other segregationists across the state. White America, Inc., a Pine Bluff–based organization, sent lawyer Amis Guthridge from Little Rock to stir up the populace. Jim Johnson, head of the newly formed White Citizens' Councils of Arkansas, followed soon after. The meeting of segregationist groups at Hoxie led to a pooling of resources and the formation of the Associated Citizens' Councils of Arkansas (ACCA). The ACCA became the main vehicle for white resistance to school desegregation in the state after the Hoxie campaign.[40]

Yet, for all the bluff and bluster of segregationists at Hoxie, they ultimately met with defeat. The school remained desegregated the following term, and the courts issued an injunction to prevent any interference.[41] Unlike other white activist groups in the South, Arkansas' White Citizens' Councils remained distinctly lacking in status. In other states, Citizens' Councils counted merchants, bankers, landowners, and politicians among their members. The groups could exert economic, political, and social influence to back up the angry rhetoric at mass rallies. In Arkansas, the radical segregationist voice came from those who had little community standing.[42] Membership figures underscored white Arkansans' lack of interest in the Citizens' Councils. Whereas Mississippi boasted 300,000 members, Arkansas recruited, at the highest and most likely overstated estimate, just 20,000 members.[43]

Despite the ACCA's overall lack of credibility, the NAACP was keenly aware of the potential dangers of growing organized white resistance in Arkansas. The standoff at Hoxie prompted an increased urgency in the ASC to step up pressure for school desegregation before similar tactics spread to other parts of the state. In December 1955, Little Rock's NAACP executive board members voted to file a lawsuit against the Little Rock school board. They contacted Tate, the LDF southwest regional attorney who had worked with them on the white primary case, for advice on how to proceed. The Little Rock NAACP was especially concerned about plans to open Horace Mann High as a segregated school in February 1956. Tate cautioned against seeking an injunction to prevent the opening of Horace Mann. Instead, he urged the branch to take the positive step of petitioning for the admission of black students to white schools when Horace Mann opened.[44]

On January 23, 1956, thirty-three black students applied for admission to four different white schools in Little Rock. All principals of the schools refused the students entry and referred them to Blossom. Daisy Bates accompanied nine of the students to Blossom's office. There, Blossom explained that he wanted to be, as he put it, "as kind as I can," but that he had to "deny their request . . . in line with the policy outlined [by the school board]." Blossom was adamant that school desegregation would take place, as planned, in 1957. Bates told reporters after the meeting, "I think the next step is obvious. We've tried everything short of a court suit."[45] On February 8, 1956, Wiley A. Branton filed suit in the federal district court against the Little Rock school board for desegregation on behalf of thirty-three students in *Aaron v. Cooper*.[46]

After graduation from the University of Arkansas in 1953, Branton had opened a law practice in Pine Bluff and had become chair of the ASC's Legal Redress Committee and a local counsel for the LDF.[47] The Little Rock NAACP branch employed Branton, since its usual lawyers, executive board members Thaddeus D. Williams and J. R. Booker, were reluctant to take the case.[48] In preparation for the trial, Branton consulted with special counsel to the NAACP Robert L. Carter and with Tate.[49]

At the trial in August 1956, the federal district court backed the modified Blossom Plan. To a large degree, this ruling reflected confusion within NAACP ranks about the nature of the trial rather than the validity of the arguments of school board attorneys. The Little Rock NAACP built its case narrowly, asking only for the enforcement of the original Blossom Plan. To reinforce the strength of the argument, branch members went to great pains to select individual examples of students who faced particular hardship under the modified Blossom Plan. Tate had different ideas about the case. As previous dealings between the national, the regional, and the local NAACP had revealed, each often had its own agenda, which could cause conflicts and misunderstandings. Tate did not confer with local branch officials before the trial. When he flew into Little Rock the day before the hearing, he claimed he was too tired to take instructions and immediately retired to his room. The next morning, Tate ignored the case built by the Little Rock NAACP and proceeded to argue the national NAACP line for the immediate and complete integration of all schools. This was the same line taken by the organization in its other sixty-five integration suits against school boards in the Upper South at the time.[50] Since Tate was senior to Branton in the NAACP legal hierarchy, the local lawyer deferred to him.[51]

Tate's line of argument lost the lawsuit by playing straight into the hands of the school board. Tate did not demand the school board live up to the promises it had already made. Rather, by demanding wholesale and immediate integration, he allowed school board attorneys to contend that their clients were acting in accordance with the "all deliberate speed" guidelines laid down by *Brown II*. Judge John E. Miller upheld their argument. Offering a shred of consolation to the local NAACP, Miller retained federal jurisdiction in the case to ensure the school board now carried out the modified Blossom Plan along the lines it had indicated in court.[52]

The Little Rock NAACP branch was naturally disappointed at the outcome of the lawsuit. In consultation with their lawyer, Branton; the director-counsel of the LDF, Marshall; and the special counsel to the NAACP, Carter, they decided to appeal.[53] The appeals court at Saint Louis heard arguments in *Aaron v. Cooper* on March 11, 1957. Again, the court upheld the modified Blossom Plan, stating that the school board was indeed operating within a timetable that was reasonable given the local problems of desegregation in the South. However, the appeals court reaffirmed Judge Miller's ruling that the school board was now obliged to carry out its modified plan, beginning with the desegregation of high schools in September 1957.[54]

Branton reported that in spite of the court defeat he was pleased by some aspects of the decision, especially the affirmation by the appeals court that desegregation must take place the following school term. Branton felt that the ruling offered an important "cloak of protection against some die-hard, anti-integration groups who might still try to delay integration."[55] In a letter to the head of the school board attorney team, Archibald F. House, Branton asserted "the plaintiffs feel just as strongly about the issues." Yet, he added, "time has made many of the problems moot and the opinion of the appellate court clarified some of the issues more favorably for us." Branton believed that the court decision left room for "give and take" that could "make for a spirit of goodwill and harmony among the students and patrons in the initial phase of school desegregation at Little Rock."[56]

Branton's confident tone despite the court defeat came within a context of continuing positive developments in Arkansas. In the schools, with Little Rock under federal court order to desegregate, four other major municipal school districts at Pine Bluff, Hot Springs, North Little Rock, and Fort Smith drew up integration plans for September 1957.[57] By then, all of the publicly supported state colleges and universities had begun to admit black students. In the political arena, six blacks were appointed to the DSC by Governor Faubus, two blacks were elected to the city councils of Hot Springs and Alexander, and two blacks were elected to school boards at Wabbaseka and Dollarway. Local groups and associations across the state made goodwill gestures promoting interracial harmony. Several religious groups integrated, with an interracial Ministerial Alliance formed in Little Rock in 1956. Some county medical societies also integrated their memberships, along with the American Association of University Women in Conway and Fayetteville and the Little Rock League of Women voters.[58]

The most striking development came in April 1956 when four municipalities, Little Rock, Hot Springs, Pine Bluff, and Fort Smith, successfully desegregated their public transportation systems. This occurred after a misunderstood Supreme Court ruling in *South Carolina Electric & Gas Co. v. Flemming* (1956), which many national newspapers reported as heralding the end of segregation in public transport. Amid the confusion, several bus companies in Upper South cities took the initiative to desegregate.[59] Even after discovering the mistake, the policy continued in Arkansas. All interstate waiting rooms for buses and trains desegregated without incident.[60] This was in direct contrast to Montgomery, Alabama, where it took a much publicized bus boycott, led by local preacher Martin Luther King Jr., and yet another Supreme Court ruling, *Browder v. Gayle* (1956), to move the city to desegregate its public transport.[61]

True, there were other developments in the state, most notably in the political arena, that appeared to counter the progress made in other areas. Many of these developments related to Governor Faubus's continuing vacillation on the school desegregation issue, a vacillation that perplexed blacks and whites alike. Throughout his first term in office, Faubus stuck to his laissez-faire policy of allowing local communities to cope with school desegregation in their own time. In his inaugural address, Faubus did not even mention race as an issue, and when the Pupil Assignment Bill passed into the legislature in 1955, he steered well clear of the controversy. When trouble flared at Hoxie, Faubus declined to intervene and allowed the protests of segregationists to fizzle out in due course. Although the governor's stance did nothing to actively help the course of school desegregation, his refusal to become embroiled in the issue at least prevented the Citizens' Council's efforts to give the race question mainstream political exposure.[62]

However, as Faubus's reelection campaign began in 1956, his relatively benign stance on school desegregation began to drift toward strong support for maintaining segregation as a result of combined national, regional, and local developments. At a national level, the impact of *Brown II* and the reluctance of either the Supreme Court, Congress, or the president to stand firmly behind school desegregation prompted a shift in southern opinion away from acceptance of implementation.[63] Across the South, it increasingly appeared that moving with shifting public sentiment on school desegregation was becoming a political necessity.[64] Alabama governor James E. Folsom's defeat by Charles W. McKay for election to the National Democratic Committee in May 1956 confirmed this. McKay, a political unknown, used Folsom's perceived moderate position on school desegregation to win a convincing victory.[65] In Arkansas, the Citizens' Councils were critical of Faubus's moderate stance, lampooning him in their publications as "Awful Faubus" and demanding he declare himself "either for the white folks or for the NAACP."[66]

Jumping on the bandwagon, head of the ACCA Jim Johnson looked to increase the political pressure on Faubus. Johnson was born and reared in Crossett, southwest Arkansas. After serving in the U.S. Marine Corps during the Second World War, he graduated with a law degree from Cumberland Law School in Tennessee and then returned to Crossett to ply his trade. At the age of twenty-five, Johnson won election to the Arkansas Senate. A self-styled agrarian radical and defender of the common man, he was regarded as a personable politician and effective speaker, employing a revivalist style of political campaigning and casting himself in the role of the battling underdog. These qualities notwithstanding, Johnson made an unsuccessful run for state attorney general in 1954, failing to translate his local and regional political support into statewide recognition. Johnson's association with the battle over integration at Hoxie and his leadership of the ACCA had significantly helped raise his political profile in the state.[67]

In 1956, staking his political career on a radical anti-integration stand, Johnson proposed an amendment to the state constitution that would uphold the idea of interposition. The largely discredited and constitutionally dubious theory of interposition contended that a state could use its position of independent sovereignty to guard its citizens from the enactment of unjust federal laws. Concerning school desegregation, Johnson's proposed amendment effectively meant that Arkansas would refuse to obey the *Brown* decision, even at the insistence of federal government that it do so. Johnson managed to garner 33,000 signatures to win a place for his proposal on the November 1956 state ballot. In May 1956, he announced he would run against Faubus in the DPA primary for governor.[68]

Faubus reacted to these developments by staking out his own segregationist credentials. In a *New York Times* interview, Faubus declared he could not "be party to any attempt to force acceptance of a change to which the people are so overwhelmingly opposed."[69] To demonstrate his revised outlook on school desegregation, Faubus appointed a five-man committee to study prosegregation measures passed by the Virginia legislature, a state at the forefront of massive resistance campaigns in the South. Faubus released a report based on the findings of the Bird Committee (named after State Board of Education chair Marvin E. Bird) on February 25, 1956. The first of the report's two main proposals involved a revision of the interposition amendment advocated by Johnson. Rather than a constitutional amendment, the Bird Committee recommended little more than a token gesture placing Arkansas on record as opposing the *Brown* decision but precluding any further action. The second proposal was a Pupil Assignment Law similar to the one already approved by the Arkansas General Assembly in 1955.[70]

Although they were by no means radical, Faubus used the Bird Committee's findings to good effect during his 1956 reelection campaign for governor. On the one hand, the report's proposals stole the thunder of Faubus's most viable opponent, Johnson, by appropriating his interposition amendment in a watered-down form. This allowed the incumbent governor to assume a segregationist mantle, declare Arkansas "solidly with the Solid South," and thereby earn segregationist support.[71] On the other hand, while courting segregationists, Faubus managed to retain support from white moderates and liberals, as well as from many black Arkansans. To them, he presented himself as a calm and reasonable figure in contrast to his opponent, portrayed by Faubus as an extremist on the race issue and a "purveyor of hate."[72]

On the campaign trail, Faubus demonstrated he could carry off the segregationist or the moderate stance to order. At a speech in Pine Bluff, he began a sentence by asserting that segregation was not an issue in the campaign, which brought boos and jeers from the audience. Faubus then finished the sentence with the assurance that there would be "no breakdown of the state's traditional segregation pattern," which brought cheers of support.[73] Faubus skillfully managed to be all things to all people. Consequently, few people were clear on exactly what he believed. Over a year after the Pine Bluff speech, a bemused *Arkansas Democrat* reader declared, "I consider the governor without peer in the art of carrying the water of segregation on one shoulder and the water of integration on the other without spilling a drop of either."[74]

Faubus went on to win a relatively easy victory over Johnson in the first DPA primary ballot, thus ensuring a return to office.[75] At the November election, the electorate voted for the Bird Committee's proposals, with the interposition resolution winning by 199,511 to 127,360 votes and the

Pupil Assignment Law proposal winning by 214,712 to 121,129 votes. Johnson's interposition amendment was also adopted, albeit by the much narrower margin of 185,374 to 146,064 votes. Although the results clearly showed that a majority of the Arkansas electorate favored measures to preserve segregation, they also indicated that voters shied away from the more radical proposal suggested by Johnson. Even Faubus's modest measures attracted a significant amount of opposition, given the heightened emotions surrounding school desegregation in the South at the time.[76]

The election certainly did not seem to mandate the passage of more hard-line segregationist legislation that emerged from the Arkansas General Assembly in 1957. However, immediate political necessities again overrode Faubus's potential voice of calm and moderation. After Faubus's reelection, his next major hurdle was to pass legislation that would set the agenda for his second administration. At the top of his list was a $22 million package that included money for socially progressive programs such as raising education standards and increasing welfare benefits. Such measures would involve controversial tax increases, and their success depended upon the willingness of east Arkansas' conservative politicians to cooperate. East Arkansas politicians, in turn, brought their own pressing agenda to the Arkansas General Assembly as they sought to stop school desegregation from proceeding in the state.[77]

Faubus used the concerns of east Arkansas politicians about desegregation to broker a compromise. In return for the passage of his measures, Faubus agreed to sign into law four prosegregation bills. The bills were far more radical than any previous legislation to circumvent desegregation. The first bill required certain organizations to submit regularly updated lists of members to the state. This measure looked to intimidate NAACP members by rendering them vulnerable to recriminations by whites. The second bill provided for an amendment to the state constitution that removed compulsory school attendance if desegregation took place. The third bill proposed to make available state money to help fund the legal costs of school districts sued for trying to avoid desegregation. The fourth bill provided for the creation of a ten-man State Sovereignty Commission to help coordinate the fight against desegregation throughout the state. The commission would comprise three members appointed by the governor, five by the legislature, with both the governor and speaker of the Arkansas House of Representatives as ex-officio members.[78]

When the package of measures for his second administration had passed safely through the legislature, Faubus failed to implement any of the prosegregation legislation. Particularly annoying to the sponsors was Faubus's reluctance to make appointments to the State Sovereignty Commission, the cornerstone of the prosegregation program. Without a quorum, the commission was unable to act upon the measures passed by the general assembly. Eventually, east Arkansas politicians launched a successful lawsuit that forced Faubus to fill the places on the commission.[79] Faubus's delay effectively undermined the prosegregation measures, since the commission was not able to hold its first meeting until August 30, just a week before school desegregation was due to occur.[80]

Faubus's move to a more moderate position on school desegregation once the immediate political necessity of hard-line rhetoric had passed was also evident in his dealings with the Citizens' Councils. They repeatedly petitioned Faubus to invoke the interposition amendment and use his authority as head of a sovereign state to prevent school desegregation from taking place. Faubus scoffed at any notion that he might intervene, telling the press, "Everyone knows no state law supersedes a federal law." "If anyone expects me to use them to supersede federal laws," he said, "they are wrong."[81]

Three years after *Brown*, the position of Arkansas toward school desegregation remained unclear. Conflicting signs from school boards, the courts, politicians, and the electorate meant there was continuing confusion over the eventual outcome of the Supreme Court ruling. A memo from the ACHR to the offices of the SRC sent less than a month before Central High was due to desegregate described sentiments as "mixed" with "defying forces . . . [as] in other sections of the South" along with "progressive affirming forces." On the side of defiance, the memo pointed to the interposition amendment to the Arkansas constitution and the prosegregation laws. On the side of progress, it pointed to the voluntary desegregation of buses, state-supported colleges and universities, five school districts, some public libraries, and several ministerial associations. The memo concluded, "[T]he defying forces and the affirming forces just now seem squared off for a tussle." Prophetically, it predicted, "In the matter of school desegregation this may prove a fateful year."[82]

The Little Rock School Crisis | 5

After three years of equivocation following the *Brown* decision, the issue of school desegregation swiftly reached its denouement at Little Rock in the latter half of 1957. Over the summer, Virgil Blossom drew up attendance zones for admission to Central High that included two hundred black students. He then asked L. M. Christophe and Edwin L. Hawkins, principals of Horace Mann High School and Dunbar Junior High, to determine how many of their students wanted to apply for transfer. Thirty-two pupils from Horace Mann and thirty-eight from Dunbar Junior High indicated interest in attending Central. Blossom asked the principals to screen each student individually and to make a judgment as to their suitability for selection, based upon a range of factors including intelligence (Blossom insisted all those selected must possess an IQ of over one hundred), personality traits, and social skills. When this process was completed, the principals forwarded the names of suitable candidates to Blossom for further screening.[1]

Blossom forged ahead with the plans for attendance zones and screening without bothering to consult the Little Rock NAACP. It learned of the new plans only through the black community grapevine. Upon hearing the news, Daisy Bates contacted the principals of the two black schools, who confirmed the selection process was already underway. The principals suggested Bates contact Blossom for an explanation of his actions. When Bates contacted Blossom, he agreed to meet with local NAACP officials.[2]

At the subsequent meeting, Blossom explained his actions by comparing the situation in the schools with the desegregation of baseball, where Jackie Robinson had been selected as the first black player because of his high personal standing, conduct, and morals. Similarly, Blossom stated, "I feel that for this transition from segregation to integration in the Little Rock school system, we should select and encourage only the best Negro students to attend Central High School—so that no criticism of the integration process could be attributed to inefficiency, poor scholarship, low morals, or poor citizenship."[3]

Questioned by local NAACP officials, Blossom admitted he could not legally turn down an application from a student simply because he or she did not meet his criteria. However, Blossom made it clear he would do everything to discourage such a candidate. With regard to the new attendance zone, which further limited the pool of potential black applicants to Central High, Blossom told the Little Rock NAACP he was prepared to invoke the Pupil Assignment Law if any complaints were raised. Furthermore, Blossom asserted that he would make any final decision on transfers to Central High. "I know it is undemocratic, and I know it is wrong," Blossom told them, "but I am doing it."[4]

Blossom's continuing manipulation of the school desegregation process angered Little Rock NAACP members, particularly as the court seemed to rule out any further modifications to the existing Blossom Plan. Efforts to screen candidates, they complained, "seem[ed] to carry persuasion and possibly pressure" and served only to instill "a feeling of inferiority, fear and intimidation" in black students. Moreover, they pointed out, the threat to use the Pupil Assignment Law clearly contradicted the "good faith" compliance demanded by ongoing court jurisdiction. Blossom responded that he already had discussed these matters with the judge and insisted that all the changes would stand.[5]

Since it was now too late to challenge the measures in court, the Little Rock NAACP reluctantly accepted the new changes to the already modified Blossom Plan. When the two black principals recommended thirty-two of their students to Blossom, he rigorously interviewed each of them again. As predicted by the Little Rock NAACP, Blossom used the selection process to dissuade students from attending Central High. In one case, he reduced a prospective female student to tears by declaring that she lacked the right "scholastic background and emotional responsibility." When two talented black high school football players turned up at his office, Blossom warned them that their careers would come to a premature end if they attended Central High. Blossom ruled, adding yet another new proviso to school desegregation, that no black students would be allowed to participate in any of the social or sports activities at Central. Upon hearing this, both students withdrew their applications.[6] Finally, after a grueling ordeal, the number of students permitted to integrate Central High School stood at just nine. They were Minnijean Brown, Elizabeth Eckford, Ernest Green, Thelma Mothershed, Melba Pattillo, Gloria Ray, Terrance Roberts, Jefferson Thomas, and Carlotta Walls.[7]

The students, later known as the "Little Rock Nine," only met as a group for the first time in August 1957, but they shared common traits. All nine students were strong-willed and fiercely independent, had made the decision to apply to Central High without pressure from either the NAACP or their parents, and belonged to families who had lived in Little Rock for many years and were relatively affluent. Furthermore, these nine students shared the same two main reasons for wanting to attend Central High. First, they lived closer to the school than to Horace Mann and wanted to attend the school nearer their homes. Second, they were academically ambitious and saw an education at Central as the best way to develop their talents. They realized that they would be pioneers in attending Central High and were taking an important step for the black community as a whole. Initially, however, the desire to integrate Central was at best a secondary consideration. For all nine students, attending the school was primarily a practical matter rather than an end goal.[8]

Individual experiences and circumstances also shaped the motives of the nine students. Ernest Green, at sixteen going on seventeen years of age, was the only senior in the group. Ernest lived with his mother, L. S. Green, and a younger brother. Ernest's father, a postal worker, had died just four years earlier. Mrs. Green was an elementary schoolteacher, and Ernest's aunt Treopia Gravely taught at Horace Mann. Ernest therefore had a good understanding of the school transfer process. In the summer of 1956, Ernest worked as a locker-room attendant at the predominantly Jewish Westridge Country Club. There, he met several white Central High students and consequently already had some acquaintances at the school.[9]

Carlotta Walls, at fourteen the youngest of the nine students, had even stronger friendships with whites, which she wanted to maintain. Carlotta lived with her mother, Juanita, thirty-two, a secretary in the office of a public housing project; her father, Cartelyou, thirty-five, a brick mason; and two younger sisters. The Walls family lived in an integrated neighborhood. Carlotta therefore had grown up with both black and white friends and, as she said, had "been playing with all my neighbors as long as I can remember." Two of her best friends attended Central High. Like many black and white children in the South, Carlotta explained, they "didn't even think about this race thing until it was time for us to start school and then they started separating us. Well, if nobody else had wanted to go to Central, I would have. I always did."[10]

Thelma Mothershed, sixteen, lived with her mother, Hosana, forty-one, who worked as a psychiatric aide at the Veterans Hospital in North Little Rock; her father A. L.; and two younger brothers. Thelma had suffered from a cardiac condition since infancy. For medical reasons alone, the ten-block journey to Central High was far preferable to the two-mile trek to Horace Mann. Additionally, Thelma's two older sisters provided inspiration in her decision to apply to Central. Lois, twenty-nine, was the first black student to enroll at Phillips University, Oklahoma, an institution supported by the Disciples of Christ of the Christian Church. Grace, eighteen, majored in nursing at the desegregated University of Arkansas. Thelma's familial experiences of desegregated education formed the backdrop for her own pioneering effort.[11]

Elizabeth Ann Eckford, fifteen, lived with her mother, Birdie, thirty-eight, who taught laundry work every weekday at the black Arkansas School for the Blind and Deaf; her father, Oscar, thirty-seven, who worked at the Little Rock railroad station as a dining-car maintenance worker; and five brothers and sisters. Elizabeth was a late applicant. When the initial screening of students began at Horace Mann in May 1957, she had not been certain whether she wanted to transfer. Elizabeth said she "thought this was a pretty important decision to make and I didn't think I could think it out in one day." After weighing her options all summer, she finally decided to transfer. When Elizabeth and her mother went to see Blossom, the final list of transfers was already complete. Although Blossom kept them waiting while he attended to whites first, they persevered, and he finally agreed Elizabeth could attend Central High when the term began in September.[12]

Terrance Roberts, fifteen, lived with his mother, Margaret, thirty-seven, who operated a catering service from home; his father, William, thirty-seven, who worked in the Dietetic Department at the Veterans

Hospital in North Little Rock; and five younger brothers and sisters. Teachers at Horace Mann rated Terrance as the most academically gifted of the nine. Terrance's older sister, Jurreta, eighteen, had been offered numerous scholarships when she graduated from Horace Mann, including one from prestigious Howard University in Washington, D.C. However, she decided to enroll at Oakwood College, Huntsville, Alabama, run by Seventh Day Adventists, the church to which the Roberts family belonged.[13]

Gloria Ray, fifteen, lived with her mother, Mary, a field worker for the state welfare department; and father, Harvey, sixty-eight, a retired agricultural extension supervisor for the Arkansas State Department of Agriculture. Gloria had an older brother and sister who no longer lived in the family home. Gloria's reason for attending Central was, she said, "quite simple. . . . I want to be an atomic scientist." Although she was "grateful for all they taught me at Dunbar [Junior High School]," she explained, "I just felt that I could get more at Central than I could at Horace Mann."[14]

Minnijean Brown, sixteen, lived with her mother Imogene, forty, a homemaker; her father, Willie Bobbie, fifty-five, a concrete finisher and stone mason; and four younger brothers and sisters. Minnijean wanted to attend Central High because it was closer to her home. "Central is only nine blocks [away]," she explained, "and Horace Mann is a mile and a half if not two miles. I can easily walk to Central."[15]

Melba Pattillo, fifteen, lived with her mother, Lois, an English teacher at Jones High School in North Little Rock; her grandmother, India; and her younger brother. Ambitious and talented, Melba wanted to be an actress and took ballet, voice, and piano lessons. For her, Central High offered the chance of a better education and therefore more opportunities to pursue her chosen vocation.[16]

Jefferson Thomas, fifteen, lived with his mother, Jessie, a nurse's aide at a private hospital; and his father, Ellis Thomas, forty-five, a farm-equipment salesman. All of Jefferson's seven older brothers and sisters, except his brother Granville, nineteen, had moved out of Little Rock. Jefferson longed to join them, especially sister Jessie, seventeen, who lived with another of his sisters, Mary Alice, twenty-four, a registered nurse in San Diego. Jessie attended an integrated school there. To Jefferson, a good education at Central took him one step closer to moving out to the West Coast.[17]

The parents of the nine black students held mixed views about the decision of their sons and daughters to attend Central High. Cartelyou

Walls provided the most outspoken support for his daughter Carlotta. "Only one thought ever crossed my mind about the whole thing" he claimed. "She had a right to go there. My tax money is not separated from the rest of the tax money. There is no reason for her to pass one school to go to another." A decorated veteran of the Second World War, he believed he had "fought as hard as anybody else. . . . So I don't see why my child should be barred from a school for which I fought. The Constitution of the U.S. gives her as much rights as anyone else." Other parents were less vociferous but still lent their support. "[I] let [Minnijean] decide," said her father, Willie Bobbie Brown, adding he was proud of his daughter's stand and the courage it took. Mrs. Green told her son Ernest that "it was up to him since he had to put up with whatever might happen there." The parents of Jefferson Thomas and Melba Pattillo also gave their approval to their offspring to attend Central High.[18]

Some parents were more ambivalent about their child's choice. "To really face up to it," admitted Terrance Roberts's mother, "I definitely didn't want Terry to go to Central." Then, "[he] convinced me it was the thing to do. So I agreed to go along with the plan." Thelma Mothershed's mother, Hosana, said she "wanted her to go to Central in a way and in another way I didn't. I kept thinking about her weak heart. . . . I just didn't know." Then she realized "[I]t was up to Thelma to pave the way for Gilbert and Michael [Thelma's younger brothers] and all the other Negro kids who would come behind her. If she went to school there now, then it would be easier for the others coming along." Elizabeth Eckford's mother knew her daughter was thinking about applying to Central, but, she said, "I was hoping she'd forget about the whole thing. In my heart, I really didn't want her to go, so I was hoping she would forget it." Elizabeth did not forget and pestered her mother continually to help her enroll at Central. After several weeks, her mother finally relented.[19]

Only Gloria Ray's parents adamantly opposed their daughter's efforts to attend. Her mother, said Gloria, "was against it from the very beginning. She put her foot down and told me not to think about it any more." Her elderly father opposed the move, too. He did not want to see his "baby" Gloria put in harm's way. Moreover, he was a wealthy, respected member of the black community. The Ray family lived in a two-story whitewashed colonial house and had both black and white friends. Harvey Ray did not want his family's comfortable life and community standing threatened because of his daughter's becoming involved in a racial controversy. Gloria ignored the wishes of her parents and registered to attend

Central High without their consent. Gloria confessed to her mother what she had done the same day. Mary Ray told Gloria not to tell her father the news, since she feared for his health. (Harvey Ray had retired in 1953 because of a heart condition.) They agreed to tell him later. As it turned out, he found out only on the first day of classes. As he was watching a television broadcast about the event, a reporter mentioned Gloria's name as one of the nine students attempting to enter the school. "I guess Daddy was a little upset about it," said Gloria. "He really put his foot down and told me I wasn't going back there no matter what happened." It took a great deal of persuasion by Gloria, her mother, who by then was resigned to her daughter's attending Central, and Daisy and L. C. Bates to change his mind.[20]

In August 1957, as the prospect of desegregation at Central High drew closer, a flurry of lawsuits sought to clarify the legality of recent proseg-regation legislation. On August 16, ten local black ministers, with the support of the Little Rock NAACP, filed suit in the federal district court to try to establish that the four segregation measures passed by the Arkansas General Assembly were unconstitutional. On August 17, a local Little Rock businessman, William F. Rector, on behalf of the school board, sought a declaratory judgment from the Pulaski County Chancery Court that the four segregation measures were legal. On August 19, Amis Guthridge, leader of Little Rock's Capital Citizens' Council (CCC), filed suit in the Pulaski County Chancery Court on behalf of Eva Wilbern and her daughter Kay, demanding white students be given the right to attend segregated classes as provided for in the Arkansas General Assembly legislation.[21] On August 20, Arkansas Attorney General Bruce Bennett intervened, asking the federal district court to put aside the suit by the ministers until after the hearing of Rector's suit in the Pulaski County Chancery Court. On August 25, lawyers acting on behalf of the Little Rock NAACP asked the court to ignore Bennett's request.[22]

On August 26, Bennett launched two new suits in Pulaski County Chancery Court clearly designed to intimidate the NAACP. The first charged that the NAACP had not registered its operation as a business concern before the previous April and therefore owed the state $350 in back taxes. The second, against the LDF, charged that it had never registered as a business with the Arkansas secretary of state and asked for the levying of a $5,000 fine.[23]

The litigation revealed the complex and divergent agendas involved in school desegregation. The minister's lawsuit merely sought to clarify that the recently passed segregation laws were unconstitutional. Rector's lawsuit apparently sought to explore the possibility that the legislation might still be used to prevent desegregation. Guthridge's lawsuit sought to force the actual implementation of prosegregation legislation. Bennett's interventions seemed to be the opening salvo in a challenge to Faubus for the office of governor the following year, staking out his segregationist credentials. Cumulatively, the lawsuits stirred a great deal of controversy and confusion over school desegregation, none of which helped ease an already tense situation.[24]

The CCC tried to exploit the unease brought about by the lawsuits by inviting two high-profile segregationists, Georgia governor Marvin Griffin and former speaker of the Georgia House of Representatives Roy Harris, to speak in Little Rock. Disturbed about the impact their presence might have on the city, Faubus telephoned Griffin to ask him not to inflame the situation with incendiary rhetoric. Griffin told him, "Naw, I'm gonna give 'em hell on the constitution and Roy is gonna give 'em hell on the civil rights thing. But nobody will advocate violence." With that assurance, Faubus invited the two Georgians to stay with him at the governor's mansion. That night, reneging on his earlier promise not to rabble-rouse, Griffin lauded the 350 persons present at a CCC fund-raising dinner as "a courageous bunch of patriots." Griffin told them that "a dedicated people, a steadfast General Assembly and an administration committed unequivocally toward preservation of our cherished institutions" assured there would be no desegregation in Georgia. Harris told the crowd Griffin would use the highway patrol to resist desegregation if necessary, and if that failed, he would enlist "every white man in Georgia."[25]

Although clearly unhelpful, neither the litigation nor the speeches by Griffin and Harris were serious enough to derail the desegregation process. The real bombshell came on August 27 when a newly formed segregationist group, the Mother's League of Central High, filed suit in Pulaski County Chancery Court. The suit sought to prevent desegregation from taking place by invoking the prosegregation laws approved by the Arkansas General Assembly.[26] Acting as spokesperson for the group, Mrs. Clyde Thomason claimed that recent events caused "uncertainty of the law, conflicting court decisions and a general state of confusion and unrest." This would lead to "civil commotion" if the school board implemented its desegregation plan. At face value, the suit appeared yet another futile bid to prevent desegregation. However, the league then dramatically called Governor Faubus as its star witness. On the stand, Faubus testified he believed violence would occur if plans for school desegregation went ahead, citing unsubstantiated reports of increased weapons sales in the city and the recent confiscation of revolvers from both white and black students.[27]

Faubus later pointed to a number of reasons for intervening in school desegregation at such a late hour. In the wake of Griffin and Harris's speeches, many people, Faubus claimed, were exerting pressure, demanding to know why Arkansas had to have school desegregation when Georgia did not. Faubus was also wary of Bruce Bennett's efforts to court the segregationist vote through his lawsuits against the NAACP. As the date for integration drew closer, Faubus felt the school board and superintendent of schools were beginning to panic and look to him to put his neck on the line by publicly supporting their desegregation plan. There were pressures from the courts, from east Arkansas politicians, from segregationists, and even from the federal government, who Faubus believed were all attempting to place the responsibility for school desegregation on his shoulders.[28]

With all these factors weighing on him, Faubus took a calculated political gamble. As he saw it, he had two options. On the one hand, he could take a stand for integration and lose his campaign for a third successive term as governor. On the other hand, he could take a stand for segregation, reap its political rewards, and face the consequences. After three years of vacillation, Faubus finally decided which side would pay the best dividends and threw his lot in with the segregationists.[29]

Chancellor Murray O. Reed, a Faubus appointee, ruled in favor of the Mother's League and issued a restraining order against the school board, preventing its desegregation plan from going ahead. Lawyers for the school board promptly petitioned the federal district court, asking it to forbid the implementation of Reed's order. On Friday, August 30, Judge Ronald N. Davies upheld the school board's petition and ordered school desegregation to proceed as planned the following Tuesday. Davies was a temporary assignee to the bench because of an unfilled vacancy and was therefore a newcomer to events. Since Arkansas was the only southern state in the Eighth Circuit Federal Court District, temporary replacements often came from northern and midwestern states. Hailing from Fargo, North Dakota, Davies was detached from the southern mores and local politics that governed issues of school desegregation and simply followed the letter of the law in his ruling.[30]

Upon hearing of Davies's decision, Faubus met with William J. Smith, his legislative counsel, and discussed the idea of calling out the National Guard to prevent desegregation from taking place. Smith counseled against doing that unless serious violence and disorder actually developed.[31] Over the weekend, a friend telephoned Blossom to warn him the National Guard was on standby. Blossom then turned to *Arkansas Gazette* assistant editor Hugh Patterson for help. Patterson attempted to contact various people to talk to the governor, including former president Truman. Since it was Labor Day weekend, many of those he tried to reach were away from home. Eventually, Patterson persuaded Winthrop Rockefeller, whom Faubus had asked to become chair of the Arkansas Industrial Development Commission (AIDC) in 1955, to talk to the governor. When they met, Faubus intimated to Rockefeller that calling out the National Guard was the only way he could keep his political ambitions alive.[32]

At 9:00 P.M. on Monday, September 2, the evening before Central High was due to desegregate, armed guardsmen began to cordon off the school buildings. At 10:15 P.M. Faubus gave a speech, broadcast by all local television and radio stations, claiming he had evidence of impending violence in the city. Therefore, he had called out the National Guard "to maintain or restore order and to protect the lives and property of citizens." Ambiguously, Faubus stated that the troops would "not act as segregationists or integrationists, but as soldiers called to active duty to carry out their assigned tasks." Clarifying his statement somewhat, he added, "it will not be possible to restore or maintain order and protect the lives and property of the citizens if forcible integration is carried out tomorrow." That being the case, Faubus said, the schools "must be operated on the same basis as they have been in the past."[33]

Shortly after Faubus finished his speech, the school board issued a statement: "In view of the situation . . . no negro students [should] attempt to attend Central or any white high school until this dilemma is legally resolved."[34] The following day, as white students began their first day of classes at Central High, the school board petitioned Judge Davies to advise them on how to proceed. Davies replied that the board should abide by Faubus's statement. National Guardsmen were neither segregationists nor integrationists but were there to preserve the peace. Desegregation, Davies declared, must proceed as planned the following day.[35]

That afternoon, Blossom called together a group of black leaders and the parents of the nine black students who were to integrate Central High. In a further demonstration of his contempt for the NAACP, Blossom did not invite Daisy Bates to the meeting, though she did attend at the request of the parents. At the meeting, Blossom said no one should accompany the students to school the following morning. Blossom reasoned that, if violence did break out, it would be "easier to protect the children if the adults aren't there." Many of the parents remained far from satisfied about the safety of their children, particularly those who remembered John Carter's lynching party roaming the streets of the city just thirty years earlier. There was further anxiety that evening when a young white reporter appeared on Bates's doorstep, imploring her not to let the students attend Central High alone because of the near-hysteria gripping many whites in the city. "I've never seen anything like it" the reporter told Bates. "People I've known all my life—they've gone mad. They're totally without reason."[36]

As a safety precaution Bates telephoned Rev. Dunbar Ogden Jr., one of the few sympathetic white clergymen in the city. Bates asked Ogden to round up a delegation of black and white ministers to accompany the students to school the next day. Ogden called several other ministers before reporting with regret that there was little enthusiasm for the plan. Nevertheless, Ogden said he would keep trying to enlist support. He arranged to meet Bates and the nine children a few blocks from the school at the intersection of Twelfth and Park Streets the next morning. Bates then telephoned the city police to ask them to meet with the students and ministers to escort them to Central High. The city police agreed, but warned that their officers could not go beyond the school limits, since the area was now out of their jurisdiction. Finally, at 2:30 A.M., Bates telephoned all the black parents (except the Eckfords, who did not have a telephone) to tell them of the plan. Exhausted, Bates decided to go to bed and to contact the Eckfords the next morning.[37]

Elizabeth Eckford had already set off for school the following morning before Bates could contact her. Leaving anxious parents behind, she caught the bus to school and alighted a block from Central High. Elizabeth saw about four hundred people gathered at the school entrance. A cordon of National Guardsmen surrounded the building. Trying to avoid the crowd, Elizabeth attempted to pass the line of guardsmen at the corner of the building. Refusing to let her through, a soldier directed her to the main entrance. Temporarily disarmed at the sight of one lone black female student, the crowd silently parted. When Elizabeth tried to enter the school, a soldier who had just allowed a white student inside the building blocked her path with his bayonet. Other guardsmen closed ranks around him.[38]

Elizabeth suddenly realized she was at the mercy of a mob. "Lynch her! Lynch her!" someone shouted. "No nigger bitch is going to get in our school. Get out of here!" another screamed. Elizabeth made for the nearest bus stop, closely followed by the mob. As Elizabeth sat at the bus stop in tears, Grace Lorch, a white woman whose husband, Lee, worked at Philander Smith College, came to her aid. With the departure of Iggers from Little Rock the previous year, the Lorches were now the only active white members in the local NAACP. Lorch turned on the mob and told them, "Leave this child alone! Why are you tormenting her? Six months from now you will hang your heads in shame." Fortunately, a city bus arrived soon afterward. Lorch boarded the bus with Elizabeth and escorted her away from the scene.[39]

Daisy and L. C. Bates were driving to meet with the students and the Reverend Ogden when they heard a radio report about the mobbing of Elizabeth at Central High. Horrified, L. C. leapt out of the car to try to find her. When Daisy arrived at Twelfth and Park, two white ministers, Ogden (accompanied by his son, David) and Rev. Will Campbell, and two black ministers, Rev. Z. Z. Driver and Rev. W. H. Bass, were with the students. A police car was there as promised. When the group arrived at Central High, the ministers chaperoned the students to the entrance, jostled and shoved by the mob on the way. Again, guardsmen refused to let the students enter. The delegation returned to its cars. The Bateses, the ministers, and the students then headed to Blossom's office, only to find him absent. Afterward they went to consult with the U.S. attorney for the Eastern District of Arkansas, Osro Cobb, who passed them on to FBI officials to make statements about what had happened.[40]

Faubus later confirmed he had given the order not to admit black students to the school, because he detected increased tension in the community. Faubus's actions placed his authority directly between a federal order and its local implementation. A terse exchange of telegrams between Faubus and President Eisenhower over the next few days contested the grounds of authority in the matter. A conference between Faubus and Eisenhower on September 14, arranged by Arkansas congressman Brooks Hays and presidential assistant Sherman Adams, produced little concrete agreement. Still Eisenhower refused to intervene, although he did verbally rebuke the governor for his actions.[41]

A resolution of the matter appeared to rest with the courts. On the same day as Elizabeth Eckford's mobbing at Central High, the school board asked Judge Davies to suspend his order to integrate, because of potential violence and disorder. The following Friday, September 6, Branton demanded that desegregation proceed as planned. On Saturday, Davies turned down the school board's request for a delay. The following Monday morning, September 9, Davies received a full report on the situation in Little Rock from U.S. Attorney General Herbert Brownell's office. After reading the report, Davies requested that both Brownell and Cobb enter the *Aaron v. Cooper* case as friends of the court. Davies indicated they should file a petition against Faubus; the commander of the Arkansas National Guard, Sherman Clinger; and the head of the National Guard unit at the school, Lieutenant Colonel Marion Johnson. Once granted, the petition would prevent the three from interfering with the implementation of the court order. After filing the petition the next day, Davies made Faubus, Clinger, and Johnson codefendants with the school board in the school desegregation case.[42]

At the following trial on September 20, Clinger and Johnson appeared in court but Faubus was absent. In an extraordinary move, Faubus's attorneys declared the governor did not recognize the authority of the court, and they asked permission to leave. Davies allowed them to do so. After the hearing, Davies granted an injunction prohibiting Faubus, Clinger, Johnson, or anyone under their orders from interfering with the school desegregation plan. Three hours later, Faubus conceded defeat and removed the National Guard from Central High. He then absented himself from events by flying away to attend the Southern Governors Conference at Sea Island, Georgia.[43]

At 8:00 A.M. the following Monday, September 23, all nine black students were with Daisy Bates at her home, waiting for news from city authorities. When the city police department telephoned, it warned that a mob of over one thousand whites had already gathered at Central High. The police agreed to meet Bates and the nine students near the school to provide an escort into the Sixteenth Street side entrance. White reporters who were camped at the Bateses set off for the school. Four black reporters remained behind to see if they could help. Bates told the black reporters that they too should go on ahead to Central High. After the black reporters left, the students divided into two cars, the first group with Daisy Bates and local black attorney Christopher C. Mercer, the second group with NAACP field secretary Frank W. Smith. The black reporters were first to reach Central High. When they arrived, the mob mistook them for the student entourage. "Here they come!" shouted someone. "Get the niggers! Get 'em." At the precise moment the mob descended upon the black reporters and started to beat them, Bates, Mercer, and Smith arrived with the nine students, who were swiftly taken into the school through the Sixteenth Street entrance. Realizing what had happened, someone from the mob yelled, "They're in! The niggers are in!"[44]

Throughout the morning, a white female student supplied a series of false reports to radio correspondents about the mobbing of black students inside the school. The unsubstantiated information was broadcast. Naturally, the reports proved terrifying for the black parents. Fortunately, white attorney Edwin Dunaway, a friend of both Daisy Bates and the assistant chief of police, acted as an intermediary to provide regular reassurance that the students were unharmed. Yet as the morning wore on, the mob refused to disperse and began to overpower the police. For their safety, the nine students were removed from the school at 11:00 A.M.[45]

The scenes of lawlessness at Central High brought an angry response from President Eisenhower. The president issued a statement condemning events as "disgraceful" and sent a proclamation commanding "all persons engaged in such obstruction of justice to cease and desist therefrom, and to disperse forthwith." Nevertheless, the next day, a mob again assembled outside Central High, defiantly intent on preventing desegregation. Eisenhower then issued an executive order. The order brought the Arkansas National Guard into federal service and sent an additional one thousand soldiers of the 101st Airborne Division to Little Rock to uphold the court-ordered desegregation plan.[46]

On the morning of September 25, federal troops arrived at the Bateses' home to take the nine black students to Central High. With tears of pride welling in their eyes, Bates and the black parents waved the students off. At the school, a crowd of segregationists gathered, waiting for the students to arrive. When a federal officer asked them to disperse, they refused. Federal troops then moved them away at bayonet-point. A host of international, national, regional, and local media representatives watched the nine students arrive and enter Central High flanked by twenty-two armed federal troops. At the end of the school day, federal troops took the students back home again. The escort would become part of the students' daily routine over the following weeks.[47]

Entry into Central High was, the nine black students soon discovered, not an end to their troubles. Over the ensuing weeks, the students were subject to "threatening notes, verbal insults and threats, crowding, bumping and jostling in the halls."[48] With the battle to keep the nine black students from attending the school lost, segregationists turned their attention to encouraging white students to make life so unbearable inside the school the black students would be forced to withdraw voluntarily. Director of NAACP branches Gloster B. Current anticipated that "there is possibly going to be a concerted attempt to conduct a war of nerves to force the Negro kids to get out." However, he warned, "We lose everything we have gained if they move out."[49] Much of the ongoing black struggle in Little Rock, and by extension in the state, would now rest on the shoulders of nine black teenagers.

On October 1, the first in a series of incidents inside the school took place. At morning recess, two white students followed Terrance Roberts and Jefferson Thomas to the locker rooms. The students attacked Terrance and Jefferson, and others started to kick their books around the hallways. A National Guardsman standing nearby did nothing to help. Finally, vice-principal of girls Elizabeth Huckaby intervened and took the two boys who had carried out the initial attack to see Principal Jess W. Matthews. The inaction of guardsmen emboldened other white students, who began to intimidate black students further. Soon after the attack on Terrance and Jefferson, Minnijean Brown and Melba Pattillo reported to the principal's office for safety. As Daisy Bates put it, "The [white] kids were having a field day all over the place." Matthews suspended the two boys who attacked Terrance and Jefferson for a period of three days. When they returned, they began to threaten the black students again.[50]

To NAACP leaders, the lack of protection afforded the students was intolerable. A central problem, they felt, was the lack of coordination between the school authorities and the soldiers. Neither would assume responsibility for looking after the black students' interests. Current complained that "no-one seems to be maintaining order, for the Guards have looked the other way and the school authorities have not moved into the breach." Meanwhile, southwest regional field secretary for the NAACP Clarence Laws bemoaned the fact that "[t]he school authorities take the position that it is the Army's position to maintain order." Compounding the problem was the elusiveness of Major General Edwin A. Walker, who was in charge of the federalized forces. After several attempts to contact him, Laws eventually spoke with two of Walker's aides, demanding a meeting with the general to "ascertain exactly what his plans are to protect the persons of these children." No satisfactory answer was forthcoming.[51]

Walker's reluctance to act reflected his own doubts about school desegregation in Little Rock. Walker carried out Eisenhower's orders only under duress. Later, in 1961, President John F. Kennedy officially admonished Walker for trying to indoctrinate his troops with right-wing literature. Walker then resigned from the army in protest, only to resurface the following year as one of the leaders of an armed mob trying to prevent James Meredith from entering the University of Mississippi in Oxford. Declaring he had been "on the wrong side" at Little Rock, Walker exhorted the mob, "Bring your flags, your tents, your skillets! It is time! Now or Never," as he led them against federal marshals and Mississippi's federalized National Guard. By the end of the day, the mob had wounded 160 federal marshals and killed two people. U.S. Attorney General Robert Kennedy charged Walker with seditious conspiracy, insurrection, and rebellion and put him in jail for five days before finally sending him for psychiatric evaluation. Walker remained an active right-wing campaigner for the rest of his life.[52]

The harassment of students continued at Central High, culminating in a vicious attack on Jefferson. On November 11, federal troops withdrew from inside Central High, leaving only six National Guardsmen on patrol. The next morning, white students stepped up their campaign of violence. At lunchtime, while Jefferson was at his locker in a school hallway, two boys jumped him from behind, and one struck a blow that knocked Jefferson out cold. A teacher in a classroom nearby heard him fall and rushed to help. Laws came to collect Jefferson from school and took him to Dr. Robinson for treatment. Fearlessly, the boy insisted on returning to school the next day over the complaints of Daisy Bates, who told him he should stay at home to recover.[53]

The same morning Jefferson returned to school, Daisy Bates and Laws went to see Blossom to complain about the continuing unrest in the school. Bates asked Blossom what he intended to do about white students who repeatedly attacked black students. Stalling, Blossom said he was not aware of a large number of incidents. Bates then showed Blossom her records outlining a series of attacks and the names of the white perpetrators. Bates told Blossom, "If you really are interested in clearing up this trouble, you should expel some of these repeated troublemakers." Flustered, Blossom shouted, "You can't tell me how to run my school." "No, I can't," Bates shot back, "but it's up to you—not the army—to maintain discipline inside the school. By not doing so, you are subjecting the children to physical torture that you will have to live with for the rest of your life." Bates and Laws then stormed out of the office.[54]

That afternoon, Bates again unsuccessfully tried to get in touch with Major General Walker. Bates then telephoned Thurgood Marshall in New York to report the latest developments. Marshall told Bates he thought Walker would not talk to NAACP officials because army regulations prevented him from doing so. Bates later telephoned Val J. Washington, director of the minorities division of the Republican National Committee, to solicit help. Washington called back with the numbers of two of the general's aides who were supposed to know his whereabouts at all times. Bates telephoned one of the aides and demanded to speak with Walker. The aide called back a few minutes later and asked if he could take a message. Bates then explained about the attacks on the students. Shortly afterward, Walker telephoned Bates to discuss the situation. Walker gave his assurance that he would look into the problem.[55]

At 9:30 the next morning, Minnijean telephoned Daisy Bates from the vice-principal's office, crying: "Come and get us. We can't take it any longer. . . . The junior mob has taken over the school." Bates told Minnijean to remain in the office. Immediately afterward, Blossom telephoned with an assurance that reinforcements were on the way. At 11:30 A.M., each black student was temporarily assigned two federal guards for protection. Consequently, the situation inside the school calmed considerably. Although minor skirmishes continued to take place, there were no more reports of serious attacks by white students.[56]

Even the petty torments took their toll. Minnijean, the most outspoken of the nine students, found herself singled out for special treatment. Despite being kicked, threatened, and insulted, Minnijean still talked back to white students. On December 17, as she was carrying her lunch to a cafeteria table, a group of boys moved their chairs to obstruct her way. As she waited, the group pulled their chairs back. When Minnijean attempted to move forward again, the boys again moved their chairs to block her. After several failed attempts to pass by, she dumped a bowl of chili on the heads of two of the boys. A watching guardsman took Minnijean and the two boys to the principal's office. Matthews sent the two boys home to change clothes and suspended Minnijean from school for six days.[57]

The following term, on February 6, 1958, a white girl kicked Minnijean on the back of her legs and called her a "black bitch." Minnijean shot back, "White trash! Why don't you leave me alone?" At lunchtime, a boy threw a bowl of hot soup over Minnijean. Both ended up in Principal Matthews's office. Matthews suspended them for three days, the boy for throwing the soup and Minnijean for calling the girl white trash. Following a recommendation from Blossom, Minnijean received an expulsion for the remainder of the school term.[58] Given Minnijean's provocation and the things white students got away with doing, Laws blasted the expulsion as "a shocking and cruel miscarriage of justice." Laws continued, "For the segregationists who have long had juvenile mobs operating within the school, this must be a day of fiendish jubilation."[59] Sure enough, white students began to wear badges, "One down and eight to go." With the help of the NAACP's national office and Kenneth B. Clark, an eminent black psychologist, Minnijean received a scholarship to attend New Lincoln High School in New York.[60]

Laws believed that there was an even more sinister side to the expulsion. The week before, Blossom indicated that the school board was planning to take the issue of school desegregation back to the courts. Laws felt that "all of these harassments against the children in the school is part of a plan to show that neither the whites nor the Negroes are ready for school integration." He even believed that there were "some important people in business here who are behind this and their plans are for getting the kids out." Laws worriedly concluded, "There are signs that point to the fact that there is a well-laid conspiracy—I shouldn't use that word, plan is better—well-laid plans to keep this thing in a state of ferment."[61]

Despite the best efforts of white students to remove them from Central High, the remaining eight black students successfully completed the school year. On May 25, 1958, Ernest Green, the only senior among the black students, attended the first integrated graduation ceremony in the history of the school. One hundred twenty-five federalized National Guardsmen, alongside city police and detectives, were on hand to make sure no trouble occurred.[62]

As the nine black students battled the taunts and torments of white students, adults in the black community fought their own war against white hostility. Anyone actively promoting integration of schools was subject to a torrent of physical violence, public insults, and economic pressure from local white segregationists. Anger focused particularly on the Bateses, their friends and neighbors, the parents of the nine black students, and other NAACP members. It was not only the radical fringe of white opposition they were forced to deal with. State-sanctioned harassment from both federal and Arkansas authorities helped assist the segregationists in their campaign of hate.

The Bates residence at 1207 West Twenty-Eighth Street became a focal point of conflict during the school crisis. Daisy and L. C. had only moved into the new home over the summer of 1956. During the school crisis, the house was subject to a barrage of incendiary bombs and gunfire from passing gangs of white hoodlums. Reinforced steel screens replaced the broken glass at the front of the building. Persons unknown burned three fiery crosses, aping the Ku Klux Klan's signature, on the Bateses lawn. The house itself was set on fire twice. Despite this abuse, appeals to the local police and the federal government for protection fell upon deaf ears. No arrests resulted from any of the attacks.[63]

In response to the terrorism and the lack of assistance from white authorities, friends and neighbors organized an armed vigil every night at the Bateses. The Bateses' position in the debate between advocates of armed self-defense and advocates of nonviolence in the struggle for civil rights was somewhat ambiguous. On the one hand, they clearly empathized with figures like president of the Monroe NAACP branch in North Carolina, Robert Williams, who defended a tradition of black violence in response to white attacks. The Bateses publicly declared that they carried firearms to deter white assailants. A *State Press* editorial pointed out that it was "pretty hard to suppress certain feelings, when all around you, you see only hate," and observed that the use of nonviolence had never prevented whites from murdering black southerners. On the other hand, the Bateses appeared equally prepared to support the nonviolent tactics of Martin Luther King Jr. Daisy Bates played a central role in the expulsion of Williams from the NAACP in 1959 when she made a speech denouncing black violence. The same year, Rajmohan Gandhi, son of Mohandas K. Gandhi, visited with the Bateses in Little Rock. They had first met in Washington, D.C., in 1958 at the Summit Conference for the Moral Re-Armament of the World. Overall, the Bateses took a pragmatic rather than a committed stance on the question of violence versus nonviolence.[64]

Although the armed guard at the Bateses home gave some degree of comfort and support, the guards themselves were the subject to intimidation. One night a car followed Jefferson Thomas's father as he left the Bateses' house. A deputy sheriff and volunteer guard, Isaac Mullen, and the Bateses next-door neighbor, Dr. Garman P. Freeman, went to investigate. Six blocks away, they found Thomas standing at the side of the road with his hands on his head being searched by two men. The men identified themselves as state policemen, though they were in plain clothes and driving an unmarked car with Georgia license plates at the time. The two men then searched Mullen and Freeman, relieved them of their guns, and charged them with carrying concealed weapons. As they were hauled into state police headquarters, one of the arresting officers told another policeman, "We made a good haul tonight. We got all of Daisy Bates' guards."[65]

Daisy and L. C. realized that the men were missing only when Thomas's wife telephoned them at 5:00 the next morning. Daisy Bates then called the city and county police, who denied any knowledge of any reported accidents or arrests. A frantic search of the city by the Bateses, their friends, and news reporters failed to find the men. At 8:00 A.M., Mrs. Mullen called to say that a recently released prisoner had forwarded a message that the men were being held at the county prison. When confronted again, the police admitted to having held them. However, they insisted, the prisoners had now been moved to a new, unknown location. Eventually, local NAACP lawyer J. R. Booker found out that the state police were holding the men for investigation. The state police then released each of the men on a $200 bond. In a telegram to President Eisenhower, Daisy Bates complained that "both local and federal authorities have declined to provide the minimum physical protection that we have requested. Now state police have begun to arrest and harass the upstanding citizens who have provided us with volunteer protection, leaving us defenseless before those who constantly threaten out lives." The reply promised "prompt and appropriate consideration." It was the last the Bateses heard on the matter.[66]

As well as using physical intimidation, segregationists looked to publicly discredit those engaged in school desegregation. One falsehood propagated by the CCC was that the nine black students in Central High were hired hands from the North, paid by the NAACP to integrate the school. In truth, all of the students belonged to families in Little Rock's black community. Nevertheless, the CCC used the myth to encourage others to send the students "home" and pointed out that once the money ran out, the NAACP could no longer afford to keep the school desegregated.[67] In November 1957, after hearing the news of Daisy Bates's Woman of the Year in Education award from the Associated Press, the CCC widely distributed a flyer identifying Bates's "arrest record," together with her mug shots. The arrests related to three charges. The first involved contempt charges filed against Bates while she was reporting for the *State Press* in 1946. The second was a minor offense pertaining to the time police raided a penny-ante poker game (described by the CCC as "gaming"). Third, there were the charges stemming from state harassment. This was hardly the record of a seasoned criminal. More significantly, the appearance of the mug shots on the flyer demonstrated a direct link between the CCC and the city police, since the photographs were the private property of the sheriff's office.[68]

Compounding the stresses and strains of local white segregationist pressure was the government harassment directed against the Bateses. The IRS, for example, sought to make life more difficult for the couple. From the time the NAACP stepped up its campaign for school desegregation after the *Brown* decision, the IRS had been, as Daisy Bates put it, "trying to get us." Fortunately, the director of the IRS in Arkansas was a friend of the Bateses who had offered help with tax returns over a number of years. But when the director died early in 1957, his replacement from Louisiana was an ardent segregationist. The new director hauled in the couple and bluntly stated he was searching for evidence of fraud. The Bateses explained that the former director had personally checked their returns over a number of years. Daisy Bates recalled, "He told us immediately that the former director was dead, and he was the director now." A week later, the Bateses received a tax bill for $1,300, with a demand for immediate payment or lien on the equipment owned by the *State Press.*[69] The NAACP national office provided the couple with a loan to prevent the seizure of *State Press* assets. Bates jubilantly reported they had "paid them [the IRS] off and thumbed their nose at them."[70]

The efforts of Arkansas Attorney General Bruce Bennett to halt the activities of Daisy Bates and to bring the operations of the NAACP within the state to a standstill proved more of an obstacle. With the authority of the state and its considerable financial resources behind him, Bennett waged a fanatical crusade against Bates and the NAACP. For seven months, Bennett pursued them through local, state, and federal courts on a variety of manufactured charges. Although Bennett ultimately failed in all his efforts to prosecute the organization and its leader, he was successful in wasting a tremendous amount of their (and Arkansas taxpayers') time and money in the process. In so doing, Bennett impaired the ability of Bates and the NAACP to use their energies and resources elsewhere.[71]

On August 28 and August 30, 1957, respectively, Bennett wrote to Daisy Bates demanding information about the operations and membership of the NAACP and the LDF in Arkansas.[72] Bennett filed his questions under legislation passed in the 1957 Arkansas General Assembly that required organizations to provide such information. Bates refused to co-operate with Bennett's requests, specifically denying him access to the names and addresses of NAACP members. Bates explained that the "current climate in the state" meant that such information would only serve to open those people to "reprisals, recriminations and unwarranted hardship."[73]

Undaunted, Bennett continued his pursuit of NAACP membership lists. Early in October 1957, he sent draft proposals for an ordinance to mayors of all Arkansas' towns and cities, calling for "certain organizations" to make public "certain information" about their activities. Little Rock adopted the Bennett Ordinance on October 14.[74] When Bates yet again failed to provide the relevant information, the Little Rock city council issued warrants for the arrest of Bates and the president of the Little Rock NAACP, Rev. J. C. Crenchaw.[75] On November 1, Crenchaw, a frail seventy-four year old, surrendered to the authorities at Little Rock police station to answer his first criminal charges ever.[76] Later that day, Daisy Bates voluntarily appeared at the police station to face charges. Both Crenchaw and Bates subsequently made bail.[77]

On December 3, 1957, Judge Harry Robinson in the Little Rock Municipal Court heard the cases against Crenchaw and Bates. The proceedings revealed the highly farcical execution of the ordinances. When Robinson called Crenchaw to the stand, Joseph Brooks, deputy city attorney, admitted the city could find no record of a letter requesting the required information from Crenchaw. Robinson ruled that if the city could not "support the case with facts," then he could not try it, and he dismissed the suit.[78] When Bates was called forward, Robinson asked the prosecution if it had any witnesses who could testify Bates had received a letter requesting the required information. The city, admitted Brooks, had none. Robinson complained about the very "loose" handling of the case, but he delayed the hearing until the prosecution could find some evidence. Eventually the city produced the secretary who had typed and mailed the letter to Daisy Bates.[79]

Local NAACP lawyer J. R. Booker told the judge that Bates openly admitted to having received the letter. However, since Bates was not the president of the Little Rock branch, she was not the person obliged to obey the ordinance. Rather, Booker told the court, Bates was president of the ASC. Robinson dismissed this argument, ruling that Bates headed "some branch or something in the NAACP." Robinson went on to fine Bates $100, ignoring the protests of Booker that the maximum amount permitted under an ordinance was only $25. Booker had his protest upheld by the Pulaski County Circuit Court, which nevertheless still maintained the verdict of the lower court on the question of Bates's guilt.[80]

Bennett's campaign of harassment against the NAACP continued on December 10 when the Arkansas Supreme Court granted him the authority to prosecute organizations for the illegal practice of law in the state.[81] Armed with this new weapon, Bennett fired what he termed his "big gun, after numerous skirmishes," with lawsuits against the NAACP and the LDF alleging illegal practice of law in Arkansas. The suits asked for the prevention of the NAACP and LDF from "engaging, either directly or indirectly, in the practice of law in any respect" in Arkansas. Such practice, Bennett argued, constituted an "invasion of the legal profession" in the state.[82] The suit proved to be Bennett's last, as all the cases crept slowly through numerous appeals. The Supreme Court eventually ruled in favor of the NAACP and LDF on all counts.[83]

The one successful campaign waged against Daisy and L. C. Bates was the economic boycott that led to the closure of the *State Press*. The Bateses had weathered numerous boycotts in the past, most notably for their reporting of the Foster shooting in 1942. After the events of September 1957, however, efforts to drive the *State Press* out of business reached new heights. At the outbreak of the school crisis, L. C. Bates estimated that the newspaper had a circulation of more than seventeen thousand, with 95 percent of its subscribers living within Arkansas. By the time the last issue came off the presses on October 30, 1959, circulation had dropped to just six thousand.[84]

The *State Press* collapsed for a variety of reasons. White merchants withdrew advertising revenue because of threatened boycotts, in some cases even threatened bombings, by segregationists. Virtually all the big advertisers, including utilities, abandoned the newspaper because they were afraid to be associated with its outspoken stance on desegregation. Political candidates refused to place campaign ads, though some did offer goodwill payments to make up for the shortfall. Certain sections of east Arkansas banned the newspaper entirely. There were even reports of blacks being beaten for just handling copies of the *State Press*. Long-term suppliers refused to deal with the Bateses, and new ones refused credit. Donations flooded in from the rest of the country to save the newspaper, and the NAACP's national office made substantial contributions to keep the publication afloat, but to no avail.[85]

Amid all the struggles over school desegregation, the Bateses suffered two intensely personal crises. The first was the loss of their foster son, Clyde Cross Bates. Although never legally adopted, Clyde lived with the couple from 1951 to 1957. The attacks on the Bateses' home by segregationists led the couple to return the boy to his natural parents for his safety. The second was the death of L. C. Bates's father in July 1958. The loss of their foster son and their continuous harassment during their period of mourning for L. C. Bates's father were two of the deepest wounds inflicted on the couple by segregationists, who probably never even knew about the tragedies.[86]

The parents of the Little Rock Nine were also subjected to pressure from white segregationists. Mostly, this took the form of threatening and obscene late-night telephone calls and economic reprisals. Mary Ray resigned from her job when white co-workers at the welfare department began to harass her after finding out her daughter was one of the Little Rock Nine. Cartelyou Walls had to seek employment out of state when building contractors in Little Rock refused to employ him. Ellis Thomas lost his job. The Arkansas School for the Blind and Deaf fired Birdie Eckford. The owner of the gas station Oscar Eckford regularly used refused him credit. The Roberts family even took the drastic step of migrating to California to escape the racial tension in the city.[87]

Blacks were not the only casualties of the Little Rock crisis. Some whites stood up for justice, although they paid a cost for doing so. Ashmore's editorials in the *Arkansas Gazette* criticizing the actions of Governor Faubus won a Pulitzer Prize in 1958 but also led to harassment. Ashmore resigned his position at the newspaper in 1959 and moved his family to California. Mayor Woodrow Mann, another Faubus critic, also left Little Rock under pressure from segregationists. Eugene G. Smith, Little Rock's assistant chief of police in September 1957 had attempted to control the white mobs and to protect black students. Smith's actions brought physical attacks and verbal criticism. In March 1960, Smith shot and killed himself and his wife at their Little Rock home. David Ogden, who accompanied his father the Reverend Ogden to enroll black students at Central High on the first day of classes, also suffered at the hands of segregationists. The Ogden family moved out of Little Rock in 1959, and David committed suicide the following year.[88]

Although some whites were prepared to take a stand against die-hard segregationists, many more whites supported them or said nothing. No white labor leaders spoke out in support of desegregation. Only a few white ministers summoned the courage to do so. Little Rock's white civic and business leadership publicly said and did nothing. All members of the Arkansas congressional delegation, including the supposedly moderate Brooks Hays, signed the Southern Manifesto denouncing the *Brown* decision. Senator John L. McClellan, from east Arkansas, openly supported Faubus and the segregationists. Senator J. William Fulbright, from northwest Arkansas, watched the unfolding of events in September 1957 in silence from Europe. Daisy Bates expressed her dissatisfaction with white liberals who called to say "I'm with you" only "from behind closed doors" and white moderates "who [were] too cowardly to say, this is the law of the land and must be obeyed."[89]

The Arkansas NAACP, personified in the efforts of Daisy Bates, provided the backbone of black organizational strength and leadership in the city during the school crisis. A study conducted by black sociologists Tilman C. Cothran and William Phillips Jr. from Arkansas AM&N revealed the extent to which Bates had become the spokesperson for the black community by 1958. Twenty-two out of twenty-six black leaders interviewed by Cothran and Phillips identified Bates as "the most influential Negro in the community," while twenty-four out of the twenty-six described her as "the most influential Negro in determining policy on educational desegregation." One interviewee described Bates as "the only outspoken Negro leader," adding that "the other Negro leaders have remained silent and have allowed her to become spokesman." A parent of one of the black students at Central High agreed that "the NAACP President is the only leader who has stood up for these children. She has been more helpful than anybody." Indicating the criticisms that many in the black community had for the inactivity of traditional community leaders, the parent added, "We have a shortage of leaders. . . . There are a lot of would-be leaders, but the problem is that when the trouble starts they won't stand up and be counted."[90] The observations of Clarence Laws bore out the claims of local people, when he admitted to Gloster B. Current, "The ball has been carried here by one person and one person alone."[91]

Bates's emergence as the sole voice of black leadership in the city was unprecedented. Nevertheless, she remained something of a maverick, her militancy far outstripping the rest of the black population. Existing black leaders respected her but were cognizant of her scathing past attacks upon them and their inactivity in the *State Press*. Undoubtedly, many felt Bates pressed whites too far. Once the crisis unfolded, however, white hostility and particularly the mobbing of black students from well-respected families galvanized the black community. Her determination not to be intimidated by whites and to protect the interests of the students were the main reasons Bates won a great deal of sympathy and support from the city's black population.[92]

Attitudes toward Bates within the NAACP's national office developed along similar lines. Even before her election as ASC president, the NAACP national office had voiced doubts about Bates's outspoken militancy. Over the following years, it remained wary about fully endorsing her leadership. The turning point in the relationship between Bates and the NAACP national office came in 1958, when the Little Rock Nine were nominated for the organization's highest award, the Spingarn Medal. NAACP executive secretary Roy Wilkins telephoned Bates with the good news, and she accepted the award on behalf of the students. However, when the nine students discovered Daisy Bates was not included in the award, they threatened to turn down their medals in protest.[93]

Facing a public-relations disaster, since the award already had been made public, Wilkins sent a memo to the members of the Spingarn Medal Award Committee. Wilkins advised the committee, chosen by the NAACP board of directors and chaired by Eleanor Roosevelt, that a similar situation had occurred in 1938 when Dr. William A. Hinton had refused the award. He noted that under those circumstances the committee had decided to make no award that year. Wilkins seriously appeared to suggest that the committee should not buckle to the demands of the nine students and that it should withdraw the offer of the award.[94]

The committee rejected Wilkins's suggestion in light of the letters they received in support of Daisy Bates. A particularly poignant appeal came from the writer, lawyer, and NAACP activist Pauli Murray. As a black woman activist, Murray identified with Bates, noting that her role in the Little Rock school crisis was "every whit as inspiring as that of the Montgomery [Bus] Boycott . . . [S]he represents the tough-minded tactical leadership in this struggle as Martin Luther King represents the moral and spiritual leadership." Murray continued, "Because of Daisy Bates, the NAACP has won friends and support throughout the nation . . . [I]n this unending battle to make human dignity the cardinal principle upon which every nation is founded, we must deal in symbols [and] Daisy Bates is such a symbol." Murray appealed for Bates's inclusion with the Little Rock Nine, since "[t]o withdraw the award would hurt the prestige and objectives of the NAACP, which is now engaged in a life-and-death struggle in parts of the South and needs thousands of leaders like Daisy Bates." Murray's comments had the desired impact. At the NAACP's annual convention in Cleveland, Ohio, in July 1958, Bates collected her Spingarn Medal along with the Little Rock Nine. Thereafter, realizing the extent of her importance to the organization, the NAACP made a far greater effort to cultivate a better relationship with Daisy Bates.[95]

The NAACP's dawning realization that supporting Daisy Bates and the struggle for school desegregation in Little Rock was important to advancing its national agenda played a vital role in the eventual triumph over segregationists in the city. Alongside the support from the NAACP's national office and the LDF was the determination of the federal government to use all means at its disposal to enforce civil rights. This ensured there would be no retreat from school desegregation in Little Rock.[96]

The day after Ernest Green's graduation from Central High, with the arrival of summer recess, federal soldiers were withdrawn from the school. By that time, the issue of school desegregation was already back in the courts. In September 1957, the NAACP bowed out of litigation in the Little Rock suit leaving LDF lawyers to assist Branton in the case. Earlier that year, the NAACP and the LDF, under continued pressure from the IRS about the LDF's tax-exempt status, had formally split into separate organizations. The Little Rock suit provided the LDF with one of its first major cases after gaining full independence. Over the course of the school year, LDF lawyers Marshall, Constance Baker Motley, and Jack Greenberg shuttled between Little Rock and New York, "taking depositions, gathering facts [and] preparing further proceedings" in anticipation of more legal battles.[97]

On February 20, 1958, the Little Rock school board asked federal district court Judge Harry J. Lemley for a two-and-half-year delay of their desegregation program. On June 21, Lemley granted the delay, using the "local problems" clause in *Brown II* to argue that the violence witnessed in Little Rock justified a cooling-off period. On August 18, Branton successfully had the delay overruled on appeal. School board attorneys then indicated they would take the case to the Supreme Court. Since the Court did not convene until October 6, it could not hear the appeal until after the Little Rock schools opened, presumably on a segregated basis, in September.[98]

On August 25, Supreme Court Chief Justice Earl Warren announced the Court would meet in special session on August 28 to hear the Little Rock case. On September 12, the Court ordered the school board to proceed with its desegregation plan. After more than four years of equivocation since the original *Brown* ruling, the Court finally set a definite timetable for school desegregation in Little Rock. Moreover, the federal government afterward indicated it was prepared to enforce the ruling by making plans to support the peaceful opening of integrated schools with the assistance of federal marshals if necessary. Everything appeared to be in place to ensure a smooth, orderly process of desegregation, in contrast to the lawlessness of 1957.[99]

Governor Faubus had other plans. While desegregation was being debated in the courts, Faubus used his political influence to turn the situation to his advantage. When the Supreme Court went into special session on August 28, Faubus presided over a special session of the Arkansas General Assembly. Defiantly waving a fist at federal law, Faubus pushed through six new state laws providing him with sweeping powers to uphold segregation in Arkansas. One of these new laws allowed Faubus to close any school forced to integrate by federal order. With the school closed, voters in the local school district would then participate in a referendum to decide if the school should reopen on an integrated basis. On the day the Court ordered integration to proceed, Faubus closed all of the city's schools. In the referendum held on September 27, the governor handily stacked the cards in his favor by providing a stark choice between keeping the schools closed or accepting "complete and total integration." By a margin of 19,470 to 7,561 votes, the electorate decided to keep the schools closed.[100]

The morning after the announcement of the referendum result, Faubus pressured the school board into leasing the public schools to the Little Rock Private School Corporation (LRPSC). Marshall and Branton later successfully petitioned the Eighth Circuit Appeals Court for an injunction against such an action. Faubus then assisted the LRPSC in purchasing private buildings with public funds to operate schools. For one term, the LRPSC provided limited schooling for some of the city's white students before finally going bankrupt.[101]

After the collapse of the LRPSC, white students variously attended private segregated schools, out-of-state schools, and schools in other Arkansas districts or took correspondence courses through the University of Arkansas. While the public schools remained closed in Little Rock, most black students attended classes in other Arkansas districts. Those who did not either went to out-of-state schools or took the correspondence course offered by Horace Mann High principal Christophe. The state retained both white and black teachers at full pay to preside over empty classrooms in closed schools.[102]

Despite the eventual folding of the LRPSC, the continued defiance of Faubus and the establishment of private schools on a temporary basis was a vote-winning combination. In November 1958, Faubus became only the second governor in Arkansas history to win a third consecutive term in office. At the same time, Jim Johnson won election to the Arkansas Supreme Court. In a dramatic political upset, Little Rock segregationist and school board member Dale Alford defeated incumbent congressman Brooks Hays, who had held the seat for sixteen years. The increased pressure from segregationists coupled with the order to continue with desegregation proved too much for the school board. In exasperation, all of its members (except for Alford, who would soon leave to take up his role as congressman) resigned. As one of their final acts in office, members voted to buy out Blossom's contract, paving the way for a new regime to take the reins of office.[103]

The election of a new board was a watershed event in the Little Rock crisis. For the first time, the election stirred one of the most potent yet hitherto somnolent forces in the white community, which had the potential to release Faubus's and the segregationists' grip on the city. Little Rock's white business elite was tight-knit and easily identifiable: owners and managers of commercial and industrial operations and a select group of accountants, lawyers, and other professionals. This elite had proved particularly adept at mobilizing community support for city projects in the past. Previous campaigns had led to the opening of an air base near Little Rock and the construction of an industrial park on the outskirts of the city in the early 1950s. The business elite was the driving force ensuring Little Rock's economic prosperity in the postwar years, when the city became an enviable example of southern affluence.[104]

For a variety of reasons, the business elite had not played a major role in the controversies over school desegregation. The Blossom Plan had insulated them from the immediate impact of integration by building Hall High in the affluent western suburbs for their sons and daughters to attend. Instead, Blossom had focused his attention on desegregating the largely working-class Central High. Moreover, Blossom eagerly took responsibility for school desegregation, even to the point of insisting no one should interfere with his plans.[105] Many businessmen also later claimed they feared boycotts instigated by segregationists would damage their companies, their clients, and their employees if they interfered in the desegregation process. At a more fundamental level, they shared the white community's sympathy with Faubus's attempts to uphold segregation and his stance against "outside interference," even if they did not necessarily agree with the way he went about it. In 1957, therefore, the business elite was prepared to take a back seat as resistance to school desegregation hardened.[106]

By December 1958, circumstances had changed considerably. There was a rising awareness of the overall effect school closings were having on the community. Teachers unoccupied in empty classrooms were leaving the public school system in droves, the education of all the city's students was being disrupted, and of more pressing concern to the businessmen, the city's economy was suffering. According to a report by Gary Fullerton in the *Nashville Tennessean*, not one new industry had chosen to locate in Little Rock since the events of September 1957. The school crisis, Fullerton estimated, had cost the city five new industrial plants, which would have brought in a revenue of $1 million and three hundred new jobs. The negative national publicity surrounding Little Rock was, Fullerton suggested, the major reason for the abrupt halting of an impressive postwar industrial record. Ongoing disruption was an embarrassment to the city, a detriment to community life, and plainly bad for business.[107]

At the school closing referendum held on September 27, a group of white women took the first community stand against segregationists by organizing a campaign to open the schools. The Women's Emergency Committee (WEC) membership included the spouses of many influential professionals in the city. At its helm was Adolphine Fletcher Terry, who came from a venerable old Arkansas family and was the wife of former Arkansas congressman David D. Terry. Although unsuccessful in getting the schools opened, the WEC remained an important lobbying force within the community.[108] At the following school board election, Terry managed to persuade five candidates to take a stand against attempts by segregationists to hijack the schools. In a closely contested election, a split ticket of three business candidates and three segregationists won positions on the school board. Though by no means a convincing victory, the election did prove it was actually possible to defeat segregationist candidates.[109]

Encouraged by the victory of the business candidates, the new president of the Little Rock Chamber of Commerce, E. Grainger Williams, questioned the closing of the schools in his inaugural speech on January 14, 1959. Williams told the audience that "no matter what our personal feelings might be," the "time has come for us to evaluate . . . the cost of the lack of public education." Despite Williams's speech, the business community remained cautious about speaking up on the school desegregation issue. Meanwhile, at the 1959 Arkansas General Assembly, Governor Faubus helped pass another thirty-two prosegregation laws, further strengthening his hand.[110]

A showdown between the business community and the segregationists finally came in May 1959. At a meeting of the new school board on May 5, segregationists attempted to push through measures to remove anyone unsympathetic to their cause from the public school system. Blocking each of these measures, representatives of business interests finally chose to withdraw from the meeting so that there would be no quorum left to make decisions. However, after they left, Ed McKinley, the segregationist president of the school board, ruled the meeting could continue as normal. Segregationists proceeded to make a series of decisions about the running of the school system. The most controversial decision was not to renew the contracts of forty-four public school employees, including seven principals, thirty-four teachers, and three secretaries.[111]

On May 8, a group of downtown business and civic leaders met to form a new organization, Stop This Outrageous Purge (STOP). The organization dedicated itself to recalling the three segregationist board members for election to allow voters to have a say on the issue of renewing teacher's contracts. On May 15, segregationists joined forces to recall business representatives on the school board in a Committee to Retain Our Segregated Schools (CROSS). On May 25, the day of the election, the vote narrowly went the businessmen's way, with all the business representatives reinstated and all the segregationist candidates dismissed from the school board. The new board, taking the election as a mandate to reopen the schools, began preparations for token desegregation to take place in September 1959 by assigning three black students to Central High and three to Hall High.[112] On June 18, the federal district court upheld the LDF's contention that the school closing laws were unconstitutional.[113]

In a surprise move designed to thwart any attempts by Faubus and the segregationists to prevent the schools from opening, the school board announced in July that the new school term would begin a month early, on August 12. The night before the schools opened, Faubus appeared on public television to deliver a final harangue against the "integrationists." Yet in decidedly more muted terms, the governor also appealed to segregationists not to cause violence and disorder but to carry on their fight through the ballot box. The next morning, three black students, Effie Jones, Elsie Robinson, and Estella Thompson, peacefully entered Hall High under city police guard. At the state capitol, one thousand whites attended a segregationist rally. Later, about two hundred segregationists marched on Central High. City policemen firmly enforced order as Jefferson Thomas and Elizabeth Eckford entered the school. The crowd dispersed and did not return. For segregationists, the battle had been lost, and the struggle to retain segregated public schools was over.[114]

Only Jefferson and Elizabeth entered Central High that morning. After her assignment to Central, Elizabeth discovered she already had enough credits to graduate. However, she attended the first day of classes so that Jefferson would not have to face the white mob alone, as she had done in September 1957. Carlotta Walls, the third black student assigned to Central by the new school board, was out of the city completing summer school in Chicago. The school board denied the requests of Thelma Mothershed and Melba Pattillo for assignment to Central. Minnijean Brown, already expelled from Central, remained in New York. Ernest Green, who graduated from Central in 1958, attended Michigan State University. Terrance Roberts and Gloria Ray had moved out of Little Rock.[115]

The reopening of Little Rock's public schools, albeit on a basis of token integration, was a landmark victory for the ASC. Emerging from the successful teachers' salary suit in 1945, the ASC throughout the 1940s and 1950s, aided by the national organization, chipped away at the legal defense of Jim Crow. It successfully challenged the white DPA primaries, pressed for an end to discrimination in higher education, and campaigned against segregation in schools. Even after the *Brown* decision, the struggle to implement the Supreme Court ruling went on. The Little Rock NAACP took legal action to force the Little Rock school board to act on *Brown* and helped blacks to stand firm against white hostility. Because of the NAACP's efforts, the federal government finally acted in a decisive manner to enforce black civil rights. Black activists demonstrated to whites that they would simply not allow them to remain ambivalent in the face of racial oppression and that ignoring black demands held a high price for the entire community.

Still, the victory did not come without significant cost, and the outcome of the school crisis held many uncertainties for the future direction of black activism in Little Rock. With the immediate crisis over, there was no longer national support from either the NAACP or the federal government to help local blacks. Local resources were threadbare. Existing black leaders and organizations demonstrated during the school crisis that they were incapable of handling black protest. The local NAACP, which had moved into the breach to provide leadership and organizational strength, was in a severely weakened state after the campaign waged by Bennett, which had drained its financial resources and reduced its membership rolls. Moreover, in an effort to recoup lost revenue after the demise of the *State Press*, Daisy Bates spent much of her time out of the city on speaking engagements and writing her memoir. This robbed the black community of a newly established spokesperson.[116]

The situation in Little Rock echoed that of many other black communities across the South at the end of the 1950s. After *Brown*, whites believed that if they could put a stop to NAACP activities, they could put an end to agitation for change. Therefore, state legislatures passed laws to harass and intimidate the NAACP. They variously tried to force local branches to reveal the names and addresses of their members, dismissed those in public employment who belonged to the organization, and barred the NAACP from challenging local segregation ordinances. Alongside this were direct acts of physical intimidation and terrorism that targeted individuals who played prominent roles in NAACP branches. Through campaigns of harassment, whites were successful at severely curtailing local NAACP activities in the region by 1959.[117]

Seeking to maintain a momentum for change, blacks in Arkansas and other southern states during the late 1950s and throughout the 1960s strove to find ways to further pressure whites to address racial grievances. Looking to build on the achievements of the NAACP, new organizations emerged to carry forward the agenda for racial change. These organizations looked to move beyond the legalistic approach to civil rights adopted by the NAACP, which the new groups increasingly viewed as a time-consuming, expensive, and long-winded process. Besides, *Brown* had already outlawed segregation in schools. The next task was to apply that ruling to other areas of community life and thereby expand the attack on segregation. Doing so would mean adopting new strategies, tactics, and methods of protest, heralding the beginning of a new direct-action phase of the black struggle.

Dismantling Jim Crow | 6

One specific area the school crisis exposed as a chink in the South's armor against segregation was the cost of racial turmoil in dollars and cents. This was particularly true in cities such as Little Rock that were anxious to court new industries and promote economic development. Business leaders only intervened in the school crisis when they realized that racial unrest struck at the economic prospects of the city. Therefore, if black activists could find some way to keep attention focused on the fact that continued segregation could not be reconciled with economic progress, the business community might begin to confront issues of racial change head-on. By employing a new battery of tactics, including sit-ins, economic boycotts, and freedom rides, civil rights activists during the 1960s fought to keep the issue of race firmly at the top of the community agenda.[1]

Achieving this in Little Rock meant tackling a white business leadership that remained reticent to use its influence to cultivate a more racially enlightened attitude. Shortly after the schools reopened, the ACHR showed a film, *Dallas at the Crossroads*, to white business leaders. The film charted the smooth process of racial change in that city because of cooperation between the black and white communities. Only ten out of seventy-five of those invited attended, and there was little progress in the discussion after the meeting. The new president of the school board and director of industrial development for the Chamber of Commerce

Everett Tucker summed up the white business community's attitude: "The best thing for Little Rock to do now is nothing."[2]

Also hindering the situation were fractious tendencies in the black community, which stalled efforts to advance an agenda for civil rights. Regional Urban League representative C. D. Coleman reported that "the one great problem facing Little Rock [is] the lack of unity, confidence and cooperation between Negro leaders and the lack of regular and orderly lines of communication between Negro organizations. . . . Disunity among Negro leaders [is of] greater concern than the school crisis."[3] The new young associate director of the ACHR John Walker observed early in 1960 that "Negro leadership is virtually nil." Yet at the same time, Walker expressed the belief that "the 'masses' of Negroes are anxious for more progressive leadership from new people." Walker blamed the timidity of existing conservative black leaders and the interference of white moderates for the lack of effective black protest.[4]

An attempt by a black candidate to run for the Little Rock school board in November 1959 provided a vivid example of the pressures that stymied local black activism. Dr. Maurice A. Jackson announced his candidacy for the school board as a representative of parents who were dissatisfied with the token integration of the schools. There was clearly support in the black community for him, as more than one thousand people signed a petition backing his action. However, established black leaders warned against the move, claiming it would help strengthen segregationist sentiment and encourage further scenes of racial violence. Members of the WEC also tried to dissuade Jackson from standing, telling him that now was "not the time" for a black candidate. There was far too much risk of stirring racial turmoil in the city, they claimed. The combined pressure of black leaders, the WEC, and ultimately Jackson's family, who feared for his safety if he became a focus for racial hostility in the city, convinced him to abandon his candidacy.[5]

Efforts by the ACHR to stimulate discussion in the black community about the need for organization and leadership met with little success. In 1960, Nat Griswold, the white director of the ACHR, wrote to John Wheeler, who had been instrumental in forming a Council on Community Organizations in Durham, North Carolina, to fight for civil rights.[6] Griswold, a native Arkansan, was an ordained Methodist minister and for twelve years had been an associate professor of religion at Hendrix College in Conway, Arkansas. Griswold had a long record of human rights activism. During the Second World War, he was director of community activities at Arkansas' Japanese-American relocation centers, and in 1954, he served as southwestern regional secretary of peace education for the American Friends Service Committee. Griswold had held the post of director of the ACHR since 1955.[7]

Griswold hoped Wheeler could persuade black leaders in Little Rock to work "together in the interest of all Negroes and . . . shift their focus above the petty views of individual leaders," to encourage a "strong united voice . . . making unequivocal the common aspirations and demands of Negroes." Though Wheeler's visit initially was planned for a day, Griswold persuaded Wheeler to stay on for a week and to confer with "individuals and small groups, especially Negro leaders," as he was "really anxious that something happen as a result of your visit."[8] Yet, nothing did happen. Divisions within the black community remained, with each black leader still reluctant to surrender his sphere of influence to work collectively for civil rights. As Griswold summed it up, "Each wanted a united voice—his."[9]

This internal factionalism had serious consequences in the ability of the black community to embrace national as well as local protest initiatives. A demonstration of this came when the student sit-in movement began to sweep across the South in 1960. The sit-ins began in Greensboro, North Carolina, when four black students from North Carolina Agricultural and Technical College asked for service at the "whites only" lunch counter of the downtown Woolworth store on February 1, 1960. Intended as a nonviolent but direct protest against segregation, their actions violated Jim Crow laws. The store refused to serve the students, but aside from the glare of a police officer and disparaging remarks from other customers, no violence occurred. Over the following weeks and months, the number of sit-in demonstrators in Greensboro grew, meeting an increasingly angry and violent reaction from the white community.[10]

Yet, the sit-ins did eventually achieve the goal of forcing the white business community into a successful dialogue about race relations, which in turn led to the desegregation of lunch counters. The successful sit-in protests at Greensboro set in motion a wave of similar demonstrations, first in neighboring towns and cities, then throughout the region. To help coordinate and sustain the burgeoning student movement, a group of young black activists attended a meeting at Raleigh, North Carolina, called by acting executive director of the SCLC Ella Baker, on the weekend of April

15, 1960. There, a new civil rights organization, SNCC—pronounced "snick"—was founded. SNCC became an influential vehicle for direct-action protests throughout the 1960s.[11]

The sit-in demonstrations embodied much of the symbolic drama and moral politics that were a hallmark of the 1960s southern civil rights movement. Black students challenged segregation at lunch counters in a dignified nonviolent manner that contrasted starkly with the thuggish behavior of white segregationists, who jeered, spat on, and beat the sit-in participants for claiming their rights as American citizens. Indeed, the spectacle was intended to elicit exactly that kind of symbolic confrontation, which would dramatize black oppression to members of the immediate community and, through the mass media, to the nation. To many onlookers, it seemed that black students, by the very moral force of their actions, managed to bring about the end of segregation.[12]

The reality was quite different. Student sit-ins represented the cutting edge of a conflict that had much deeper roots in the black community. Students were often in the front line, because they did not have the economic and familial responsibilities that precluded many others from taking similar action. Their actions had a catalytic effect, sharply focusing previously blurred racial issues in the community. Ultimately, their success was dependent on winning wider support from the local black adult community and local black organizations. It was no coincidence Greensboro became the launching pad for a successful sit-in movement. Greensboro's large concentration of black colleges, an active local NAACP branch, and the presence of established black churches all provided vital interrelated networks of support. Similarly, at other places where sit-ins were successful at bringing an end to segregation, networks of support already existed, which student activists could build upon and which they in turn stimulated to greater efforts.[13]

In contrast to successful sit-ins that have drawn the attention of scholars, the first sit-ins at Little Rock reveal another side of the story. Philander Smith College students, whose numbers had grown to about seven hundred in 1960, launched the sit-in movement in Little Rock. However, their attempts to stage sit-ins to force the white business community into making concessions for racial change failed dismally. With little coordination or cooperation between existing leaders and organizations in Little Rock, the necessary support networks to sustain such protests were not in place and could not be mobilized. In the absence of the necessary infrastructure for a sit-in campaign, whites rode roughshod over student demonstrations, handing out harsh fines and sentences that swiftly ground the movement to a standstill.[14]

The first sit-ins in Little Rock took place on March 10, 1960, when fifty Philander Smith students protested against segregated lunch counters at the downtown F. W. Woolworth. Woolworth officials refused to serve the students and immediately alerted Chief of Police Eugene Smith. Smith advised the store manager to shut down the lunch counter and to ask the students to leave. When the counter closed, all but five students left the premises. Those remaining were Charles Parker, twenty-two, from Saint Louis; Frank James, twenty-one, from Oklahoma City; Vernon Mott, nineteen, from Little Rock; Eldridge Davis, nineteen, from Malvern, Arkansas; and Chester Briggs, eighteen, from Hot Springs, Arkansas. Smith arrested all under a state statute that made it unlawful for a person to refuse to leave a business premise when requested. Shortly after arriving at the police station, the five arrested made bail of $100 each, funded by the Little Rock NAACP.[15]

White authorities were determined to stamp out the sit-ins quickly by taking a hard-line approach to the demonstrations. Arkansas attorney general Bennett advised Chief Smith to charge the students with two other offenses besides the state statute for loitering. The first charge was under Act 17, passed in the 1958 special session of the Arkansas General Assembly, which made it a misdemeanor to enter public school property or a public place of business to create a disturbance. The second charge was under Act 226, passed in the 1959 Arkansas General Assembly session, which specifically made sit-in demonstrations illegal. A breach of either act carried a fine of up to $500 and/or a six-month jail sentence.[16]

At the hearing before the Little Rock Municipal Court the following morning, the students' counsel, Harold B. Anderson from Little Rock, asked for a continuance. J. Frank Holt, the state prosecutor, demanded an early trial, because the state viewed the acts of the defendants "as a deliberate attempt . . . to disturb the peace of the community." By bringing swift, decisive retribution on the students, the state believed it could stall further demonstrations. Judge Quinn Glover complied with Holt's request and set a trial date for March 17. Glover warned Anderson there would be no continuances issued and advised him to use his influence with the students to make sure there were no further demonstrations. Glover was also adamant that he would not rule on the constitutionality of the acts, which local NAACP lawyers believed to be illegal, but solely on the innocence or guilt of those charged with the offenses.[17]

As the students awaited trial, their actions predictably received widespread condemnation from whites. An impromptu poll of white community leaders by the *Arkansas Democrat* revealed that most rejected the sit-ins as an acceptable form of protest. Many white leaders also believed the protests would prove detrimental to the black community in the end. An appeal by students for support from the adult black community proved unsuccessful. Typical of the cautious responses from black leaders were the comments of I. S. McClinton, who claimed he was "neither for or against the sit-down." A much more hostile reaction came from Philander Smith president M. Lafayette Harris, who told the press the college did not and would never "subscribe to mass action in dealing with difficult problems."[18]

Ignoring the lack of support from the college and the city's black leadership, students continued with the protests. On March 17, the five students arrested in the sit-in appeared for trial at Little Rock's Municipal Court. Other Philander Smith students packed the courtroom. Judge Glover found the students guilty under Act 226. The court handed each student a $250 fine and a thirty-day jail sentence. The students' lawyers, Anderson and George Howard Jr., from Pine Bluff, indicated that both fines and sentences would be appealed.[19]

When the Little Rock NAACP sought talks with the Little Rock Chamber of Commerce about desegregating lunch counters to halt the protests, it received a noncommittal response. The reluctance of whites in Little Rock to enter a dialogue with black activists mirrored the initial reactions to sit-ins in many other communities across the South. Public announcements by chain stores such as F. W. Woolworth, S. S. Kressage, S. H. Kress, and W. T. Grant declared that the policy of segregation would continue. In light of this, the NAACP's national office called for a boycott of stores to support the aims of the sit-in demonstrators. On March 31, the Little Rock NAACP formally adopted what it termed a "Racial Self-Defense Policy" against discrimination in local stores. In a memorandum designed to elicit widespread support for a boycott of white businesses that refused to end segregation, the local NAACP pleaded with "all religious institutions, fraternal organizations, fraternities, sororities, civic and political groups" to withdraw patronage from targeted stores. The memorandum called for a rallying of the black adult community to help support the students. "HE NEEDS OUR HELP," it appealed. "[W]e have the family purse and we have the ballot, and the NAACP is asking 'DO YOU HAVE THE WILL?'" The answer, seemingly, was no. Within just a week, the boycott collapsed.[20]

Despite the boycott's lack of success, the students continued with their sit-in campaign. On April 13, police arrested two Philander Smith students, Frank James Lupper, nineteen, and Thomas B. Robinson, twenty, at Blass Department Store. A further six students, Sammy J. Baker, eighteen, Winston Jones, eighteen, McLoyd Buchanan, eighteen, William Rogers Jr., nineteen, Melvin T. Jackson, twenty, and Eugene D. Smith, twenty-one, were arrested at Pfeiffer department store. The police charged the six students at the Pfeiffer sit-in under Act 226. Additionally, Lupper and Robinson were charged under Act 17 for their refusal to leave Blass when requested to do so. At the trial on April 21, Judge Glover, reflecting the growing annoyance and irritation of the white community about the turn of events, handed down tougher penalties than in the first sit-in cases. Glover gave the six students charged under Act 226 a $250 fine and a sixty-day jail sentence each and the two students additionally charged under Act 17 a $400 fine and a ninety-day jail sentence each.[21]

At the appeal of the five students arrested for the first sit-in, Pulaski County Circuit Court Judge William J. Kirby handed them each a $500 fine and sixty days in jail, thereby doubling the initial sentences. When Kirby heard the second batch of sit-in appeals on May 31, he again doubled all the penalties for the students, awarding them each the maximum fine of $500 and sixty-day jail sentences. At the trial of Lupper and Robinson on June 17, Kirby handed each a $418 fine and a ninety-day prison sentence. In all cases, Anderson indicated that his clients intended to appeal.[22]

The summer recess at Philander Smith effectively ended the sit-ins, since many students left Little Rock to return home.[23] At the beginning of the fall semester, in the absence of college president Harris, who had moved to Atlanta over the summer, a new group of Philander Smith students attempted to revive sit-in protests. The students went under the banner of the Arkansas SNCC or "Arsnick" for short. Rev. William E. Bush of Toledo, Ohio, chaired the new organization, and Frank James, who had been arrested in the earlier sit-ins, was its executive secretary.[24] One new leader behind the sit-in movement was Worth Long, a Philander Smith student who also worked at a nearby air base. At twenty-four, Long was one of the older students on campus. According to an observer in the ACHR, Long had a "good public relations sense," which resulted in the demonstrations being "well coordinated and managed."[25]

The major obstacle to the protests remained the difficulty in winning support from the wider black community, which hampered efforts to extend the sit-ins to a boycott of stores. The ACHR lamented the lack of "coordinated support from the adult community which is showing its usual fragmentation and divisiveness." With the initial momentum for demonstrations waning and uncertainty about the position of those still involved in protracted courtroom battles and facing large fines and jail sentences, protests were intermittent and eventually ground to a halt. The lack of support from the Little Rock black community, together with pressure exerted by whites through the courts, meant that the city's brief flirtation with 1960s-style direct-action protest achieved very little in the way of concessions.[26]

Little Rock's experiences with the Freedom Rides, another direct-action tactic employed in the southern struggle for civil rights during the 1960s, proved equally inauspicious. Freedom Rides were initiated by the Chicago-based CORE, under the direction of its president James Leonard Farmer, Jr. In 1947, members of CORE had successfully traveled on the interracial Journey of Reconciliation through a number of Upper South states after the *Morgan v. Virginia* (1946) ruling outlawed segregated seating on interstate bus routes. In *Boynton v. Virginia* (1960), the Supreme Court extended the *Morgan* ruling to include the desegregation of bus terminal facilities. Farmer, in the wake of the sit-in movement and increased civil rights activity across the South, proposed to renew the Freedom Rides to test facilities throughout the region. As with the sit-ins, it was hoped that creating a symbolic confrontation would show the nation the ugly face of white southern bigotry, which CORE hoped might bring some federal response.[27]

On May 4, 1961, thirteen Freedom Riders, comprising veterans from the Journey of Reconciliation and younger activists, divided into two groups and boarded buses in Washington, D.C. The first leg of their journey, through Virginia, North Carolina, South Carolina, and Georgia, was largely incident free. On May 13, the two groups set off from Atlanta on what they knew would be the most difficult part of their journey, across Alabama to their final destination of Jackson, Mississippi. At Anniston, Alabama, a white mob attacked the first group, savagely beating the Freedom Riders and firebombing their bus. The next day, whites attacked the second group of Freedom Riders as they pulled into Birmingham. Because of the violence, the bus companies involved refused to transport any more Freedom Riders, and CORE halted the campaign.[28]

Unperturbed, SNCC declared that it would continue with the Freedom Ride. President John F. Kennedy responded to SNCC's decision to head for Montgomery, Alabama, by sending federal representatives to try to ensure the riders' safety. Nevertheless, when the riders reached Montgomery, whites again besieged the bus, and the situation rapidly descended into lawlessness and violence. Kennedy then sent four hundred federal marshals to ensure a safe passage for the Freedom Riders on their last leg of the journey to Jackson and arranged a National Guard escort, accompanied by police cars and helicopters. Upon their arrival in Jackson, the Freedom Riders were arrested by police, but in accordance with an agreement worked out between U.S. Attorney General Robert Kennedy and Mississippi senator James O. Eastland, there was no violence.[29]

The Freedom Ride campaign ultimately proved successful. The national publicity about the issue of segregated public transportation led the Kennedy administration, through the Interstate Commerce Commission (ICC), to order the integration of all interstate buses and bus terminals. Meanwhile, CORE, SNCC, and the SCLC set up a Freedom Ride Coordinating Committee (FRCC) to keep pressure on the federal government as well as to encourage black communities to confront segregation in their own localities.[30]

On July 10, 1961, Little Rock's first Freedom Riders arrived in the city as part of the FRCC follow-up campaign to enforce bus terminal desegregation. Sponsored by the Saint Louis branch of CORE, the group comprised Rev. Ben Elton Cox, thirty, a black preacher from High Point, North Carolina; Bliss Anne Malone, twenty-three, a black schoolteacher from Saint Louis; Annie Lumpkin, eighteen, a black student from Saint Louis; Janet Reinitz, twenty-three, a white homemaker from New York; and Rev. John Curtis Raines, twenty-seven, a minister from Long Island, New York. The group began their journey in Saint Louis and had already successfully tested bus facilities in other parts of Arkansas. As they had anticipated, they encountered little opposition in the Upper South state. The journey through Arkansas was seen simply as a prelude to what they believed would be the much harder task of testing facilities in the Lower South state of Louisiana.

A crowd of more than four hundred white civilians and around a dozen police officers met the bus carrying the five Freedom Riders into Little Rock. As the Freedom Riders disembarked, they met with jeers from the crowd but moved unmolested to the waiting rooms. The facilities at the bus terminal in Little Rock already technically complied with the letter of the law, which called only for the desegregation of interstate travel facilities. Accordingly, the bus terminal had a waiting room for "Inter-state and Colored Intra-state" passengers. Yet the bus terminal retained segregation in intrastate travel, which the ICC did not have jurisdiction over, by providing a segregated "White Intra-state" waiting room. The Freedom Riders headed for the segregated intrastate waiting room.[31]

As the Freedom Riders sat in the waiting room, Chief of Police Paul Glascock approached and asked them to move, stating they were "threatening a breach of the peace." When they remained silent, Glascock, to the delight of the crowd, charged the Freedom Riders under Arkansas' Act 226, and arrested them. Local lawyer Thaddeus D. Williams acted as legal counsel for the Freedom Riders. Williams informed the press his clients had refused bail and would spend the night in jail with an intention to plead "not guilty" the following morning.[32]

Although the city viewed the sit-ins as a local matter, the manhandling of the Freedom Riders raised the possibility of national publicity, which set alarm bells ringing in Little Rock. Many in the city were wary of drawing attention to civil rights issues because of the damage already done by the school crisis in 1957. The *Arkansas Gazette* warned that Little Rock was only just managing to recover from the events of 1957 and that the presence of Freedom Riders held the potential to damage its "record of recovery." The paper criticized police handling of the matter, arguing officers should not have allowed the crowd to gather at the bus terminal in the first place. The solution the newspaper offered was to "dispose" of the Freedom Riders as quickly as possible before reinforcements arrived to cash in on the media coverage and the city again began to grab national attention. "The quicker the defendants can be freed, the better for the community," read an *Arkansas Gazette* editorial. If "common sense" prevailed, "then Little Rock may reassert to the nation that the resurgence of law and order, which we have so proudly been proclaiming, is fact and not illusion."[33]

The trial held the following day in the Little Rock Municipal Court demonstrated the desire of the city to rid itself of the Freedom Riders as quickly as possible. Williams argued that the Freedom Riders' arrest violated the federal interstate commerce clause, which guaranteed citizens free and unmolested transit, and that Act 226, under which they were being tried, was unconstitutional. Refuting these arguments, Judge Glover ruled that the case had nothing to do with interstate commerce, but that the defendants faced charges under a state act. As to the constitutionality of that act, the Arkansas Supreme Court had yet to declare on the matter. Glover, indicating that he viewed the Freedom Riders as outside agitators, pointed out that the defendants "seem unwilling to wait until the Arkansas Supreme Court has ruled on the validity of this law." Glover then handed each of the Freedom Riders the maximum sentence, a $500 fine and a six-month prison term. However, to get the Freedom Riders out of the city, Glover told the defendants that he would suspend their sentences if they agreed to "leave the state of Arkansas and proceed to their respective homes." After discussions with Williams and calls to the Saint Louis branch of CORE, the Freedom Riders accepted the terms of the court. Glover then ordered the Freedom Riders released from custody.[34]

The deft handling of the matter appeared to have achieved the city's goal of dispatching the Freedom Riders with the minimum amount of fuss. Yet later the same afternoon, the plan went awry when the Freedom Riders announced that they were refusing to accept the agreement. In particular, they were alarmed by the news that when Judge Glover had told them to "return home," he had actually meant they were to return to their doorsteps rather than just leave the state. The Freedom Riders had accepted the terms of the court only in the belief they could continue their journey to Louisiana. Cox declared that they would not leave with the city believing they "came here, got spanked and are going back home." For his part, Glover confirmed that the phrase "return home" meant exactly what it said and insisted that if the Freedom Riders wanted to go to jail instead, "[T]hat's alright with me." That evening, police rearrested Cox and the others and placed them in jail, resulting in increased media coverage. Cox was now telling newspaper reporters he would "much rather be dead and in my grave" than be "a slave to segregation" and threatening to go on hunger strike.[35]

For the first time since the school crisis, the city's businessmen were prompted to intervene. Thirteen business leaders met at First National Bank to discuss the situation and formed an ad hoc Civic Progress Association. In a statement to the press, the leaders diplomatically backed the city authorities in their handling of the matter. At the same time, they suggested the city could learn from the incident how to better deal with similar occurrences in the future. The following morning, Judge Glover capitulated. In court, he admitted he did not have the legal authority to prevent the Freedom Riders from continuing their journey. Instead, Glover ordered there should be no more demonstrations in Arkansas and declared that he was turning "the other cheek in this matter, hoping it to be for the good of all," albeit "very, very reluctantly." Cox and the others rode out of Arkansas the same day to test bus terminal facilities in Louisiana.[36]

Though the Freedom Ride failed to make the desired impact on whites in Little Rock, it did act as a catalyst for a significant new black community initiative. Dismayed by the events of the sit-ins and embarrassed by the city's treatment of the Freedom Riders, a cadre of young black medical professionals—Dr. William H. Townsend, Dr. Maurice A. Jackson, Dr. Garman P. Freeman, and his wife, Dr. Evangeline Upshur—decided to act. The four had recently set up a joint practice in the city, after working in the offices of Dr. J. M. Robinson on West Ninth Street for several years. In the 1960s, their new offices on Wright Avenue became the headquarters of COCA. COCA dedicated itself to providing the type of coordinated black community leadership needed to mobilize an assault on the city's segregated order.[37]

This new group was careful to foster good relations with older leaders and existing organizations and was thus able to persuade them to pool their resources in pursuing civil rights. COCA achieved this seemingly impossible task by appointing black leaders to committees that met to formulate policy but then reported to an executive board for consultation on all decisions. By incorporating all factions within the black community under one umbrella, COCA managed to temper rivalries between different leaders and organizations. As with Arkansas' earlier prototype civil rights organization, the CNO, COCA's explicit aim was to create an organization of organizations providing unity and direction of purpose to black activism in the city.[38]

Dr. Townsend was COCA president and its most influential figure. Born on a farm near West Point, Mississippi, in 1914, the eldest of eleven children, he moved with his family to Earle in east Arkansas when he was four. There he was reared and received his early education. After attending school in Memphis for a year, he enrolled at Tuskegee Institute. Townsend earned a high school diploma and graduated with a bachelor of science degree in agriculture from Tuskegee in May 1941. Early the following year, Townsend entered the army, where he served a total of forty-five months, most of them overseas. During that time, he studied for six months at the University of Nottingham, England, where he first experienced integrated classes. At the end of his military service, Townsend enrolled at Howard University. After a year of premedical study at Howard, he moved to Northern Illinois College of Optometry in Chicago, where he graduated in 1950. Later that year, he opened a practice in Little Rock and became the first licensed black optometrist in Arkansas.[39]

Much as Flowers had done when he had formed the CNO some twenty years earlier, Townsend built extensive links with black organizations and institutions in his locality and in the state. Townsend was a member of the Executive Committee and treasurer of the ACHR and a member of the executive boards of the Little Rock NAACP and the Little Rock Urban League. He belonged to various professional associations, including local, state, and national optometry associations, and he was vice president of Plaza Enterprises, a local black-owned chain of grocery stores and service stations. Townsend was also a member of the Mount Zion Baptist Church board of trustees, a member of the Pi Lambda Chapter of the Alpha Phi Alpha fraternity, a member of the Parent-Teacher Association, a member of the American Legion, a thirty-second-degree Mason and chair of the Pulaski division of the Boy Scouts. Townsend drew upon his contacts within the black community, as well as his life experiences that reached beyond Arkansas and the United States, to provide a new direction, purpose, and leadership within the black community. Amiable and amenable (his instantly recognizable opening line was "How's the family?"), he was respected and well liked by blacks and whites. Townsend's ability to mediate between various factions in the black community and to negotiate effectively with the white community made him a key figure in efforts to end segregation.[40]

Townsend's younger medical colleagues played important roles in COCA. Jackson, thirty-eight, was a native of Little Rock. He was a graduate of Philander Smith College and one of the first blacks to graduate with a doctor of medicine degree at the integrated medical school in Little Rock. Jackson had first sought to promote black activism after the school crisis by running for the Little Rock school board in 1959. However, dissenting white moderates and black conservatives had led him to withdraw his candidacy. Like Townsend, Jackson had extensive local contacts with black organizations and institutions and served as chair of COCA's Coordinating Committee. Freeman, thirty-nine, and his wife, Evangeline Upshur, both dentists, were also already well acquainted with black activism in the city. The couple had been next-door neighbors of Daisy and L. C. Bates throughout the school crisis, and Freeman had been one of their armed guards. Freeman, born in Fargo, east Arkansas, had resided in

Little Rock for fifteen years. He chaired COCA's Political Affairs Committee. In this capacity, Freeman played an important role in directing efforts by members of the black community to stand in elections.[41]

Other talented, young black professionals joined Townsend's colleagues in COCA. Ozell Sutton, thirty-seven, was born in the east Arkansas town of Gould and reared in Little Rock. A graduate of Philander Smith College, Sutton in 1948 was the first black reporter hired by the *Arkansas Democrat*. In 1957, he left the paper to take up a post at Winthrop Rockefeller's cattle ranch at Petit Jean Mountain, sixty-five miles northwest of Little Rock. In June 1962, Sutton became associate director of the ACHR. As COCA's public relations director, he played an influential role in developing its overall strategy for racial change. Dr. Jerry D. Jewell, thirty-two, another east Arkansan, was born on a sharecropping farm in Crittenden County. Jewell attended Arkansas AM&N College before graduating from Meharry Medical College at Nashville, Tennessee, in 1957. He then spent two years in the Army Dental Corps in east Texas, followed by two years at a training base in Missouri, and he opened a dental practice in North Little Rock in 1961. Jewell became president of the Little Rock branch of the NAACP in 1962, having been a member of the organization since high school. He chaired COCA's Housing Committee. George I. Henry, thirty-seven, yet another east Arkansan, hailed from Gurdon and was a graduate of Philander Smith College. Henry worked as a salesman of office supplies for thirteen years before taking the position of executive director of the Little Rock Urban League. He chaired COCA's Employment Committee.[42]

Representing the clergy in COCA were Rev. Negail Riley and Rev. Rufus K. Young. Riley, thirty-two, was pastor of the Wesley Chapel Methodist Church, located on Philander Smith's campus. A native of Oklahoma City, he received his bachelor's degree from Howard University and was one of the first black students to enroll at the Perkins School of Theology at Southern Methodist University in Dallas. Riley graduated with a bachelor of divinity degree and undertook resident studies toward a doctorate in theology at Boston University. In 1962, he moved to Little Rock to work on his dissertation. Riley chaired COCA's Education Committee. Young, fifty-two, was pastor of Bethel AME Church in Little Rock. Hailing from Drew County in east Arkansas, he was a graduate of Shorter College in North Little Rock and of Payne Theological Seminary at Wilberforce University, Ohio. Young was president of the Greater

Little Rock Ministerial Association and represented the older, more established clergy as chair of COCA's Committee on Religion.[43]

Two other important figures linked COCA's new guard with past black activism in the city and state. One was L. C. Bates, who chaired COCA's Health and Welfare Committee. The other was W. L. Jarrett, COCA treasurer, who had been an influential member of the CNO during the 1940s and had been temporary president of the ASC in 1951.[44]

The first issue COCA sought to address was the lack of existing communication and cooperation between the black and white communities. On July 21, 1961, COCA representatives met with the city board and informed them that a failure to confront racial issues fostered a potentially explosive situation. Only through tackling racial problems head-on could the city repair its tarnished image after the school crisis. This approach would eliminate the need for sit-ins, boycotts, Freedom Rides, and other demonstrations. COCA believed that through interracial cooperation the process of desegregation in Little Rock could proceed in a relatively painless and civilized manner, without the turmoil and costly litigation seen in other communities.[45] In light of the divisions whites knew previously existed in the black community, the city board did not take COCA seriously and refused to act.[46]

After several months, having exhausted all channels of dialogue and cooperation, COCA resolved to demonstrate its strength. On March 8, 1962, twenty-two members of COCA filed a collective suit in the federal district court against the city board of directors for the desegregation of "public parks, recreational facilities, Joseph T. Robinson Auditorium and all other public facilities." Wiley A. Branton, hired by COCA as legal counsel, was confident of victory, telling reporters, "Without question, the court has always ordered desegregation of all facilities. The day of separate but equal is out." Apparently, a number of factors had resulted in the suit's being filed, but the final straw came when Duke Ellington cancelled a scheduled show at the Joseph T. Robinson Auditorium in response to criticism by the NAACP about performing for a segregated audience.[47]

Members of the city board of directors admitted that the desegregation of public facilities was "a foregone conclusion" if the case went to court. Nevertheless, there was an absolute commitment to fight the lawsuit, if only to buy time to devise other methods to avoid desegregation.[48] In an effort to exert further pressure, COCA arranged to meet with Little Rock

Downtown Limited, a group comprising some of the city's most influential businessmen. At the meeting, COCA demanded the desegregation of rest room facilities in the city's stores, an end to segregated lunch counters, and better job opportunities for blacks. COCA leaders, having already proved they were willing to take their grievances to court, felt confident the group would take the requests seriously. The businessmen, however, refused to budge. Like the city board, they seemed prepared to prolong litigation to delay desegregation as long as possible.[49]

The earlier student protests had failed without the backing of a unified black community leadership. Now the efforts of COCA, in the absence of such direct-action protests, met with little success. Only through a two-pronged approach, direct action coupled with a support network that could help sustain such protests and articulate the demands of the local black community, would whites respond to black activism. With the student movement at Philander Smith ravaged by the harsh sentences and fines imposed by the courts, a potential base for direct action was lacking. Thus, in an effort to revive the sit-ins, the ACHR asked SNCC's national office in Atlanta, Georgia, if it would lend assistance in revitalizing protest in the city. SNCC responded by sending civil rights activist Bill Hansen to Little Rock.[50]

When the twenty-three-year-old white activist arrived in Little Rock on October 24, 1962, he was already a veteran of the civil rights movement. In 1961, he had traveled from his hometown of Cincinnati, Ohio, to Montgomery, Alabama, as a CORE delegate in one of the first Freedom Rides. Arrested en route, Hansen spent one and a half months in a Mississippi jail. After his experience in Mississippi, he became even more heavily involved in civil rights protests, helping to organize sit-in demonstrations in Maryland at Baltimore, Annapolis, and Cambridge. While he was organizing protests, friends introduced Hansen to SNCC. He then began to travel south, helping SNCC to organize campus action groups at black colleges in Virginia. In 1962, Hansen was at Albany, Georgia, helping SNCC and SCLC to organize mass demonstrations. In one demonstration, local police jailed and beat Hansen, which resulted in four broken ribs and a broken jaw. Shaken by this encounter, he moved to New York to recover. After several weeks of recuperation, Hansen traveled to SNCC's national office. There he met with SNCC communications director Julian Bond, who told him about a telegram the office had received from the Little Rock-based ACHR. Bond told Hansen that Little Rock was already on the verge of negotiating an end to desegregation and that the assignment should only take a "couple of weeks to a month."[51]

When Hansen arrived at the ACHR office in Little Rock, he spoke with director Nat Griswold and associate director Ozell Sutton. Both believed the city was ready to capitulate to demands for desegregation if blacks could apply sufficient pressure. The businessmen's fear of unwanted publicity after the school crisis was, they believed, "the most vulnerable point in Little Rock's armor." The only drawback was a lack of direct action in the city, which might persuade downtown businessmen to act. Griswold and Sutton told Hansen they hoped he would use his organizational skills to help reinvigorate the student movement at Philander Smith to provide the needed catalyst for change.[52]

Later that afternoon, Hansen contacted Philander Smith student Worth Long, whom Hansen had met at national SNCC conferences.[53] Long offered to take Hansen to a meeting of student activists on campus that evening. At the meeting, Hansen witnessed firsthand the threadbare state of the student movement. Only seven people attended. Among those present, he failed to detect any "ground-swell of . . . enthusiasm." Attempting to generate some interest, he explained the work of SNCC and what the organization had already done and achieved. The meeting ended on a positive note when Hansen persuaded a couple of the students to accompany him downtown the following day to try to get service at a segregated lunch counter.[54]

Hansen used the sit-in to gauge community feeling among whites in Little Rock. Accompanied by the chair of SNCC at Philander Smith, Rev. William E. Bush, Hansen entered Woolworth, sat at the lunch counter, and ordered coffee. When the waitress refused to serve Bush, Hansen asked the store manager whether it was the policy of his store to refuse to serve blacks. The manager replied that it was not store policy but city policy. In a field report about the incident, Hansen noted "the absolute lack of tension at the counter when Bush was sitting there," in contrast to the hysteria and violence similar demonstrations had encountered in other communities. He concluded, "[T]he whole incident gives an indication that there would be no widespread consternation among the white community if Negroes were served at the lunch counters." Hansen advised students to avoid demonstrations, which might risk a white backlash, and instead encouraged them to talk with managers of downtown stores to persuade them it would be in their best interests to desegregate without a fuss.[55]

The following Monday morning, four black students went to Woolworth to talk to the store manager. Attempting to stall the students, he asked them to return in a couple of weeks. The students demanded an answer by Wednesday and left the store. On Wednesday, the manager told the students he was trying to work out a solution with other downtown businessmen. When pressed for details, the manager refused to set a specific date for desegregation. In response, the students sat down at the lunch counter, which the manager then closed. Hansen called newspapers and television and radio stations to publicize the event, bringing further pressure on the business community to meet the students' demands. When the police arrived, the manager refused to press charges against the students. By midafternoon, they left of their own accord.[56]

The sit-ins had the intended impact on the business community. Shortly after the outbreak of new demonstrations, the executive director of Downtown Little Rock Limited, Willard A. Hawkins, contacted Long. Hawkins informed Long that a group of businessmen had formed a Downtown Negotiating Committee (DNC), headed by James Penick, president of Worthen Bank and Trust, and the group was willing to meet with students. Alongside Penick on the DNC was Will Mitchell, who had been instrumental in organizing the STOP campaign during the school crisis; Arthur Phillips, president of Cohn department store; and B. Finley Vinson, president of First National Bank. Before meeting with students, Penick, a well-respected and powerful figure in the Little Rock business community, met with downtown merchants and professional leaders to pave the way for negotiations. Penick informed them that they must face the choice of risking further demonstrations or ending segregation. During the first two weeks in November 1962, a delegation from the black community, comprising two Philander Smith students, Long and Burt Strauss, and two COCA leaders, Henry and Sutton, met with the DNC to discuss desegregation. Although both sides agreed segregation should end, talks stalled over the timing involved, with the black delegation pressing for change within a matter of weeks and whites talking about gradual desegregation over a number of years.[57]

Disillusioned with the results of the negotiations, Philander Smith students expanded sit-in demonstrations to the Walgreen, McClellan, and Blass stores. At Walgreen, nine students asked for service at a segregated lunch counter. The manager closed the counter, but the students refused to leave. When Hansen and Long sat at the lunch counter and refused to leave, the manager called the police and had them arrested. The arrests helped muster more support from campus, with more than one hundred Philander Smith students holding a march downtown the following day. At a rally that evening, COCA offered its backing for the demonstrations by providing the $1,000 bond for the release of Hansen and Long.[58]

The new burst of demonstrations brought the city's businessmen back to the negotiating table. Rather than risk the potential damage of a prolonged battle over desegregation, they decided to broker a compromise. Eventually, after further haggling, businessmen reached an agreement with black representatives to desegregate downtown lunch counters in the early months of 1963. Penick took charge of the operation. He first approached the manager at Woolworth, opposite Worthen Bank's downtown headquarters. Penick explained that the DNC had reached an agreement with students that lunch counters would desegregate in return for an end to demonstrations. The manager at Woolworth agreed to go along with the plan if other stores were willing to participate.[59]

Penick used this tentative agreement to persuade other stores to adhere to the arrangements for desegregation. When the major downtown stores agreed to cooperate, store managers, businessmen, and representatives from the black community met to discuss arrangements. Representatives from each constituency agreed that initially a small delegation from the black community would ask for service at particular stores at a set date and time. At first, the black groups would stay only for a short time, then over the course of the next few weeks, increase the numbers of those served and the length of their stay. They agreed to notify the local police and the staff at lunch counters in advance to avoid any confusion.[60]

On January 2, 1963, Woolworth, McClellan, Walgreen, and Blass all desegregated their lunch counters.[61] The only dissent in the whole process came from Amis Guthridge of the CCC, who led a handful of die-hard segregationists in a picket of stores. When the picketing had no effect, the demonstrations ceased. Indeed, many in the white community actually went out of their way to eat at desegregated lunch counters to ease the process.[62] The whole event took place under a blanket of media silence to avoid stirring up widespread opposition. The lack of local newspaper, television, or radio coverage came at the request of the city's businessmen, and in the perceived interests of the community, the owners of the media agreed to comply.[63] Not until January 20 did the first reports of desegregation emerge in a Pine Bluff newspaper, which revealed the "secret."[64]

The successful desegregation of the major lunch counters prompted many smaller businesses to follow suit shortly after. Moreover, by the end of January several major hotels, motels, and a downtown bowling alley had desegregated.[65] On February 15, federal judge J. Smith Henley ruled in favor of the COCA desegregation lawsuit filed in March 1962. The ruling ordered an end to racial segregation in all public facilities, except public swimming pools, which COCA did not specifically mention in the lawsuit. COCA had left out a request to desegregate the swimming pools as it touched upon the issue of interracial bathing and the white fears of miscegenation.[66] In June, the city's movie theatres and Robinson Auditorium admitted blacks. By October, most of the city's restaurants had desegregated, as, by the end of the year, had all city parks, playgrounds, golf courses, the Little Rock Zoo, and the Arts Center. At the end of 1963, Little Rock had desegregated most of its public and some of its private facilities.[67]

The changes taking place in Little Rock captured media attention precisely because of the notable absence of tension. Little Rock's rediscovered image of racial progress contrasted starkly with major upheavals over desegregation in other southern cities. For example, at Birmingham, Alabama, in 1963, Chief of Police Eugene "Bull" Connor used police dogs and fire hoses to break up black demonstrations.[68] An article in *Jet* about peaceful desegregation in Little Rock contrasted events there with violence in other communities across the South. James Forman, executive secretary of SNCC, heralded the city as "just about the most integrated . . . in the south." Local black leaders indicated they were pleased with progress in the city. Both Townsend and Sutton agreed that the major change in the city since 1957 was the newfound unity in the black community. "Negroes realize they can do things on their own behalf," Sutton said. He added that it was this fact that had forced the white community to confront the racial situation.[69]

In direct contrast to the rising fortunes of new groups dedicated to black advancement such as COCA and SNCC, the NAACP faced a much tougher time during the early 1960s. A number of problems beset Arkansas' oldest civil rights organization. For a start, there was the massive task of rebuilding NAACP membership within the state. As the controversy over school desegregation had intensified, membership in the NAACP brought with it the threat of physical intimidation and economic reprisals. Consequently, from 1955 to 1957, NAACP membership figures in Arkansas dropped from 2,086 to 992. By the end of the school crisis, because of rising racial tension in general and Attorney General Bennett's campaigns in particular, almost half of the thirty-three local NAACP branches in the state had disbanded. The branches that remained often operated in a makeshift fashion. Only the Little Rock and Pine Bluff branches contained more than one hundred members.[70]

The absence of Daisy Bates was a major blow to NAACP activities in Little Rock and throughout the state. After the *State Press* closed in October 1959, Bates spent most of the following two years either in New York, writing her memoir of the school crisis, or on the road for numerous speaking engagements. She reveled in her role as one of the civil rights movement's first nationally recognized women and enjoyed a series of high-profile positions. Bates was a member of the NAACP and the SCLC boards of directors, she was appointed by President Kennedy to the Democratic National Committee, and she worked as an adviser on President Lyndon B. Johnson's antipoverty programs. In 1963, Bates was the only woman asked to speak at the March on Washington. She attended the march as part of a Tribute to Women, alongside heroine of the 1956 Montgomery bus boycott Rosa Parks, SNCC activist Diane Nash Bevel, and the leader of the Cambridge Nonviolent Action Committee in Maryland, Gloria Richardson.[71]

In the absence of Daisy Bates, her husband, in his new role as Arkansas' NAACP field secretary, helped take care of the day-to-day business of the organization. The NAACP's national office established the post of field secretary in 1956, when it sent Frank W. Smith to Little Rock to assist in running the state branches. However, Smith's ill-defined role led to criticism from Arkansas NAACP members, who regularly expressed dissatisfaction about his inactivity to the national office. Other intermittent appointments were made, but those fared little better. The NAACP's national office gave L. C. Bates the position in January 1960, partly as recompense for the collapse of the *State Press*.[72]

L. C. Bates struggled to revive the fortunes of the NAACP in the state. The Bateses had been the solid foundation of the organization's activities in Arkansas for almost a decade. In a reversal of traditional gender roles, Daisy took the leadership role while L. C. more often acted as nurturer and supporter, in part due to the thirteen-year age difference between the two. Without his younger, more energetic partner, L. C. Bates failed to provide the driving force the NAACP needed.[73]

Compounding these difficulties were the Bateses' personal problems. After the school crisis, their paths diverged, with Daisy attracting national attention and L. C. staying behind in Arkansas. The distance placed a great deal of strain on the relationship. Matters came to a head in December 1962 when Daisy Bates filed for divorce, alleging "abuse, contempt and studied neglect." L. C. did not contest the action. The couple reconciled and remarried within the space of eight months. Nevertheless, they continued to live virtually separate lives throughout most of the 1960s.[74]

One potential new source of NAACP leadership was Dr. Jerry D. Jewell, who became president of the Little Rock NAACP branch with the support of Daisy Bates in 1962. Bates persuaded long-serving existing president Rev. J. C. Crenchaw that the NAACP needed "new blood and new persons" to reinvigorate the organization. Despite the reservations of some branch members, who felt that the recently arrived Jewell did not know enough about local affairs, Crenchaw agreed to step down in favor of the younger man. Jewell's forthright activism cast him in the Daisy Bates mould. He worked closely with NAACP field secretary L. C. Bates in Little Rock and provided the organization with a link to fresh developments in black activism through his association with COCA.[75]

Another possible new source of NAACP leadership was Pine Bluff lawyer George Howard Jr., who succeeded Daisy Bates as president of the ASC in November 1961. Howard, a graduate of the University of Arkansas, represented parents in the *Dove v. Parham* (1959) school desegregation suit in Pine Bluff's Dollarway school district. *Dove* was the only school desegregation suit in the state outside of Little Rock. However, in succeeding Bates, Howard faced the impossible task of trying to live up to her achievements. Complicating matters further was the fact that the former ASC president often revisited Arkansas and still took an active interest in the state NAACP activities. When Howard managed to escape the long shadow cast by Daisy, her husband loomed over his shoulder, holding a position that appeared in many ways to conflict with Howard's role as ASC president. That Howard was based in Pine Bluff and L. C. Bates and Jewell were based in Little Rock only served to further blur the division of responsibility within the Arkansas NAACP. Although never as openly antagonistic as the struggle between Flowers and Taylor in the 1940s, the reemergence of distinct NAACP camps in Pine Bluff and Little Rock was an ominous development.[76]

One obstacle all potential leaders of the NAACP faced was competition from other civil rights groups operating in the state. During the 1940s and 1950s, the NAACP had been the main vehicle for black advancement. The emergence of groups such as COCA and SNCC threatened that dominance. Although the NAACP was part of COCA's coalition, it stubbornly continued to cultivate its own influence and prestige. For example, when delicate secret negotiations were taking place between white businessmen, black students, and COCA to end downtown desegregation in 1963, the NAACP openly demanded separate talks. Governor Faubus exploited this rift in his newspaper *The Arkansas Statesman* to alert the public to the negotiations, to try to stop them, and to embarrass white businessmen. Fortunately, the negotiations were at such an advanced point that Faubus's intervention proved little more than a token gesture. The *Arkansas Gazette* assured its readers the NAACP was definitely not involved in the discussions. The episode only added to the perception that the NAACP was out of touch with new efforts to promote civil rights.[77]

Even old allies appeared to be leaving the NAACP behind. In June 1962, Branton moved to Atlanta to head the Voter Education Project (VEP). The VEP, part of a regionwide effort to bolster the black vote across the South, was endorsed by all major national civil rights groups and run under the tax-exempt auspices of the SRC. Despite this new role, Branton continued to represent plaintiffs in the ongoing Little Rock school desegregation suit. Aware of the stigma attached to the NAACP in Arkansas, Branton encouraged parents to deal directly with the LDF. Increasingly, his contact point in Little Rock was Sutton, not the Bateses. Branton also represented COCA in its suit demanding the desegregation of Little Rock's public facilities. Daisy Bates chastised Branton for working with those who did "not feel any moral or financial responsibility to the NAACP," believing his actions had "devastating effects," which "added nothing to our campaign for members and funds." Yet, Branton was not being disloyal to the NAACP. He was simply being pragmatic about the increasing need to work through a variety of different channels to secure black advancement.[78]

Events at a local level echoed national and regional developments in the NAACP in the late 1950s and early 1960s. In a rapidly changing black struggle, the NAACP often appeared unable to adapt or to relate to new circumstances. NAACP executive secretary Roy Wilkins clung to the organization's reliance on legal strategies, while new organizations such as the SCLC increasingly believed that "the courts are secondary to direct action by the masses." Wilkins shied away from the idea of cooperation and coordination with other groups. In that respect, Wilkins shared the view of others in the organization: "We need only one national organization to speak for Negroes and all other organizations and leadership should rally around the NAACP." In particular, Wilkins appeared jealous of the popularity of younger leaders, such as Martin Luther King Jr., and newer organizations, such as the SCLC and SNCC. The NAACP leader lacked the charisma and dynamism to appeal directly to the black masses. The antagonistic stance of Wilkins only served to hasten the sidelining of the NAACP in the national civil rights struggle during the 1960s.[79]

Notwithstanding the difficulties that beset the NAACP, by the mid-1960s, the black struggle for civil rights was at floodtide in Arkansas, in the South, and in the nation. Some hitherto recalcitrant white communities had begun to forge ahead with a program of desegregation that would have been unthinkable just five years before. Black communities, in turn, appeared to have undergone a transformation, evidencing a new determination and unity in addressing racial issues. Public sentiment outside the South swung decisively for civil rights. The media aided the cause by graphically depicting barbarous incidents of southern white racism. Southern black leaders such as Martin Luther King Jr. assured whites that blacks simply wanted their share of the American dream. Consequently, the federal government showed more conviction than ever in the cause of civil rights, leading to the passage of the 1964 Civil Rights Act and the 1965 Voting Rights Act.[80]

Despite exuberance over these developments, a great deal of work for civil rights activists lay ahead. Although legislation granted notional rights, the task of testing and implementing those rights at a local level still remained. Moreover, the spectacular advancements won by civil rights activists by the mid-1960s only partly addressed the problems blacks faced. True, the gains removed the overt barriers of discrimination in public places by outlawing Jim Crow and further empowered the black community with an extended protection of voting rights. Yet, the more fundamental bases of discrimination, in areas such as employment and housing, remained largely untouched. In the mid- to late-1960s, civil rights activists in Arkansas and across the South sought to maintain momentum for further racial change. They worked to extend the goals already achieved in some communities uniformly across the region and began to turn their attention to the problems of discrimination blacks still encountered.

New Challenges   7

During the latter half of the 1960s, black activism expanded dramatically across Arkansas. SNCC moved on from its successful demonstrations in Little Rock, accruing more volunteers to extend the organization's activities into the Arkansas Delta. Across the Delta, SNCC waged campaigns to end segregation and to mobilize the black vote until its departure from the state in 1967. Taking over from SNCC as the main vehicle for black activism in 1967 were various community organizations established by President Johnson's War on Poverty legislation. However, by the end of the 1960s, there was growing disillusionment with the progress of the antipoverty programs and the slow pace of change in other areas of concern to blacks. This led to a wave of protest and violence, which emerged hand in hand with a new movement of "black power."

The very nature of the struggle began to change. In the past, a small cadre of committed black activists had drawn upon local black support and outside help to issue demands to whites. During the late 1960s, mass black support for civil rights began to emerge in some localities, which translated into mass black activism. The class basis of the movement began to shift as a coalition of young and poor blacks began to challenge the priorities of established middle-class black leaders. This in turn led to a shift in the focus of black protest. Although voter registration and the desegregation of public facilities remained important issues, progress in areas such as employment and housing were additionally demanded. Mass activism also impacted the tactics and methods of redress adopted by blacks. Litigation and nonviolence began to give way to mass demonstrations and threats of violence to try to force concessions from whites. Taken together, these changes forged a new and explosive period of race relations in Arkansas.

In many ways, the expansion of black activism in Arkansas represented the fulfillment of the ambitions of Flowers and the CNO back in the 1940s to mobilize the black population in the state. In the 1940s, Flowers had insisted that Little Rock blacks would have to take the lead in achieving this goal. Since then, Little Rock blacks had successfully campaigned for the equalization of teachers salaries, the appointment of black police officers, black participation in the Democratic Party primaries, and the desegregation of public schools and other facilities. Moreover, Little Rock had proved an important gateway for introducing and promoting both local organizations, such as ANDA and COCA, and national organizations, such as the NAACP and SNCC, that were essential vehicles for statewide black organization and mobilization. As black activism expanded in the state, it built on the foundations of these earlier struggles in Little Rock.

However, as the struggle for civil rights spread in Arkansas during the 1960s, local conditions and personalities profoundly shaped the development of local black activism. In some areas, most notably in the cities and the larger towns of east Arkansas, mass black movements began to emerge. In other areas, attempts to mobilize the black population were more sporadic. There were even some rural areas in the farther reaches of the state that the civil rights movement bypassed altogether. A full understanding of the complexities of black activism across Arkansas in the 1960s warrants more detailed attention than can be given here. Nevertheless, it is important to understand the broad contours and trends of those struggles, since they represented the culmination of earlier black activist efforts and provided the context for new directions in black protest in Arkansas' capital city.

After the sit-ins in Little Rock, SNCC moved its headquarters to Pine Bluff. The organization then used its new base of operations to extend its influence into the Delta towns of Helena, Forrest City, and Gould. In turn, when SNCC had established itself in those towns, it began to penetrate the smaller villages and settlements scattered across the region. Early Delta campaigns mirrored those at Little Rock in successfully using direct-action protests, such as sit-ins, as a focal point to stimulate community discussion about and action on racial issues. By the time SNCC left Arkansas in 1967, most public facilities in the state's major towns and cities had integrated, and efforts were underway to end segregation in other parts of the state. SNCC's campaigns ensured that legally mandated Jim Crow, a physically and psychologically potent part of white discrimination, was finally banished from Arkansas.[1]

Later SNCC efforts switched attention to strategies that offered the possibility of making fundamental long-term changes within black communities. One major SNCC innovation in this respect was the establishment of Freedom Schools, which taught basic classes in literacy and numeracy to all age groups in the black community. Alongside this practical instruction, SNCC held citizenship classes, which provided information about voting rights and the machinery of government in the state. Freedom Schools therefore provided both the day-to-day means for black advancement and encouraged collective discussions about the needs, aims, and goals of the community.[2] Classes were often instrumental in establishing new indigenous organizations that would form the bedrock of black activism in the Delta in future years. The emergence of the Pine Bluff Movement, the Saint Francis County Achievement Committee, and Gould Citizens for Progress was directly related to SNCC's success in encouraging local communities to draw upon their own resources to press for racial change.[3]

SNCC also made a concerted effort to raise black political consciousness in the state and to register black voters. Like Flowers and the CNO before, SNCC saw widespread political participation through increased voter registration as crucial to black advancement. Tirelessly, SNCC workers retraced the steps of Flowers and the CNO, reviving and extending the previous areas of influence. This helped almost double the number of blacks who were registered to vote, from 34 percent in 1962 to 67.5 percent in 1968.[4]

SNCC's voting rights campaigns drew widespread white opposition. Attempts to run black candidates for elective offices encountered numerous examples of fraud at the polls. In the 1965 school board elections, for example, thirty-two black candidates ran for office in the Delta and all but one, who ran against another black candidate, were defeated. SNCC workers monitoring events reported illegal voting by whites, harassment and arbitrary disqualification of black voters, destruction and manipulation of black voters' ballots, and the practice of maintaining segregated lines and ballot boxes at the voting booths. One SNCC report concluded,

"[I]llegal practices do not represent isolated, accidental instances, but a deliberate policy, the purpose of which is to render Negro votes meaningless."[5]

Nevertheless, SNCC persevered with its voting rights campaign and had its first significant breakthrough in the 1966 elections. The announcement that year by Faubus that, after an unprecedented six consecutive terms in office, he would not run for reelection threw the race for governor wide open. The two new candidates who contested the post offered the electorate a stark choice for the future direction of the state. For the Democrats, Jim Johnson won the nomination. From the outset, Johnson made it clear he would not be campaigning in the black community, and he even refused to shake hands with blacks on the election trail.[6]

The Republicans again nominated Winthrop Rockefeller, who had unsuccessfully run for governor against Faubus in 1964.[7] Born in New York in 1922 and the grandson of Standard Oil founder John D. Rockefeller, Winthrop Rockefeller had a privileged northern background that could not have been more different from Johnson's folksy, southern, good-old-boy image. Rockefeller attended Yale, then worked in the Texas oil industry before enlisting in the army in the Second World War, where he rose to the rank of lieutenant colonel. Returning from the war to the high life in New York, Rockefeller developed a reputation as a wealthy playboy. In 1948, he married Barbara "Bobo" Spears, though the marriage ended in a much-publicized acrimonious divorce in 1954. Partly to escape the adverse publicity of the divorce and to cut his ties with New York, Rockefeller moved to Arkansas in 1953. In Arkansas, Rockefeller ran a cattle ranch at Petit Jean Mountain, near the town of Morrilton. Faubus had first persuaded Rockefeller to enter Arkansas political life when he appointed him as chair of the AIDC in 1955.[8]

Rockefeller's views on the race issue were somewhat ambiguous, although he had taken an active interest in race relations in the past and he had joined the executive board of the National Urban League in 1940. The fact that a black friend from the North, Jimmy Hudson, ran Rockefeller's ranch demonstrated a clear disregard for the established racial etiquette of the state. One of Rockefeller's chief campaign managers, John Ward, suggested that his candidate's views on race relations were "color-blind." By this, Ward meant that Rockefeller did not have any definite or specific program to better the position of blacks, but would run for office on a nondiscrimination basis.[9]

SNCC was initially unenthusiastic about throwing its support behind

Rockefeller, who described himself as "somewhere between my brother Nelson [liberal Republican governor of New York, who lost the 1964 Republican nomination for president and would serve as vice president under Gerald Ford, 1974–77] and Barry Goldwater [right-wing 1964 Republican presidential candidate] but closer to Goldwater" on the political spectrum.[10] Yet, Winthrop Rockefeller was certainly preferable to Jim Johnson, and SNCC, the NAACP, and other civil rights groups in the state believed it was imperative to prevent the stalwart segregationist from winning office.[11] Moreover, supporting Rockefeller meant gaining access to the considerable personal funds of the wealthy candidate, who indicated an interest in harnessing the support of black voters eschewed by his opponent.[12]

Rockefeller's gubernatorial election victory in 1966 depended heavily on the efforts of SNCC, as well as other groups such as the NAACP, COCA, and a Democrats for Rockefeller organization made up of white Democratic opponents of Johnson.[13] These groups drew upon Rockefeller's considerable resources, along with those channeled from the VEP through the Arkansas Voter Project (AVP), to mobilize the black vote statewide. Demonstrating the continuing importance of COCA and its willingness to cooperate with other groups, Ozell Sutton was director of the AVP, Dr. Townsend was chair, and W. L. Jarrett was treasurer. The VEP, headed by native Arkansan Wiley A. Branton, already had strong connections with the state.[14]

Changes to the voter registration law significantly aided the effort to increase the number of black voters. In 1964, the passage of Amendment Twenty-Four to the U.S. Constitution outlawed the use of the poll tax in federal elections. In 1965, Arkansas abolished the poll tax as a requirement for voting and introduced a permanent voter registration system. This new system simply required a free, one-time registration, which in most cases lasted a lifetime. Qualifying to vote therefore became much easier, and the number of black and white electors in Arkansas rose rapidly.[15]

Despite the reservations of SNCC workers voiced privately during the campaign, Rockefeller's election and subsequent reelection as governor in 1968, when he polled 88 percent of the state's black vote, marked a sea change in Arkansas politics. Before the Democrats recaptured the office in 1970, the DPA, a bastion of white supremacy for many years, undertook a thorough reexamination of its ideals and priorities. No longer would it consider a candidate like Johnson as a nominee for governor. The successful Democratic candidate in 1970, Dale Bumpers, was the first in a line of Democratic governors of Arkansas to embrace racially enlightened ideals and to make open and active efforts to court the black vote.[16]

By 1972, Arkansas boasted ninety-nine black elected officials, the second-highest number of any southern state. The same year, Jewell, who in 1965 succeeded Howard as head of the ASC, became the first black member of the Arkansas Senate. Townsend became one of three blacks elected to the Arkansas House of Representatives. Lawyer Perlesta A. Hollingworth became the first black member of the Little Rock board of directors. Throughout the state, blacks won elective offices as aldermen, mayors, justices of the peace, school board members, city council members, city recorders, and city clerks. These gains further stimulated black voter registration. By 1976, 94 percent of Arkansas' voting-age blacks were registered, the highest percentage of any state in the South. As on the national level, Democrats became the party of civil rights in the state. In the 1980s, the support of black Arkansans was as vital in securing the post of governor for William Jefferson Clinton as the national black vote was in his two campaigns for president of the United States during the 1990s.[17]

However, at the very point that the civil rights struggle reached its zenith in the mid-1960s, it began to suffer what historian Adam Fairclough refers to as a "crisis of victory." Fairclough points out that by this point, the civil rights movement had largely achieved its two central goals, desegregating public facilities and securing federal protection for the registration of black voters. Having achieved those goals, it "lacked a program or plan for translating the notional equality of the law into the social actuality of shared wealth and power." Meanwhile, "white prejudice [remained] a persisting fact." With the two common goals achieved, confusion and division over how to next proceed threatened to splinter civil rights activists.[18]

SNCC was the first casualty of this crisis of victory. In June 1966, James Meredith, the first black student to enter the University of Mississippi in 1962, began a march across Mississippi to assert the right of blacks to move freely in the state. Just a few hours into his journey, Meredith was shot and wounded. Shortly afterward, civil rights leaders from SNCC, SCLC, and CORE arrived to continue the march. As the march resumed, SNCC activist Willie Ricks began to popularize the slogan of "black power." Although the meaning of the slogan remained ambiguous, it quickly became a rallying cry for blacks who were dissatisfied with the pace and extent of racial change in America. New SNCC chair Stokely Charmichael embraced the black power slogan and called for blacks to take control of the organization's operations. As elsewhere, this departure fostered schisms within Arkansas SNCC ranks over the future direction of its activities and played a major role in its eventual disbanding.[19]

One person glad to see the back of SNCC in Arkansas was L. C. Bates, who viewed the organization as unwelcome competition for the NAACP. Bates described east Arkansas counties as "infested with SNCC." Particular problems emerged in Lincoln County, where Bates reported that SNCC had "infiltrated" the NAACP branch. Officers of the Lincoln County NAACP were participating in SNCC protests, which resulted in a court injunction against both SNCC and the NAACP. When Bates investigated, he found that the Lincoln NAACP president and secretary were desperately trying to stop its members from participating in SNCC activities. Bates backed them, telling NAACP dissenters that if they wanted to support SNCC, they would have to leave the NAACP first. Several weeks later, Bates reported that he had "heard no complaints since" and that he believed "the branch has won a victory over its enemies." Contrary to Bates's view, SNCC's presence in the state had a positive effect on the NAACP. After SNCC left Arkansas, the interest in black activism it had stimulated led to a brief NAACP renaissance. Branch membership started to grow again in precisely those areas where SNCC had been active.[20]

The NAACP's national office appeared far more concerned with the activities of Bates than of SNCC. In particular, it expressed concern over an article appearing in the *New York Times* about Bates's role as "special advisor" to Faubus. According to the report, in 1965 Bates had demanded Faubus hire more blacks in federally funded state agencies. Faubus agreed, in compliance with federal nondiscrimination regulations. Faubus then asked Bates and two other blacks to make nominations for the positions. This led to the appointment of more than one hundred blacks to state agencies. Faubus shrugged off the arrangement, contending, "I've always been on a friendly basis with L. C." For his part, Bates claimed Faubus had changed "[n]ot his attitude, but his practices. He plays politics, we know that. But while he is playing politics, we are getting some of the things that we've been fighting for."[21]

NAACP director of branches Gloster B. Current questioned Bates about the article. "How does this new posture in Little Rock, Arkansas, square with our image as a militant organization?" he asked. The militant record he had built in Arkansas since 1941 was the very basis, said Bates, "for the recognition I now enjoy in helping the economic condition of the

Negro." "How do we avoid the criticism that the NAACP is now collaborating with its former enemies?" asked Current. Bates replied that he had been criticized for many things in the past, including trying to desegregate Central High School. That did not concern him. Bettering the position of black Arkansans did. Bates noted, "My effort is responsible for some 100 Negroes in good paying dignified jobs where federal funds are being used." "Are you in a position to support the view that this type of advisorship is consonant with the policy and program of the NAACP?" Current asked. "Yes," replied Bates. It was in line with item five on his NAACP membership card to "secure equal job opportunities based upon individual merit without regard to race, religion or national origin." Bates admitted he was "guilty of overstepping bounds" only insofar as insisting on the first choice of jobs going to NAACP members. Bates stressed, "The NAACP *is not* working with the Faubus administration. The NAACP *is not* involved in politics in Arkansas."[22]

In some ways, Bates's defense was viable enough. Faubus worked with a range of black leaders throughout his political career, before, during, and after the school crisis. Moreover, as Bates pointed out, just two years earlier Current had asked Bates, "If you can't get rid of him [Faubus], can't you use him?" Bates claimed he was simply trying to secure black advancement any way he could. In other ways, Bates's role was deeply worrisome. From a public-relations standpoint, it did not look good for an officer of the NAACP to work with Faubus but to oppose SNCC. Moreover, Bates's insistence on hiring only NAACP members smacked of nepotism. Worse still, the arrangement had uncomfortable overtones of paternalism and made Bates appear to be an unscrupulous black leader trading influence with a white politician, a practice he had previously criticized in the *State Press*. Whatever his intentions, Bates's actions were clearly out of step with the prevailing mood of the times.[23]

Dissatisfaction with the work of Bates as Arkansas' NAACP field secretary had been growing in the state for some time. Jewell believed Bates's lack of "aggressive activity" had allowed SNCC to eclipse the NAACP in the state, and he had alerted the NAACP national office about Bates's relationship with Faubus, expressing his misgivings about it. The decline of the NAACP in Little Rock, where the field secretary's office was located, reflected the organization's inactivity statewide. In 1966, the NAACP branch in the state capital reported only seventy-two members. By 1969, the ASC was actively pushing for Bates's retirement. Current admitted, "We would be glad to do something along these lines," but practical considerations needed to be taken into account. "We have no place to put L. C. and we have to make sure that his retirement will be effective in terms of insurance funding," Current reported.[24]

Finally, in May 1971, the NAACP national office unceremoniously unloaded the seventy-year-old Bates. Bates was far from happy with the decision and described the letter from the NAACP demanding his retirement as "the most shocking missive that I have ever received." Bates could not believe "that any reputable organization would notify an employee with over 11 years service . . . that he would be retired the following month. Since you made it emphatically clear that my retirement pay would start [then] I felt like an impostor. I felt that we were advocating a doctrine of fairplay [sic], that we, ourselves could not support." Certainly, it seemed an unbefitting exit for someone who had contributed so much to the NAACP and the struggle for civil rights in Arkansas.[25]

Meanwhile, Daisy Bates's career of black activism took an unpredictable turn. In 1965, she suffered a debilitating stroke, which cut short her involvement with the national civil rights struggle. Bates moved back to Little Rock to recover. In 1968, she moved into a mobile home at Mitchellville, an impoverished, predominantly black settlement in Desha County, southeast Arkansas. There, Bates returned to grassroots community activism as director of the Mitchellville OEO Self-Help Project, one of Arkansas' many community initiatives funded by the federal War on Poverty. Over the following six years, Bates successfully campaigned for the installation of new water and sewage systems, for paved streets, and for the building of a community center and swimming pool.[26]

Bates's efforts in Mitchellville formed part of a broader wave of new black activism founded on federal antipoverty legislation. The War on Poverty played a central role in the president's desire to create a Great Society. Building upon and extending antipoverty programs initiated by the Kennedy administration, Johnson successfully persuaded Congress, over stiff Republican opposition, to pass the Economic Opportunity Act (EOA) in 1964. The EOA created the Office of Economic Opportunity (OEO) to coordinate Community Action Programs (CAPs) run through Community Action Agencies (CCAs). Each state set up its own OEO to coordinate CCAs that operated variously at county and local levels. The CCAs, as a requirement of federal legislation, promoted "maximum feasible participation" by the poor in the antipoverty programs. The CCAs oversaw attempts by CAPs to assist the poor by targeting improvements in areas such as social services, health services, and employment. Although the antipoverty programs were controversial in terms of their cost and administration, they did contribute to decreasing levels of poverty in the United States between 1964 and 1974.[27]

In the absence of SNCC's organizational support, federal antipoverty programs unwittingly nurtured growing black activism in the state and provided it with new points of mobilization. Although they aimed to address the problems of all the state's poor, black and white alike, the programs became virtually synonymous with black advancement in many areas. The appointment of the South's first black state OEO director, William "Sonny" Walker, in 1967, further underscored the racial orientation of the War on Poverty in Arkansas. Over the course of a decade, a plethora of government-sponsored programs had a far-reaching impact on black activism.[28]

In strongly advocating maximum feasible participation by the poor, the federal government ensured that new initiatives perpetuated the SNCC ethos of enabling black communities to define and address their own problems. At one end of the spectrum, antipoverty programs in Arkansas encompassed neighborhood projects that specifically targeted areas such as social services, health, and education for improvement. At the other end were large-scale projects such as the Health Advocate Program, which sought to provide health care for six of the poorest, most heavily black-populated east Arkansas counties. On the surface at least, antipoverty projects appeared to offer the possibility of addressing the problems of the black poor.[29]

Ultimately, however, the most discernible effect of the programs was their radicalizing impact on black activism. The effects of the War on Poverty in the 1960s in many ways echoed the effects of the New Deal in the 1930s. The antipoverty programs highlighted the potential for government-sponsored improvement in the black community while demonstrating the large gap between the promise of a better life and the reality of existing conditions. When the federal government subsequently failed to provide many of the promised funds to sustain the initiatives, there was a great deal of resentment among Arkansas' black poor. The lack of funding for the antipoverty programs only served to increase black frustration at the slow pace of change in key areas such as employment, housing, and school desegregation. During the late 1960s, this frustration began to manifest itself in open conflict between blacks and white authority figures.[30]

Developments in Little Rock underscored black concerns about the persistence of second-class citizenship in Arkansas despite the battles won for civil rights. Black employment opportunities, for example, remained extremely limited. Little appeared to have changed in the city since the publication of the 1941 *Survey of Negroes* by the Greater Little Rock Urban League. Black men remained overwhelmingly concentrated in menial, unskilled jobs, and most black women still worked as domestic servants in white homes. Revealingly, the percentage of the median family wage earned by blacks in comparison to whites had actually dropped since the 1940s.[31] Black-owned businesses were still in relatively short supply. The 254 that did exist comprised many of the same small-scale neighborhood services that had appeared in the original survey. With integration, white stores and establishments began to welcome the patronage of blacks, placing a further strain on black business interests.[32]

Progress in housing for blacks was virtually nonexistent. Segregation, both as a matter of public policy and private practice, actually accelerated during the 1960s. This trend continued despite President Kennedy's 1962 executive order outlawing such practices. Up until then, the Little Rock Housing Authority (LRHA) had openly followed a policy of segregation in its public housing projects. Afterward, the LRHA relied on established housing patterns to maintain segregation. The LRHA argued that the existence of exclusively black and white housing projects was not evidence of discrimination. Rather, the LRHA claimed, blacks and whites simply chose to stay near areas where their race constituted a majority and near public facilities they already used.[33]

Blacks fared little better in reversing racial trends in private housing. Any inroads made were due to the efforts of a few individuals who were willing to buck existing racial residential patterns. Doing so usually meant going through a long, arduous ordeal. First, prospective black homeowners had to make the difficult decision to move away from the security of living in a predominantly black neighborhood. Next, they had to find a willing seller in a white neighborhood. Because of the fear that blacks moving into a white area would send house prices plummeting, there was a great deal of peer pressure on whites not to sell their homes to blacks.[34]

Those blacks who did find a white seller then faced the prospect of intimidation from their new neighbors. John Walker, who in September 1965 became the first Little Rock black to move his family into the all-white residential district of Broadmoor, soon discovered this fact. Walker bought his house from a resident looking to make a quick sale because he was moving to California. Even before arriving at their new home, the

Walkers had their front window smashed by a can of paint and their shrubbery set on fire. When they finally moved in, the neighbors ostracized them. As one put it, "If no one says anything to them I think it will only be a matter of time until they move somewhere else." Though the Walkers persevered for several years, they eventually tired of the situation and moved to another neighborhood.[35]

After the Walkers, the next person to move into a white neighborhood was Joe Anderson Jr. A self-employed carpenter, Anderson bought his home in March 1966 from the executive director of the Arkansas Council on Churches, Rev. Sam Allen, who was moving to Louisiana. Just over a year later, in April 1967, Anderson moved out of his home because of harassment from zoning ordinance officers after a complaint by neighbors that he was using his garage as a workshop. When Janice Marie Spencer, along with her three children and elderly mother, moved into a white district in central Little Rock in 1967, neighbors firebombed the Spencers' home twice in the first week. They moved out shortly afterward. Such episodes ensured that there were few other blacks willing to risk moving into a white neighborhood.[36]

Efforts to desegregate Little Rock's schools remained an important barometer for the pace and extent of racial change. From August 1959 to the mid-1960s, the Little Rock school board maintained a policy of token integration.[37] The 1964 Civil Rights Act sought to stimulate action on school desegregation by involving the Department of Justice and the Office of Education (part of the Department of Health, Education, and Welfare) in the process. In April 1965, the Office of Education drew up new guidelines for school desegregation. Although these were more prescriptive than in the past, they still permitted geographical zoning and the so-called "freedom-of-choice" plans some southern school boards had already adopted to limit further integration. Shortly afterward, the Little Rock school board introduced its own freedom-of-choice plan. This allowed all new students at entry-level grades to choose the school they wanted to attend. Under the plan, the proximity of students to their chosen school and the availability of places there would form the basis of pupil assignments.[38]

The apparent simplicity of the freedom-of-choice plan belied its more insidious intent. Local black lawyer Harold B. Anderson, along with director-counsel of the LDF, Jack Greenberg, and LDF-affiliated lawyers James M. Nabrit III and John Walker, challenged the new plan in the federal district court. They argued that a freedom-of-choice plan unfairly placed the burden of desegregation on the black community. It was clear from the outset that few whites would choose to attend a majority black school. This meant black students had to apply to white schools for integration to proceed. Given the history of school desegregation in Little Rock, many black students and their parents were reluctant to take the offer. Another drawback of the plan was that it limited the choice of schools to entry-level students. It therefore did not allow transfers within the school system for the majority of students who were in other grades. Essentially, the plan relied on existing social pressures to leave black and white students with practically no choice at all.[39]

The school board persevered with the freedom-of-choice plan over the objections of the black community, since it provided yet another useful temporary stalling tactic. Yet just as the school board had feared, in March 1966, the Office of Education issued new and bolder guidelines for school desegregation. The new guidelines indicated that using a freedom-of-choice plan as a delaying tactic was unacceptable and that such plans needed to take into account "the extent to which Negro . . . students have in fact transferred from segregated schools." In effect, this meant that school boards had to prove that freedom-of-choice plans were actually making an impact on the numbers of children attending integrated schools.[40]

Responding to the new guidelines, in August 1966, the Little Rock school board commissioned the University of Oregon to draw up an independent plan for the integration of the city's schools. In June 1967, the University of Oregon report claimed that with the right investment, it would take just two years to establish "an integrated high-quality educational program for all children" in the city. The Oregon Plan encountered fierce opposition, especially from the affluent white western suburbs of Little Rock, whose schools would encounter a significant degree of integration under its guidelines. After two months of bitter wrangling, the Little Rock school board agreed to adopt some of the report's suggestions, but rejected the bulk of the plan. The responsibility for school desegregation then fell on the shoulders of the new superintendent of schools, Floyd Parsons. The Parsons Plan, devised in December 1967, focused mainly on the city's high schools and shifted the emphasis from a freedom-of-choice plan to a policy of geographical zoning to achieve school desegregation. When voters failed to ratify a tax increase to facilitate the plan, it too fell by the wayside. In the 1966–67 academic year, only 16.7 percent of black students in Little Rock attended school with whites. This figure was just below the 18 percent of black students attending school with whites across the South. Moreover, the public school system in Little Rock still contained seven all-white schools and a dozen all-black schools.[41]

By 1967, ten years after the school crisis, Central High School had made more progress than many other schools in Little Rock, with 415 black students accounting for 19 percent of the total enrollment. However, a glimpse of life inside Central demonstrated that the statistics failed to do justice to the complex issues involved in school desegregation. An article in *Life* updating the integration story in Little Rock declared, "Central High reflects the surprising progress of Negro education all across the South." A series of color photographs provided illustrations of the progress. Opal Harper, one of five black teachers at Central, taught English to a class of black and white students. Cora Lee Mercer, the first black student to join the Central High cheerleaders, the High Steppers, instructed two white students vying for selection. Black student Henry Hall played alongside white students in Central High's school band. Bill Brooks was one of a number of black athletes at Central High starring on the running track and in the football team. Black and white students stood next to one another in the line at the school cafeteria. At the senior prom, fifty black couples shared the dance floor with white couples. All of these scenes indicated that Central High was a much different place than it had been a decade before.[42]

Yet, the glossy photographs did not reveal the entire picture of life at Central. Though black and white students studied together in classrooms, they clustered in racially exclusive enclaves at recess. They stood in line together at the school cafeteria, but they sat at different tables. At the senior prom, white students danced with other white students, and black students danced with other black students; there was no racial mixing. As the evening wore on, white students moved on to parties at homes to which black students were not invited. At the end of the night, there were more black couples left on the dance floor than whites. True, reported *Life*, different groups of students traditionally stuck together in cliques, but this was "stronger and uglier." Central High was, black and white students concluded, "desegregated but not integrated."[43]

David Baer, a white student who was editor of the Central High newspaper *The Tiger*, explained, "We don't associate with them. We don't invite them to our parties. We just both go to the same school, that's all. If you did become pals with one, I don't think you'd be well accepted in your own group. I think you would be pretty lonely." From a black perspective, student Ed Whitfield lamented conditions at Central: "I was in the band and during practice it was the nicest group I'd been with. But afterward kids who'd played and joked with me during practice didn't even know me. When we first came to school, whites were polite when we sat down at their lunch tables. They stayed to themselves but they didn't get up and leave. But after a few months they started moving when we sat down. That'll get you a little. You can have a half-way decent opinion of yourself until people leave the table when you approach."[44]

As in the past, Central High reflected the wider racial climate in Little Rock. As the legal barriers to desegregation fell, one formal regime of state-sanctioned racial discrimination gave way to more informal racial practices based on social exclusion. Indeed, as Whitfield's testimony indicated, the more blacks began to enjoy the fruits of changes in the law, the stronger the impulse of whites became to draw other firm distinctions between the races. After many years of fighting to remove Jim Crow, the new barriers that emerged to limit black freedom and citizenship only fueled black frustration and disillusionment.

As in many other parts of the South, the assassination of civil rights leader Martin Luther King Jr. in Memphis, Tennessee, in 1968, served as a focal point for black anger over the seemingly stalled process of racial change in Arkansas. Many blacks saw King's death as a decisive end to the nonviolence that had been a hallmark of the southern civil rights movement in the early- to mid-1960s. In the wake of King's death, fires broke out in black neighborhoods in Hot Springs and North Little Rock, and conflict between demonstrators and police in Pine Bluff led to the shooting and wounding of four blacks. Increasingly, scenes of racial unrest punctuated race relations in the state. In August 1969, eighty blacks marched on the city hall in Benton after the shooting of a black youth by a white restaurant owner. In August 1970, the white owner of a grocery store in Blytheville shot and killed a black picketer, leading to major unrest there. In September 1971, there was a shootout between local blacks and members of the Ku Klux Klan at Parkin. In the heartland of the Delta, at places like Forrest City, Marianna, and Earle, demonstrations, shootings, and racial violence became part of the fabric of everyday life.[45]

The period saw a sprouting of new radical black organizations that embraced the psychologically potent, if somewhat ideologically and philosophically ambiguous, slogan of black power. These organizations were prepared to take to the streets to protest against continuing discrimination. The emergence of such groups reflected the steady erosion of faith in the efficacy of nonviolent direct-action protest to adequately address racial problems. The Crittenden County Improvement Association (CCIA) at Earle and the Council for the Liberation of Blacks (CLOB) at Hot Springs were representative of this new wave of indigenous protest. The Invaders, a black-power group based in Memphis, urged local blacks in nearby Forrest City to take a more determined stance against whites there. Self-appointed "prime minister" of the Invaders Lance Watson (alias "Sweet Willie Wine") organized a much-publicized march across the Arkansas Delta in 1969, as did the Community Organization Methods Build Absolute Teamwork (COMBAT) at Cotton Plant a year later.[46]

Reactions to King's death in Little Rock paralleled the situation across the state. White officials in the city were quick to condemn the shooting of King and praise his message of nonviolence. Blacks in Little Rock placed a very different interpretation on events. "They killed a man who advocated nonviolence," said appliance repairman Robert L. Worsham when interviewed by a white reporter. "Now the racial situation has developed into another phase." Echoing these remarks, a speaker at Philander Smith's memorial service for King told students, "We tried to be nice [but the] white man had his chance to make this thing equal and he blew his chance. . . . If you let the white man beat on you, and not do anything about it, he'll beat on you again." At an interracial memorial service held at the state capitol on Sunday April 7, Dr. Jerry D. Jewell warned, "The youth of today no longer will accept the old order. Let's change the old order . . . In a riot, we all lose somewhere, but they say Negroes have nothing to lose. You figure that one out."[47]

A series of meetings between black and white community leaders attempted to calm tensions by addressing ongoing black grievances. At these meetings, a new, young black voice began to assert itself. This new voice sought to articulate the problems of black youth and the black poor, insisting they were not prepared to accept the racial conditions and mores of their elders. Younger black representatives warned whites that if vital issues remained ignored, there was a real risk of major unrest in the community. Figures such as Bobby Brown (brother of Minnijean Brown, who helped integrate Central High in 1957) and Duff Rogers claimed to speak for the interests of the black unemployed and underprivileged. Both Brown and Rogers worked with antipoverty agencies in the state and were therefore constantly in touch with this segment of the black community. This constituency, said Rogers, no longer had faith in "talk, talk, talk." He insisted, "[T]he time has come for government to prove that nonviolence will work so we don't have to go out on the streets."[48]

The concerns articulated by black youths led to the formation of a new black organization for those who felt that existing groups did not adequately represent them. Black United Youth (BUY), fronted by Brown, formed the single most important expression of growing black militancy in Little Rock in the late 1960s. Deeply rooted in the antipoverty programs in the state, with which many of its leading members were directly involved, BUY was, according to Brown, "an eyeball to eyeball organization," dedicated to "direct confrontation with white people for making changes." Among its membership, BUY included "schoolteachers [and] professional people," as well as "street people [and] gangsters" from the local neighborhoods. Within this broad constituency was a common goal of obtaining what blacks felt was a fair share of access to schools, jobs, homes, and other community resources. Most important of all, BUY was steadfast in refusing to accept white inaction on issues of importance to the black community.[49]

The unresolved tensions and continuing resentment over the treatment of blacks in the aftermath of King's assassination simmered over the summer months. The situation finally reached boiling point in August after the death of Curtis Ingram, an inmate at the Pulaski County Penal Farm. Police arrested Ingram on July 22, 1968, on suspicion of possessing barbiturates he claimed were for a medical disorder. On July 31, the court found Ingram guilty, fined him $110.50, and handed him a six-month suspended sentence. Under an 1875 state law, the court sent Ingram to the penal farm to work off his fine at the rate of $1.00 a day. Just two days later, on August 2, Ingram was battered over the head with a three-foot stick wielded by a white trusty, a fellow prisoner assigned the responsibility of overseeing work on the farm. Ingram died because of the beating later that day.[50]

The official version of events was that Ingram had first attacked the trusty, who then defended himself against the prisoner. However, BUY member Bob Broadwater, a disc jockey with black-oriented Little Rock radio station KOKY, discovered a different story. Broadwater produced two anonymous witnesses who said that the white trusty had attacked Ingram on the orders of one of the paid guards after the prisoner had complained of feeling ill. The state attorney's office subsequently investigated the incident and brought charges against the trusty. The state attorney's office won a conviction at the trial despite conflicting testimony provided by black and white prisoners. Lingering doubt in the case helped bring a conviction of manslaughter rather than murder.[51]

Ingram's death was not an isolated incident but part of a series of complaints about the treatment of black prisoners in Arkansas' archaic penal system. In a letter to the *Arkansas Gazette* in September 1966, a group of black prisoners protested conditions at the penal farm. They were "worked from sun-up until sundown at time [*sic*]," they claimed, "in rain, cold, snow until we are soaking wet and half frozen, like human machines." In particular, they singled out the trusty system as especially corrupt, since it invariably gave white inmates license over blacks. The prisoners levied allegations of trusties running rackets of extortion, vice, alcohol, and drugs, as well as participating in beatings and forced sexual encounters with inmates. Prisoners endured whippings despite the fact that the State Penitentiary Board had officially abolished the practice in June 1964. When inmate Winston Talley filed a petition against the use of the whip, the federal district court declared such punishment was permissible if administered as "dispassionately as possible by responsible people." This hardly seemed likely within the racial power hierarchy that existed at the farm.[52]

To BUY members, the death of Ingram symbolized the arbitrary power whites continued to exercise over blacks and highlighted the inability of existing black leaders to do anything about it.[53] BUY demonstrated its anger over the events at a protest march on Friday, August 9. In what they intended as a determined but peaceful protest, two hundred BUY members marched in columns four abreast from Dunbar Community Center, in the heart of the city's black residential district, through downtown Little Rock to the city courthouse. At the courthouse, BUY held a rally under the scrutiny of city police and armed National Guards, who closely monitored events from nearby Robinson Auditorium. For just over thirty minutes, marchers heard speeches from Dora Ingram, the mother of Curtis Ingram; Ben Grinage, former director of SNCC in Arkansas; and BUY president Bobby Brown. Afterward, protestors assembled for the march back to Dunbar Community Center.[54]

As the marchers made their way through the downtown streets, some of them began to throw bricks and stones at police and newsmen as the mood of the demonstration began to sour. Events reached crisis point when, back at Dunbar Community Center, armed guardsmen entered the picture. Though black leaders were dispersing the crowd at the time, guardsmen began to prod marchers into obedience. Black youths scuffled with the police and the National Guard. In the ensuing fight, a police patrolman was hurt, and a black youth was shot and wounded. The conflict then erupted into a full-scale riot. Over the weekend, there were reports of firebombings, gunshots, and widespread unrest in black areas. With the situation escalating beyond control, the state enlisted more troops to quash the disturbances. Governor Rockefeller imposed a curfew from Friday to Monday night and banned all sales of alcohol in the city. After several days of unrest, an uneasy calm began to return the following Tuesday.[55]

Although BUY leaders were disappointed their intended peaceful protest had ended in violence, the actions of the city and state authorities further infuriated the group's members. Articles in BUY's newsletter declared, "Brother get your gun because it will soon be kill or be killed. Let us arm ourselves and join together to stop whitey from misusing us." This rhetoric only served to alienate established black and white community leaders. Brown tried to explain that the BUY newsletter was uncensored and did not necessarily reflect the views of the group as a whole, but many people remained unconvinced. BUY was embroiled in yet another controversy when Brown supported the main tenets of the Black Manifesto advocated by former SNCC chair James Forman and adopted in August 1969 at Detroit by the National Black Economic Development Conference. The controversial manifesto called for churches to pay reparations for wrongs done to blacks under slavery. Brown demanded such payments from white clergymen in Arkansas, but the call fell largely on deaf ears.[56]

Conflicting interests between black youths and white officials culminated in the arrests of Brown and another BUY member, James Edward Perkins, in July 1969. Brown and Perkins, it was alleged, had robbed a white couple, Mr. and Mrs. James Leonard, at gunpoint. As the trial unfolded in Little Rock Municipal Court, it transpired that the items allegedly stolen by Brown and Perkins were in fact already stolen property in the hands of the Leonards. Indeed, the Leonards were already facing charges of burglary and grand larceny at Sheridan, Arkansas, where James Leonard had escaped from jail. John Walker, attorney for Brown and Perkins, asked the prosecution if the Leonards were reliable witnesses. The prosecution told Walker that Mrs. Leonard probably was, but that James Leonard probably was not.[57]

Another of the contentious issues at the trial was how police knew to search the homes of Brown and Perkins, where they found the supposedly stolen items. The prosecution told the court that they had been alerted by a black male informant "of average height and build in his mid-20s" who had infiltrated BUY on their behalf. When the prosecution failed to identify the informant or to let him take the stand, Walker moved for a dismissal, since the constitutional rights of his clients had clearly been violated by an illegal search. Judge Quinn Glover refused to dismiss and instead referred the case to grand jury. Eventually, the state cut a deal to suspend the sentences of Brown and Perkins if they left Arkansas.[58]

The arrest and departure of Brown and Perkins, and thereafter the demise of BUY, was in keeping with a growing nationwide trend of suppressing black militancy. Republican Richard M. Nixon, who won the race for president in 1968, championed a white backlash against racial unrest by employing a rhetorical stance of "law and order" that promised to put a halt to future demonstrations. Nixon's southern strategy contrasted sharply with that of fellow Republican Winthrop Rockefeller. Instead of cultivating black votes, Nixon actively appealed to the inherent conservatism and racial fears of the white population. In so doing, he was successful in winning the region over to the Republican cause. After winning the election, Nixon delivered on his promise to restore law and order by supporting and extending strong-arm law enforcement tactics. Nixon deployed the Counter Intelligence Program (COINTELPRO), the Department of Justice, the FBI, and state agencies to break up and eradicate what the president perceived to be radical black organizations. By the early 1970s, a black uprising in the United States had been effectively subdued.[59]

Events in the 1960s marked the end of one black struggle and the beginning of another. From 1940 to 1970, the central focus for black activists was the goal of legal and political advancement. Blacks insisted that as citizens of Arkansas, they deserved the same rights under the law as whites. Efforts to organize and mobilize the black population as a political force underpinned this goal. Since the 1940s, black activists such as Flowers viewed the vote as an essential instrument in improving the condition of the race in the state. During the 1940s and 1950s, through the offices of the NAACP, Flowers and the Bateses focused on courtroom battles to remove Jim Crow barriers to black advancement in higher and secondary education. In the 1960s, a new wave of black activists used direct-action protests to challenge the segregated order head-on, bringing about the desegregation of public facilities. Through these campaigns for equality, black activists were successful at ending legally mandated discrimination and removing impediments to black voting rights.

The next phase of the black struggle in Arkansas would involve imple-menting those newfound legal and political rights. There was a need to consolidate existing gains. Alongside this was the ongoing task of translat-ing victories in politics, in the courts, and in the streets into tangible day-to-day changes that would affect the lives of all of Arkansas' black popula-tion. Most important, there was still the enormous task of seeking black economic advancement, the most vital issue now affecting the black com-munity. Though blacks had gained political and social equality with whites under the law, the crippling economic impact of slavery and segre-gation remained largely unaddressed.[60]

Exactly how to achieve these new goals divided black activists. In the late 1960s, various black groups across the state came forward with visions for the future of the black struggle. Out of these many different points of view, there were two broadly discernable schools of thought. On the one hand, existing black leaders, invariably drawn from the expanding black middle class, looked to pursue black advancement through mainstream methods of redress, building upon and extending the gains already made in the courts and through the ballot box. On the other hand, a coalition of young and poor blacks grew increasingly disillusioned with the continu-ing discrimination they experienced in employment, housing, and educa-tion. Their faith in the ability of litigation, politics, and nonviolent direct action to correct the situation began to subside. Consequently, they advo-cated a struggle that demanded immediate changes and used any means necessary to attain them, including, as one BUY member put it, "[r]iots, disorders, disturbances, or whatever."[61] Whites clearly indicated which brand of black activism they preferred by upholding black legal and politi-cal rights while moving decisively to crush more militant expressions of black protest.

Of course, disagreements and divisions over how best to achieve black advancement predated the earliest campaigns for civil rights run by Flow-ers and the CNO in the 1940s. However, there was an important differ-ence in the nature of the divisions within the black community in 1940 and in 1970. In 1940, a central issue for blacks was the question of whether they should press for social and political equality at all. In 1970, the cen-tral issue was not whether blacks should press for equality but how. This indicates a legacy of black activism that reached beyond its victories in the courtroom and at the ballot box. Just as importantly, black activists had successfully championed a fundamental transformation in the perceptions of black individuals, institutions, and organizations, about their capacity to resist white oppression. The black community was simply no longer prepared to accept second-class citizenship and was ready to take a stand for what the people believed to be rightfully theirs.

Therefore, whatever the differences in opinion over the future direction of black activism, there was a least one point of agreement: blacks could not rest until they had fully realized the goal of freedom and equality in Arkansas. In an era of new challenges and more complex and ambiguous race relations, this ensured that the black struggle would not end in 1970, but that it would continue in the decades that followed.

Notes

Introduction

1. Eisenhower, *Waging Peace;* Hays, *Southern Moderate* and *Politics Is My Parish;* Faubus, *Down from the Hills* and *Down from the Hills II;* Blossom, *It Has Happened Here;* Mann, "Truth about Little Rock"; Ashmore, *The Negro and the Schools, Epitaph For Dixie,* and *Hearts and Minds;* Alford and Alford, *Case of the Sleeping People;* Huckaby, *Crisis at Central High;* Reed, *Faubus;* Bartley, "Looking Back at Little Rock"; McMillen, "White Citizens' Council"; Campbell and Pettigrew, *Christians in Racial Crisis;* Jacoway, "Taken by Surprise"; Murphy, *Breaking the Silence;* Gates, "Power from the Pedestal"; Freyer, *Little Rock Crisis.*

2. Bates, *Long Shadow;* Beals, *Warriors Don't Cry.*

3. For example, see Bennett, *What Manner of Man;* Bishop, *Days of Martin Luther King;* Miller, *Martin Luther King;* Reddick, *Crusader Without Violence.*

4. Fairclough, *Race and Democracy,* xi.

5. Quote from Chafe, *Civilities and Civil Rights,* 3. Other important local and state community studies include Colburn, *Racial Change and Community Crisis;* Dittmer, *Local People;* Eskew, *But for Birmingham;* Fairclough, *Race and Democracy;* Gavins, "NAACP in North Carolina"; Norrell, *Reaping the Whirlwind;* Payne, *I've Got the Light of Freedom.*

6. Dittmer, *Local People;* Fairclough, *Race and Democracy;* Gavins, "NAACP in North Carolina."

7. Mitchell, "Analysis of Arkansas' Population," 117, 121.

8. Fletcher, *Arkansas,* 1–9; Yates, "Arkansas," 233–34.

9. Fletcher, *Arkansas,* 1–9; Whayne, *New Plantation South.*

10. Mitchell, "Analysis of Arkansas' Population," 118–20.

11. On east Arkansas history, see Whayne and Gatewood, eds., *Arkansas Delta*. On the shared racial traditions of the Arkansas and Mississippi Delta, see Woodruff, "African-American Struggles." On lynching, see Lewis, "Mob Justice."

12. Holmes, "Arkansas Cotton Pickers Strike."

13. On the Elaine Race Riot, see Cortner, *Mob Intent on Death;* Waskow, *From Race Riot to Sit-In;* Dunaway, *What a Preacher Saw;* Rogers, "Elaine Race Riots"; Taylor, "'We Have Just Begun'"; Whayne, "Low Villains"; Butts and James, "Underlying Causes." The exact number of black casualties is uncertain, with estimates ranging from 25 to 856. Most accounts suggest a figure of somewhere between 200 and 250.

14. On the Southern Tenant Farmers Union, see Grubbs, *Cry from the Cotton;* Mitchell, *Mean Things Happening.* Quotes from Kester, *Revolt among the Sharecroppers,* 81–85, quoted in Tucker, *Arkansas,* 79.

15. Yates, "Arkansas," 234–35.

16. Ibid.; Fletcher, *Arkansas,* 326–27.

17. Fletcher, *Arkansas,* 1–9; Mitchell, "Analysis of Arkansas' Population," 119–20.

18. Reed, *Faubus,* 9.

19. Angelou, *I Know Why,* 47. See also replies to questionnaires sent by Bernie Babcock to northwest Arkansas counties, box 6, folder 2, WPA Papers.

20. Key, *Southern Politics,* 183–204.

21. Ashmore, *Hearts and Minds,* 118.

22. Writers' Project, WPA, *Arkansas,* 174–76.

23. On black slave life in Little Rock, see Lack, "Urban Slave Community"; Gatewood, *Aristocrats of Color,* 92–93.

24. Gatewood, *Aristocrats of Color,* 92–95; Gatewood, "Negro Legislators"; Graves, *Town and Country,* chap. 6.

25. Dillard, "Perseverance."

26. Jacoway "Introduction," 2; Lewis, "Mob Justice," 156–84.

27. Tucker, *Arkansas,* 77.

28. Ibid., 81–82.

29. Blair, *Arkansas Politics,* 89.

30. Fletcher, *Arkansas,* 394.

31. Tucker, *Arkansas,* 87.

32. Fletcher, *Arkansas,* 394.

33. U.S. Census Bureau, *Sixteenth; Seventeenth; Eighteenth; Nineteenth.*

34. Tucker, *Arkansas,* 87–88.

35. Peirce, *Deep South,* 147–54.

36. Arsenault, *Wild Ass of the Ozarks,* 11.

37. Peirce, *Deep South,* 147–54.

38. On class issues in Little Rock, see Bartley, *Rise of Massive Resistance,* chap. 14; Daniel, *Lost Revolutions,* chap. 12; Williams, "Class."

39. Jacoway, "Taken by Surprise"; Vinson interview.

Chapter 1. Founding a Movement

1. Mitchell, "Analysis of Arkansas' Population," 121; Writers' Project, WPA, *Arkansas,* 171.

2. Writers' Project, WPA, *Survey of Negroes,* 43; Taylor, "Negroes of Little Rock—Outline," 3–4.

3. Writers' Project, WPA, *Survey of Negroes,* 42; Taylor, "Negroes of Little Rock—Outline," 4.

4. Writers' Project, WPA, *Survey of Negroes,* 42; Taylor, "Negroes of Little Rock—Outine," 4–5.

5. On the early history of Arkansas AM&N, see Rothrock, "Joseph Carter Corbin," and Wheeler, "Isaac Fisher."

6. Writers' Project, WPA, *Survey of Negroes,* 38–40; Taylor, "Negroes of Little Rock—Outline," 1–3; Anderson, *Education of Blacks in the South,* 206–11.

7. Writers' Project, WPA, *Survey of Negroes,* 47–50; Taylor, "Negroes of Little Rock—Outline," 7.

8. Writers' Project, WPA, *Survey of Negroes,* 26–27.

9. Taylor, "Negroes of Little Rock—Outline," 16.

10. Bussey interview.

11. Gatewood, *Aristocrats of Color,* 92–95. On the slave community in Little Rock, see Lack, "Urban Slave Community."

12. Gatewood, *Aristocrats of Color,* 93–94; Dillard, "Golden Prospects"; Smith, "John E. Bush." On blacks in Little Rock during Reconstruction, see Graves, *Town and Country,* chap. 6.

13. Gatewood, *Aristocrats of Color,* 93–95; Graves, "Negro Disfranchisement."

14. Writers' Project, WPA, *Survey of Negroes,* 35–46.

15. Ibid., 30–34.

16. Ibid., 21–34.

17. Ibid., 10, 17–18, 56, 64, 73; Taylor, "Negroes of Little Rock—Digest," WPA Papers.

18. Writers' Project, WPA, *Survey of Negroes,* 5–20; Haiken, "The Lord Helps Those."

19. Writers' Project, WPA, *Survey of Negroes,* 61–64.

20. Ibid., 66–75; Walls, "Some Extinct Black Hospitals."

21. Writers' Project, WPA, *Survey of Negroes,* 55–60; Taylor, "Negroes of Little Rock—Outline," 13–14.

22. Writers' Project, WPA, *Survey of Negroes,* 82–89.

23. Ibid., 35–46.

24. Ibid., 90–94. On the Little Rock Urban League, see Urban League of Arkansas, *Golden Anniversary Celebration.*

25. Washington's *Negro in Business* names members of Little Rock's black elite as successful examples of his philosophy of "accommodation." On Washington, Tuskegee, and accommodation, see Harlan, *Booker T. Washington.*

26. On black community leadership in the 1940s, see Myrdal, *American Dilemma,* 689–705, 720–35 and 768–80.

27. On Du Bois and the formation of the NAACP, see Lewis, *Biography of a Race.*

28. Meier and Bracey, "NAACP as a Reform Movement," 13–30. For a more detailed account, see Cortner, *Mob Intent on Death.*

29. "Application for Charter and Official Authorization," reel 4, frames 0785–0787, NAACP Papers, Little Rock, microfilm.

30. Telegram from William Pickens to Carrie Sheppherdson, January 5, 1925, reel 4, frame 0879, NAACP Papers, Little Rock, microfilm.

31. Mrs. H. L. Porter to Roy Wilkins, November 14, 1933, reel 5, frames 0039-0041, NAACP Papers, Little Rock, microfilm.

32. Bush and Dorman, *Mosaic Templars.*

33. Gatewood, "Negro Legislators," 220–33.

34. Dillard, "Scipio Jones," 201–19; Dillard, "Perseverance," 62–73.

35. Dillard, "Scipio Jones," 201–19; Dillard, "'To the Back of the Elephant,'" 3–15.

36. Key, *Southern Politics,* 183.

37. "Special Investigation of the John Carter Lynching, Little Rock, Ark.," group I, series C, container 349, in "Sub-File-Lynching-Little Rock, Ark., 1918–1927" folder, NAACP Papers, Library of Congress; *Arkansas Gazette,* May 4, 5, 6, 7, 1927.

38. Jacoway "Introduction," 2; Lewis, "Mob Justice," 156–84.

39. *Arkansas Gazette,* May 4, 5, 6, 7, 1927.

40. Writer's Project, WPA, *Survey of Negroes,* 95.

41. Text of speech delivered by Dr. J. M. Robinson to the Jefferson County Democratic Association, Pine Bluff, Arkansas, July 18, 1952, Robinson Papers.

42. On Robinson and ANDA, see Kirk, "Dr. J. M. Robinson."

43. Key, *Southern Politics,* 183.

44. Dr. J. M. Robinson to J. F. McClerkin, August 6, 1928, Robinson Papers; John A. Hibbler to William T. Andrews, September 27, 1929, group I, series D, container 44, in "Cases Supported—Arkansas Primary Case, 1928–1929" folder, NAACP Papers, Library of Congress; Hine, *Black Victory,* 72–85.

45. John A. Hibbler to William T. Andrews, September 27, 1929, and William T. Andrews to John A. Hibbler, June 12, 1930, both in group I, series D, container 44, in "Cases Supported—Arkansas Primary Case, 1928–1929" folder, NAACP Papers, Library of Congress.

46. Walter White to Arthur Spingarn, November 7, 1929, miscellaneous correspondence, 1917–25, 1928–32, NAACP Papers, Fayetteville, microfilm.

47. *Arkansas Gazette,* November 27, 1928, clipping in PCDC Scrapbooks.

48. William T. Andrews to John A. Hibbler, July 19, 1930, group I, series D, container 44, in "Cases Supported—Arkansas Primary Case, 1928–1929" folder, NAACP Papers, Library of Congress; Hine, *Black Victory,* 115.

49. For the national and regional impact of the New Deal on blacks, see Daniel,

"Legal Basis of Agrarian Capitalism"; Sitkoff, *New Deal for Blacks*. For the local impact of the New Deal on blacks, see Writers' Project, WPA, *Survey of Negroes*.

50. Mitchell, "Analysis of Arkansas' Population."

51. On blacks and the Second World War, see Blum, *V Was for Victory;* Dalfiume, *Desegregation of the U.S. Armed Forces;* Dalfiume, "'Forgotten Years'"; Reed, *Seedtime for the Modern Civil Rights Movement;* Sitkoff, "Racial Militancy"; Wynn, *Afro-American and the Second World War.*

52. William Pickens to W. H. Flowers, May 10, 1940, group II, series C, container 10, in "Pine Bluff, Ark., 1940–1947" folder, NAACP Papers, Library of Congress.

53. Angelou, *I Know Why,* 47; *Arkansas Gazette,* July 31, 1988.

54. For a portrait of black Pine Bluff in the age of segregation see Lipsitz, *Life in the Struggle,* 15–38.

55. W. H. Flowers to Walter White, October 31, 1938, Flowers Papers.

56. Charles Houston to W. H. Flowers, November 22, 1938, and Thurgood Marshall to W. H. Flowers, April 14, 1939, both in Flowers Papers.

57. Tushnet, *NAACP's Legal Strategy,* 100; Tushnet, *Making Civil Rights Law,* 27; Greenberg, *Crusaders in the Courts,* 19–21.

58. Press Release, n.d., Flowers Papers.

59. *CNO Spectator,* July 1, 1940, Flowers Papers.

60. Morris, *Origins,* 40–76, 100.

61. *CNO Spectator,* July 1, 1940, Flowers Papers.

62. Ibid.

63. Ibid; Dunaway interview.

64. *CNO Spectator,* July 1, 1940, Flowers Papers.

65. *Arkansas Gazette,* July 31, 1988.

66. *CNO Spectator,* July 1, 1940, Flowers Papers.

67. Partial Text of Keynote Address, W. H. Flowers, First Conference on Negro Organization, Lakeview, Arkansas, September 27, 1940; CNO Press release, October 12, 1940; Flowers to William H. Nunn, October 5, 1940; all in Flowers Papers.

68. Press Release, September 11, 1941, Flowers Papers.

69. *Arkansas State Press* (hereafter *State Press*) September 19, 1941.

70. Ibid.

71. Press Release, September 11, 1941, Flowers Papers.

72. Ibid.; *State Press,* May 15, 1942.

73. *State Press,* May 15, 1942.

74. Ibid., March 6, 1942.

75. Patterson, *Arkansas Teachers Association,* 89–91.

76. On the teachers' salary suits, see Tushnet, *NAACP's Legal Strategy,* chaps. 4–7; Tushnet, *Making Civil Rights Law,* chap. 8.

77. Mrs. H. L. Porter to William Pickens, June 9, 1940, group II, series C, container 9, in "Little Rock, Arkansas, 1940–1947" folder, NAACP Papers, Library of Congress.

78. W. H. Flowers to Ella Baker, August 18, 1945, group II, series C, container 11, in "Arkansas State Conference, April 1945–December 1948" folder, NAACP Papers, Library of Congress.

79. Kirk, "Dr J. M. Robinson"; Smith, "Politics of Evasion," 40–51.

80. Lawson, *Running for Freedom,* 85.

81. Bussey interview.

82. Hawkins interview.

83. Kirk, "Dr. J. M. Robinson," 39–40.

84. *Arkansas Gazette,* July 31, 1988; Walker interview. On Branton's civil rights career, see the brief biography in "Scope and Contents," 1–4, finding aid, Branton Papers.

85. Nichols, "Breaking the Color Barrier," 3–21.

86. *State Press,* July 15, 1949.

Chapter 2. War, Race, and Confrontation

1. *Arkansas Gazette,* December 8, 1940, clipping in PCDC Scrapbooks.

2. Hine, *Black Victory,* 202–7.

3. Ibid.

4. *Arkansas Gazette,* April 12, 1942, clipping in PCDC Scrapbooks.

5. Ibid., July 22, 1942.

6. Ibid., July 24, 25, 27, 1942.

7. Ibid., July 29, 1942.

8. Text of speech, Dr. J. M. Robinson, National Voters League, Birmingham, Alabama, April 4, 1945, Robinson Papers; *Arkansas Gazette,* August 4, 1942, clipping in PCDC Scrapbooks.

9. Text of speech, Dr. J. M. Robinson, National Voters League, Birmingham, Alabama, April 4, 1945; Hine, *Black Victory,* 212–29.

10. *Arkansas Gazette,* April 4, 1944, clipping in PCDC Scrapbooks.

11. Ibid., April 11, 1944.

12. Ibid., April 22, 1944.

13. Text of speech, Dr. J. M. Robinson, National Voters League, Birmingham, Alabama, April 4, 1945; *Arkansas Gazette,* May 17, 1944, clipping in PCDC Scrapbooks.

14. *Arkansas Gazette,* May 18, 1944, clipping in PCDC Scrapbooks.

15. Dr. J. M. Robinson to Sam Rorex, July 18, 1944, group II, series B, container 210, in "Voting, Arkansas, 1943–47" folder, NAACP Papers, Library of Congress; *Arkansas Gazette,* June 4, 1944, clipping in PCDC Scrapbooks.

16. Text of speech, Dr. J. M. Robinson, National Voters League, Birmingham, Alabama, April 4, 1945; Smith, "Politics of Evasion," 47.

17. *Arkansas Gazette,* July 20, 1944, clipping in PCDC Scrapbooks.

18. Text of speech, Dr. J. M. Robinson, National Voters League, Birmingham, Alabama, April 4, 1945; J. R. Booker to Thurgood Marshall, March 21, 1945; Thurgood Marshall to J. R. Booker, March 27, 1945; Thurgood Marshall to Dr. E. A. Dennard, April

23, 1945; all group II, series B, container 210, in "Voting, Arkansas, 1943–1947" folder, NAACP Papers, Library of Congress; *Arkansas Gazette,* July 26, 1944, clipping in PCDC Scrapbooks; Alexander, "Double Primary"; Smith, "Politics of Evasion," 48–49.

19. *Arkansas Gazette,* September 17, 1944, clipping in PCDC Scrapbooks.

20. Ibid., September 23, 1944.

21. *State Press,* November 17, 1944.

22. Tushnet, *Making Civil Rights Law,* 21.

23. Ibid., 13, 20–21.

24. Ibid.

25. Ibid., 20–26, 116–22.

26. Ibid.

27. Ibid., 119–20.

28. Miss Solar M. Caretners to Melvin O. Alstin, February 20, 1941; Miss Solar M. Caretners to Walter White, February 22, 1941; both in group II, series B, container 174, in "Teachers Salaries" folder, NAACP Papers, Library of Congress.

29. Writer's Project, WPA, *Survey of Negroes,* 41.

30. Scipio Jones to Thurgood Marshall, August 12, 1941; Frank D. Reeves to Scipio A. Jones, August 15, 1941; J. L. Wilson to Thurgood Marshall, December 9, 1941; all in group II, series B, container 174, in "Teachers Salaries" folder, NAACP Papers, Library of Congress.

31. Thurgood Marshall to J. L. Wilson, February 11, 1942; J. L. Wilson to Thurgood Marshall, February 16, 1942; Thurgood Marshall to Roy Wilkins, February 28, 1942; all in group II, series B, container 174, in "Teachers Salaries" folder, NAACP Papers, Library of Congress.

32. Thurgood Marshall to Roy Wilkins, February 28, 1942, group II, series B, container 174, in "Teachers Salaries" folder, NAACP Papers, Library of Congress.

33. Thurgood Marshall to WW and WHH (probably Walter White and William Henry Hastie), September 30, 1942, group II, series B, container 174, in "Teachers Salaries" folder, NAACP Papers, Library of Congress; Morris interview.

34. *Arkansas Gazette,* March 1, 1942.

35. Ibid., May 21, 1942.

36. Ibid., October 3, 1942; Thurgood Marshall to WW and WHH, September 30, 1942, group II, series B, container 174, in "Teachers Salaries" folder, NAACP Papers, Library of Congress.

37. Thurgood Marshall, memorandum to WW, WHH, and Thomas, September 19, 1942, group II, series B, container 174, in "Teachers Salaries" folder, NAACP Papers, Library of Congress.

38. Thurgood Marshall to Messrs. White and Thomas, October 3, 1942, and Thurgood Marshall to Miss Consuelo Young, June 21, 1945, both in group II, series B, container 174, in "Teachers Salaries" folder, NAACP Papers, Library of Congress; *Arkansas Gazette,* October 3, 1942; *State Press,* October 9, 1942; Tushnet, *Making Civil Rights Law,* 120.

39. Morris interview.

40. John H. Lewis to Thurgood Marshall, July 19, 1943; Thurgood Marshall to J. R. Booker, May 29, 1945; both in group II, series B, container 174, in "Teachers Salaries" folder, NAACP Papers, Library of Congress; *State Press,* May 28, 1943; Patterson, *Arkansas Teachers Association,* 90.

41. *Arkansas Gazette,* January 6, 1944.

42. Ibid.

43. The U.S. Eighth Circuit Federal Court District covers Arkansas, Iowa, Minnesota, Missouri, Nebraska, North Dakota, and South Dakota.

44. *Arkansas Gazette,* January 6, 1944; Press Release, June 21, 1945, group II, series B, container 174, in "Teachers Salaries" folder, NAACP Papers, Library of Congress; Tushnet, *NAACP's Legal Strategy,* 90.

45. *Arkansas Democrat,* September 21, 1944.

46. *Bulletin of the Arkansas Teachers Association,* January 1947, 1.

47. Sitkoff, "Racial Militancy," 661–81.

48. Ibid.

49. Burran, "Racial Violence," 51–55.

50. Ibid.

51. "Investigation Concerning the Death of Sergeant Thomas B. Foster, June 10, 1942," 3, Records of the Office of the Secretary of War.

52. Virgil L. Peterson to Adjutant General, April 24, 1942, Records of the Office of the Secretary of War.

53. Ibid.; "Investigation Concerning the Death of Sergeant Thomas B. Foster," 3, Records of the Office of the Secretary of War; *Arkansas Gazette,* March 23, 1942.

54. "Investigation Concerning the Death of Sergeant Thomas B. Foster," 4, Records of the Office of the Secretary of War.

55. Virgil L. Peterson to Adjutant General, April 24, 1942, Records of the Office of the Secretary of War.

56. "Investigation Concerning the Death of Sergeant Thomas B. Foster," 4, Records of the Office of the Secretary of War.

57. Ibid., 6.

58. Virgil L. Peterson to Adjutant General, April 24, 1942, Records of the Office of the Secretary of War.

59. "Investigation Concerning the Death of Sergeant Thomas B. Foster," 7, Records of the office of the Secretary of War; *Arkansas Gazette,* March 23, 1942.

60. *(Little Rock) Arkansas Gazette,* March 23, 1942.

61. Ibid., March 24, 1942.

62. Ibid., March 26, 1942.

63. Smith, "From 'Separate but Equal' to Desegregation," 254–56; Brynda Pappas, "L. C. Bates: Champion of Freedom," *Arkansas Gazette,* October 19, 1980, 3–4; Bates, *Long Shadow,* 33; Williams, *Arkansas Biography,* 20–21.

64. Bates, *Long Shadow*, 6–31.

65. Ibid., 33–34.

66. On the role played by the black press during the Second World War, see Finkle, *Forum for Protest.*

67. Smith, "From 'Separate but Equal' to Desegregation," 254–56.

68. Wassell, "L. C. Bates," 36.

69. Freyer, *Little Rock Crisis,* 27. Only a few scattered copies and clippings of the *Southern Mediator Journal* exist.

70. *State Press,* March 27, 1942.

71. Ibid.; *Arkansas Gazette,* March 24, 1942.

72. "Report of Citizens Committee of Greater Little Rock, Arkansas, March 29, 1942," 2–4, group II, series B, container 152, in "Soldier Killing Foster, Thomas B. 1942" folder, NAACP Papers, Library of Congress; *Arkansas State Press,* March 27, 1942.

73. "Report of Citizens Committee of Greater Little Rock, Arkansas, March 29, 1942" 3–4, group II, series B, container 152, in "Soldier Killing Foster, Thomas B. 1942" folder, NAACP Papers, Library of Congress; *State Press,* April 5, 1942.

74. "Report of Citizens Committee of Greater Little Rock, Arkansas, March 29, 1942," 4, group II, series B, container 152, in "Soldier Killing Foster, Thomas B. 1942" folder, NAACP Papers, Library of Congress; *State Press,* April 5, 1942; *Arkansas Gazette,* March 30.

75. Roy Wilkins to Wendell Berge, April 10, 1942; Thurgood Marshall to Scipio Jones, April 30, 1942; Thurgood Marshall to John A. Hibbler, May 1, 1942; all in group II, series B, container 152, in "Soldier Killing Foster, Thomas B. 1942" folder, NAACP Papers, Library of Congress; *State Press,* April 10, 24, 1942; May 1, 8, 1942.

76. Capeci, "Lynching of Cleo Wright."

77. Virgil L. Peterson to Adjutant General April 24, 1942; Records of the Office of the Secretary of War.

78. Ibid.

79. *Arkansas Gazette,* June 11, 1942.

80. *State Press,* June 12; *Arkansas Gazette,* June 12, 1942.

81. Wendell Berge to Maj. Gen. J. A. Ulio, June 17, 1942, Records of the Office of the Secretary of War.

82. Bates, *Long Shadow,* 36–37; *Arkansas Gazette,* March 30, 1942, August 24, 1980.

83. *Arkansas Democrat,* March 23, 1942.

84. *Arkansas Gazette,* August 13, 1942.

85. *State Press,* August 21, 1942; *Arkansas Gazette,* August 19, 1942.

86. Lawson, *Running for Freedom,* 31–40.

87. Bloom, *Class, Race, and Civil Rights,* 74.

88. Tushnet, *NAACP's Legal Strategy,* chaps. 4, 5; Tushnet, *Making Civil Rights Law,* chaps. 9, 10.

Chapter 3. Postwar Reform and Its Limitations

1. *State Press,* November 5, 1948; McMath interview. On the "GI revolt" and southern liberalism, see Badger, "Fatalism." On the McMath administrations, see Lester, *A Man for Arkansas.*

2. Harry S. Truman to Sid McMath, January 5, 1949, series 1, box 1, folder 1, McMath Papers, Fayetteville; Badger, "Fatalism"; Lester, *A Man for Arkansas.*

3. On the NAACP lawsuits in higher education, see Tushnet, *Making Civil Rights Law,* chaps. 9, 10.

4. Ibid.

5. Nichols, "Breaking the Color Barrier," 5–6. Nichols was dean of the College of Arts and Sciences at the time the University of Arkansas, Fayetteville, desegregated in 1948.

6. Ibid.

7. Kirk, "He Founded a Movement," 36.

8. Nichols, "Breaking the Color Barrier," 8; Leflar, *One Life in the Law,* 83.

9. "Admission of Blacks to the University of Arkansas," Herbert L. Thomas Sr.; "Admission of the First Black Students to the University of Arkansas," Lewis Webster Jones; both in Thomas Papers.

10. "Admission of Blacks to the University of Arkansas," Herbert L. Thomas Sr., Thomas papers.

11. Nichols, "Breaking the Color Barrier," 10–11.

12. Ibid., 12–13; Cohodas, *Strom Thurmond,* 130, 157–58, 167–68; Leflar, *One Life in the Law,* 83.

13. Nichols, "Breaking the Color Barrier," 12–13; Leflar, *One Life in the Law,* 84.

14. Nichols, "Breaking the Color Barrier," 13–14.

15. "Text as given by Wiley A. Branton," quoted in Goodwin, "Silas Hunt," 15–16; Nichols, "Breaking the Color Barrier," 14.

16. "Admission of Blacks to the University of Arkansas," Herbert L. Thomas Sr., Thomas Papers.

17. Nichols, "Breaking the Color Barrier," 15.

18. On the *Arkansas Gazette,* see Ashmore, *Hearts and Minds,* 118–20, 272–74; Ashmore, *Civil Rights,* 63–69. The *Arkansas Democrat* bought out the *Arkansas Gazette* in 1991. For a useful short overview of the history of the *Arkansas Gazette* and *Arkansas Democrat,* see the *Arkansas Democrat Gazette* web site article "Arkansas' Past Entwined with Newspapers' Vivid Story," <http://www.ardemgaz.com/info/history.html>.

19. On Ashmore, see Ashmore, *Hearts and Minds;* Ashmore, *Civil Rights.*

20. Ashmore, *Hearts and Minds,* 273; Reed interview; *Arkansas Democrat-Gazette* web site article in note 18.

21. Nichols, "Breaking the Color Barrier," 15–16.

22. Goodwin, "Silas Hunt," 7–9.

23. Woods interview; Williams, *Arkansas Biography,* 35–36.

24. Reed interview; Greenberg, *Crusaders in the Courts,* 228; Williams, *Arkansas Biography,* 35–36.

25. "Biographical Sketch," 1, finding aid, Branton Papers.

26. Nichols, "Breaking the Color Barrier," 16; Williams, *Arkansas Biography,* 146–47.

27. "Text as given by Wiley A. Branton" quoted in Goodwin, "Silas Hunt," 14–15.

28. Nichols, "Breaking the Color Barrier," 16.

29. "Text as given by Wiley A. Branton," quoted in Goodwin, "Silas Hunt," 18–19; Leflar, *One Life in the Law,* 84–85.

30. "Text as given by Wiley A. Branton," 19; Nichols, "Breaking the Color Barrier," 18–19; Leflar, *One Life in the Law,* 82, 85; Mercer interview.

31. "Admission of the First Black Students to the University of Arkansas," Lewis Webster Jones, Thomas Papers; "Arkansas Med. School Opens Its Doors," *Ebony,* January 1949, 13–16; *State Press,* August 27, 1948; Jackson interview.

32. Morgan and Preston, *Edge of Campus,* 13–14, 25–30, 41, 54–66, 155–62.

33. Smith, "Localism and Segregation," 52–53, 80, 94–95; Dunaway and Sutton interviews.

34. Smith, "Localism and Segregation," 14–28.

35. Bussey and Hawkins interviews.

36. Bussey, Hawkins, Hollingworth, McClinton, and Walker interviews.

37. Bussey, Hawkins, McClinton, and Patterson interviews.

38. *State Press,* December 29, 1950.

39. Ibid., November 30, 1951; Bates interview.

40. *State Press,* September 17, 1948.

41. *Arkansas Gazette,* November 23, 1934; *Arkansas Democrat,* November 23, 1934; clippings in Wassell Scrapbooks.

42. Spitzberg, *Racial Politics,* 125.

43. Little Rock City Council and Board of Directors Minutes, November 25, 1935, January 6, 1936, May 11, 1936, December 11, 1936, January 28, 1937.

44. Little Rock City Council and Board of Directors Minutes, September 26, 1938.

45. Ibid., February 19, 1940, July 7, 1941.

46. *Arkansas Gazette,* June 14, 1940, clipping in Wassell Scrapbooks.

47. Ibid., June 29, 1941.

48. *State Press,* June 13, 1947.

49. Ibid., November 28, 1947.

50. Ibid., June 25, 1948.

51. *Arkansas Democrat,* August 15, 1948, clipping in Wassell Scrapbooks.

52. *Arkansas Gazette,* December 3, 1948, clipping in Wassell Scrapbooks; McClinton interview.

53. *Arkansas Gazette,* December 4, 1948, clipping in Wassell Scrapbooks.

54. Ibid., February 9, 1947.

55. Little Rock City Council and Board of Directors Minutes, December 27, 1948.

56. Smith, "Localism and Segregation," 46–50.

57. *Arkansas Gazette,* February 2, 1949; *Arkansas Democrat,* February 2, 1949, clippings in Wassell Scrapbooks.

58. *State Press,* December 16, 1949.

59. *Arkansas Gazette,* May 13, 1949, clipping in Wassell Scrapbooks; Little Rock City Council and Board of Directors Minutes, May 16, 1948.

60. *Arkansas Gazette,* September 12, 1949, clipping in Wassell Scrapbooks; Vinson interview. See also the articles on slum clearance in the *Arkansas Gazette,* May 3–10, 1950.

61. Souvenir Program, Gillam Park Swimming Pool Opening, Sunday, August 20, 1950; *Arkansas Gazette,* August 21, 1950, clipping; and *Arkansas Democrat,* August 21, 1950, clipping, all in Wassell Scrapbooks; *State Press,* August 25, 1950.

62. *State Press,* August 25, 1950.

63. *Arkansas Gazette,* June 5, 1951, clipping in Wassell Scrapbooks.

64. *State Press,* August 29, 1952.

65. Ibid., July 8, 1954.

66. Ibid., June 4, 1950.

67. Ibid.

68. Ibid., June 7, 1950; *Arkansas Gazette,* June 8, 1950.

69. *Arkansas Democrat,* June 13, 1950.

70. Ibid., June 15, 1950.

71. Ibid., June 16, 1950.

72. Ibid., July 6, 1950.

73. *State Press,* September 1, 1950.

74. Ibid., September 23, 1950; Text of speech delivered by Dr. J. M. Robinson, Chicago, Illinois, October 29, 1950, Robinson Papers. On Guthridge's later career, see McMillen, "White Citizens' Council."

75. Rev. Marcus Taylor to Ella Baker, December 4, 1945, group II, series C, container 9, in "Little Rock, Arkansas, 1940–1947" folder, NAACP Papers, Library of Congress.

76. Ibid.

77. Memorandum, Gloster B. Current to Thurgood Marshall, n.d., group II, series C, container 11, in "Arkansas State Conference, April 1945–December 1948" folder, NAACP Papers, Library of Congress.

78. Lucille Black to W. H. Flowers, January 15, 1948, group II, series C, container 10, in "Pine Bluff, Ark., 1948–1955" folder, NAACP Papers, Library of Congress.

79. Ibid.

80. Memorandum, Donald Jones to Gloster B. Current, n.d., group II, series C, container 11, in "Arkansas State Conference, April 1945–December 1948" folder, NAACP Papers, Library of Congress.

81. Mrs. L. C. Bates to Miss Mary W. Ovington, December 9, 1948, group II, series C, container 10, in "Little Rock, Ark., 1948–1955" folder, NAACP Papers, Library of Congress.

82. Gloster B. Current to Mrs. L. C. Bates, January 19, 1949, group II, series C,

container 10, in "Little Rock, Ark., 1948–1955" folder, NAACP Papers, Library of Congress.

83. Donald Jones to Gloster B. Current, February 24, 1949, group II, series C, container 10, in "Arkansas State Conference, 1949–1950" folder, NAACP Papers, Library of Congress.

84. Resolution, September 3, 1949, group II, series C, container 10, in "Pine Bluff, Ark., 1948–1955" folder, NAACP Papers, Library of Congress.

85. Walter White to Pine Bluff NAACP, February 25, 1949, Roy Wilkins to Arkansas Branches of the NAACP, May 10, 1949, group II, series C, container 10, in "Pine Bluff, Ark., 1948–1955" folder, NAACP Papers, Library of Congress.

86. Lulu B. White to Gloster B. Current, November 1, 1950, group II, series C, container 11, in "Arkansas State Conference, 1949–1950" folder, NAACP Papers, Library of Congress.

87. Memorandum, Gloster B. Current to the Staff, Branches and Regional Offices, August 7, 1951, group II, series C, container 11, in "Arkansas State Conference, 1951–1952" folder, NAACP Papers, Library of Congress.

88. U. Simpson Tate to Gloster B. Current, August 20, 1952, group II, series C, container 11, in "Arkansas State Conference, 1951–1952" folder, NAACP Papers, Library of Congress.

89. For an extensive account of the background to *Brown v. Board of Education* see Kluger, *Simple Justice.*

90. Chafe, *Civilities and Civil Rights,* 43.

91. Bates, *Long Shadow,* 47–48.

92. Wilkinson, *From Brown to Bakke,* 62–63.

Chapter 4. *Brown v. Board of Education*

1. Goldfield, *Black, White, and Southern,* 75–76; Memorandum, Harry Ashmore to Phil Coombe, Phil Hamer, and Harold Fleming, May 18, 1954, reel 39, frames 1176–1177, SRC Papers, Library of Congress, microfilm; Lambright and Ray interviews.

2. *Southern School News,* September 1954.

3. *Arkansas Gazette,* May 18, 1954; Patterson interview.

4. *Southern School News,* October 1954.

5. Ibid., September 1954, October 1954, December 1956.

6. Ibid., September 1954.

7. Ibid., October 1954.

8. Faubus interview. For a more detailed account of Faubus's upbringing and political career, see Reed, *Faubus.*

9. *Southern School News*, March 1955, 2. On the reactions of liberal southern politicians to *Brown,* see Badger, "Fatalism." On Faubus, see Reed, *Faubus.*

10. *Southern School News,* March 1955.

11. Ibid., April 1955.

12. Muse, *Ten Years of Prelude,* 64–72.

13. *Southern School News,* December 1956.

14. Rev. J. C. Crenchaw to Frank W. Smith, April 11, 1957, group III, series C, container 4, in "Arkansas State Conference, 1956–57" folder, NAACP Papers, Library of Congress; Daisy Bates to Wiley A. Branton, August 28, 1962, series 1, box 1, folder 2, Bates Papers, Fayetteville; Georg C. Iggers to Tony Freyer, September 17, 1980, letter provided by Iggers; Freyer, *Little Rock Crisis,* 26–27.

15. Iggers, "Arkansas Professor," 284–85.

16. Georg C. Iggers to Tony Freyer, September 17, 1980; Charles C. Walker and Mrs. W. Floyd Bates to Friend, September 17, 1954, Fred K. Darragh to George S. Mitchell, March 25, 1955, and Nat Griswold to Christopher C. Mercer, April 9, 1955, all in series 1, box 15, folder 151, ACHR Papers; Dunaway, Reed, and Sutton interviews.

17. Georg C. Iggers to Tony Freyer, September 17, 1980.

18. Ibid.; Harry A. Little to Little Rock School Board, February 20, 1952, Blossom Papers.

19. Iggers, "Arkansas Professor," 285.

20. Blossom, *It Has Happened Here,* 4–7, 11–13.

21. Ibid., 11–13.

22. A. F. House to Arthur B. Caldwell, July 21, 1958, box 5, folder 7, Caldwell Papers.

23. On massive resistance, see Bartley, *Rise of Massive Resistance.* On Blossom's attitude to school desegregation, see Blossom, *It Has Happened Here,* 13–15.

24. Iggers, "Arkansas Professor," 286; Little Rock Board of Education to Legal Redress Committee, NAACP, Arkansas, September 9, 1954, Blossom Papers.

25. Iggers, "Arkansas Professor," 286–87.

26. "The Status of Desegregation in Arkansas—Some Measures of Progress," group II, series B, container 136, in "Schools, Arkansas, 1946–55" folder, NAACP Papers, Library of Congress; *Southern School News,* May 1955.

27. On *Brown II* and its aftermath, see Wilkinson, *From Brown to Bakke,* 61–95.

28. Ibid.; Goldfield, *Black, White, and Southern,* 81; Mayer, "With Much Deliberation."

29. *Southern School News,* July 1955; Iggers, "Arkansas Professor," 287.

30. Iggers, "Arkansas Professor," 287.

31. Ibid., 287–88.

32. *Southern School News,* September 1955; Wiley A. Branton to William G. Cooper, August 21, 1954, box 4, folder 10, Bates Papers, Madison.

33. *Southern School News,* July 1955, August 1955, September 1955.

34. Mildred L. Bond to Roy Wilkins, August 6, 1955, box 4, folder 10, Bates Papers, Madison.

35. *Southern School News,* August 1955.

36. "A 'Morally Right' Decision," *Life,* July 25, 1955.

37. Ibid.

38. "Integration: Battle of Hoxie, Arkansas," *New York Times Magazine,* September 25, 1955.

39. *Southern School News,* September 1955.

40. McMillen "White Citizens' Council," 97–100; Vervack, "The Hoxie Imbroglio," 22.

41. Arthur Brann Caldwell, "The Hoxie Case—The Story of the First School in the Old South to Integrate in the Wake of the *Brown* Decisions," 6–20, manuscript provided by William Penix, attorney for the Hoxie school board.

42. The best guide to the White Citizens' Councils is McMillen, *Citizens' Council.* On the composition of the ACCA, see "Race Relations in Little Rock before 1957," series 1, box 20, folder 197, ACHR papers.

43. Blair, *Arkansas Politics,* 65.

44. Iggers, "Arkansas Professor," 288–89.

45. *Southern School News,* February 1956.

46. Ibid., March 1956; Branton, "Little Rock Revisited," 253.

47. Branton, "Little Rock Revisited," 252; Greenberg, *Crusaders in the Courts,* 228; Williams, *Arkansas Biography,* 35–36; Reed interview.

48. Freyer, *Little Rock Crisis,* 43.

49. Branton, "Little Rock Revisited," 254.

50. Iggers, "Arkansas Professor," 290.

51. Freyer, *Little Rock Crisis,* 52.

52. Branton, "Little Rock Revisited," 254; Freyer, *Little Rock Crisis,* 56–58.

53. Rev. J. C. Crenchaw, "Our Reason for Appeal," n.d., box 4, folder 10, Bates Papers, Madison; Branton, "Little Rock Revisited," 255–56.

54. *Southern School News,* May 1957; Branton, "Little Rock Revisited," 255–56.

55. "Statement by Rev. J. C. Crenchaw," n.d., box 4, folder 10, Bates Papers, Madison; *Southern School News,* May 1957.

56. Wiley A. Branton to A. F. House, July 10, 1957, Blossom Papers.

57. *Southern School News,* July 1957.

58. "What Is Happening in Desegregation in Arkansas," January 1957, series 1, box 29, folder 302, ACHR Papers.

59. Barnes, *Journey from Jim Crow,* 118–19; Sutton and Young interviews.

60. "What Is Happening in Desegregation in Arkansas," January 1957, series 1, box 29, folder 302, ACHR Papers.

61. On the Montgomery bus boycott, see Branch, *Parting the Waters,* 143–205; Fairclough, *To Redeem the Soul of America,* 11–35; Garrow, *Bearing the Cross,* 11–82.

62. Faubus interview.

63. Aucoin, "Southern Manifesto," 173–93.

64. Freyer, *Little Rock Crisis,* 75.

65. *Southern School News,* June 1956.

66. Ibid., September 1955; McMillen, "White Citizens' Council," 108.

67. Freyer, *Little Rock Crisis,* 68–71; Reed, *Faubus,* 170.

68. Freyer, *Little Rock Crisis,* 68–71, 80–81; Reed, *Faubus,* 175.

69. *Southern School News,* February 1956.

70. Ibid., June 1956; Freyer, *Little Rock Crisis,* 79–80; Reed, *Faubus,* 177–78.

71. *Southern School News,* July 1956.

72. Ibid., August 1956; Reed, *Faubus,* 178–79; Faubus interview.

73. *Southern School News,* August 1956.

74. *Arkansas Democrat,* August 3, 1957.

75. *Southern School News,* September 1956.

76. Ibid., December 1956; Reed, *Faubus,* 180.

77. Wallace, "Orval Faubus," 320–21.

78. Ibid.; *Southern School News,* March 1957.

79. *Southern School News,* August 1957.

80. Ibid., July 1957, August 1957.

81. McMillen, "White Citizens' Council," 104; Reed, *Faubus,* 188.

82. "A Request to the Southern Regional Council," ca. Sept. 1957, reel 141, frames 0823–0830, SRC Papers, Library of Congress, microfilm.

Chapter 5. The Little Rock School Crisis

1. "Report of Conference between Little Rock School Superintendent and NAACP Representatives, May 29, 1957," group II, series A, container 98, in "Desegregation of Schools, Arkansas, Little Rock, Central High, 1956–1957" folder, NAACP Papers, Library of Congress.

2. Ibid.

3. Ibid.

4. Ibid.; *State Press,* June 7, 1957.

5. "Report of Conference between Little Rock School Superintendent and NAACP Representatives, May 29, 1957," group II, series A, container 98, in NAACP Papers, Library of Congress.

6. Mrs. L. C. Bates to Mr. Robert L. Carter, August 2, 1957, group II, series A, container 98, in "Desegregation of Schools, Arkansas, Little Rock, Central High, 1956–1957" folder, NAACP Papers, Library of Congress; Blossom, *It Has Happened Here,* 19–21.

7. Bates, *Long Shadow,* 59.

8. Ibid., 113–60; "Nine Kids Who Dared," *New York Post Daily Magazine,* October 21–31, 1957, clippings in Bates Scrapbooks; interview with Green, Murphy Papers.

9. Green interview, Murphy Papers; "Nine Kids Who Dared," *New York Post Daily Magazine,* October 24, 1957, clipping in Bates Scrapbooks; Bates, *Long Shadow,* 145–50.

10. "Nine Kids Who Dared," *New York Post Daily Magazine,* October 29, 1957, clipping in Bates Scrapbooks; Bates, *Long Shadow,* 130–32.

11. "Nine Kids Who Dared," *New York Post Daily Magazine,* October 27, 1957, clipping in Bates Scrapbooks; Bates, *Long Shadow,* 134–38.

12. "Nine Kids Who Dared," *New York Post Daily Magazine,* October 23, 1957, clipping in Bates Scrapbooks; Bates, *Long Shadow,* 133–34.

13. "Nine Kids Who Dared," *New York Post Daily Magazine,* October 31, 1957, clipping in Bates Scrapbooks; Bates, *Long Shadow,* 138.

14. "Nine Kids Who Dared," *New York Post Daily Magazine,* October 28, 1957, clipping in Bates Scrapbooks; Bates, *Long Shadow,* 139–45.

15. "Nine Kids Who Dared," *New York Post Daily Magazine,* October 25, 1957, clipping in Bates Scrapbooks; Bates, *Long Shadow,* 116–22.

16. "Nine Kids Who Dared," *New York Post Daily Magazine,* October 22, 1957, clipping in Bates Scrapbooks; Bates, *Long Shadow,* 139.

17. "Nine Kids Who Dared," *New York Post Daily Magazine,* October 30, 1957, clipping in Bates Scrapbooks; Bates, *Long Shadow,* 122–30.

18. "Nine Kids Who Dared," *New York Post Daily Magazine,* October 22, 24, 25, 29, 30, 1957, clippings in Bates Scrapbooks.

19. "Nine Kids Who Dared," *New York Post Daily Magazine,* October 23, 27, 31, 1957, clippings in Bates Scrapbooks.

20. "Nine Kids Who Dared," *New York Post Daily Magazine,* October 28, 1957, clipping in Bates Scrapbooks; Bates, *Long Shadow,* 139–45.

21. *Southern School News,* September 1957.

22. Ibid.

23. Ibid., October 1957.

24. Reed, *Faubus,* 196, 203, 245, 261.

25. *Southern School News,* September 1957; Reed, *Faubus,* 196–97; Sherrill, *Gothic Politics,* 105–6.

26. On the Mother's League, see Cope, "'A Thorn in the Side.'"

27. Warren Olney III to Arthur B. Caldwell, September 13, 1957, box 5, folder 2, Caldwell Papers; Reed, *Faubus,* 199; Silverman, *Little Rock Story,* 6–7.

28. Warren Olney III to Arthur B. Caldwell, August 30, 1957; Warren Olney III to Arthur B. Caldwell, September 13, 1957, both in box 5, folder 2, Caldwell Papers; Faubus interview.

29. Warren Olney III to Arthur B. Caldwell, September 13, 1957, box 5, folder 2, Caldwell Papers; Faubus interview.

30. Branton, "Little Rock Revisited," 259–60; Reed, *Faubus,* 199–200; Silverman, *Little Rock Story,* 7.

31. Spitzberg, *Racial Politics,* 65.

32. Ibid., 65–66; Warren Olney III to Arthur B. Caldwell, September 13, 1957, box 5, folder 2, Caldwell Papers; Reed, *Faubus,* 202–3; Ward, *Arkansas Rockefeller,* 4–5.

33. Telephone Report, Assistant U.S. Attorney James E. Gallman, Little Rock, Arkansas, September 3, 1957, box 5, folder 2, Caldwell Papers; Reed, *Faubus,* 208.

34. Telephone Report, Assistant U.S. Attorney James E. Gallman, Little Rock, Arkansas, September 3, 1957, box 5, folder 2, Caldwell Papers; Branton, "Little Rock Revisited," 260.

35. *Southern School News,* October 1957.

36. Bates, *Long Shadow,* 62–64.

37. Ibid., 64–66; Branton, "Little Rock Revisited," 261.

38. Bates, *Long Shadow,* 70–75; Branton, "Little Rock Revisited," 261–62.

39. See note 38.

40. Bates, *Long Shadow,* 66–67.

41. Adams, *First Hand Report*, 268–74; Hays, *Southern Moderate*, 140–45; Reed, *Faubus*, 217–21.

42. Branton, "Little Rock Revisited," 262–63; Silverman, *Little Rock Story*, 11.

43. Bates, *Long Shadow*, 83–84; Branton, "Little Rock Revisited," 262–63; Reed, *Faubus*, 222; Silverman, *Little Rock Story*, 13–14.

44. Bates, *Long Shadow*, 88–91; Reed, *Faubus*, 224.

45. Bates, *Long Shadow*, 90–92; Dunaway interview.

46. Branton, "Little Rock Revisited," 264; Silverman, *Little Rock Story*, 15–16, 35.

47. Glenn E. Smiley, "Report on Little Rock," box 6, folder 60, ACHR Papers; Bates, *Long Shadow*, 104–6.

48. Statement by Clarence Laws, November 13, 1957, box 5, folder 2, Bates Papers, Madison.

49. Transcript, telephone conversation between Gloster B. Current, Daisy Bates, and Clarence Laws, Wednesday, October 2, 1957, box 5, folder 2, Bates Papers, Madison.

50. Ibid.; Bates, *Long Shadow*, 125.

51. Roy Wilkins to Wilbur M. Brucker, March 14, 1958, group III, series A, container 98, in "Desegregation Schools Arkansas Little Rock Central High 1958 Jan-June" folder, NAACP Papers, Library of Congress; Transcript, telephone conversation between Gloster B. Current, Daisy Bates, and Clarence Laws, Wednesday, October 2, 1957, box 5, folder 2, Bates Papers, Madison.

52. Branch, *Parting the Waters*, 656; Clark, *Schoolhouse Door*, 189; Cohodas, *Strom Thurmond*, 325; Lesher, *George Wallace*, 166. For a more extensive analysis of Walker, see Cravens, "Edwin A. Walker."

53. Transcript, telephone conversation between Daisy Bates and Gloster B. Current, November 13, 1957, box 5, folder 2, Bates Papers, Madison; Bates, *Long Shadow*, 125–26.

54. Bates, *Long Shadow*, 126–27.

55. Ibid., 127–29.

56. Ibid., 129–30.

57. "Ordeal of Minnie Jean Brown," group III, series A, container 98, in "Deseg., Schools, Arkansas, LRCH 1958, Jan-Jun" folder, NAACP Papers, Library of Congress; Clarence Laws to Roy Wilkins, December 18, 1957, box 4, folder 10, Bates Papers, Madison; Bates, *Long Shadow*, 117.

58. Bates, *Long Shadow*, 119–20.

59. Statement, Clarence Laws, February 12, 1958, box 4, folder 10, Bates Papers, Madison.

60. Bates, *Long Shadow*, 120–22.

61. Transcript, telephone conversation between Gloster B. Current, Clarence Laws, Christopher Mercer, and Mrs. L. C. Bates, February 13, 1958, box 5, folder 2, Bates Papers, Madison.

62. *Southern School News*, June 1958.

63. Telegram, Daisy Bates to United States Attorney General, July 8, 1959, box 4, folder 10, Bates Papers, Madison; Bates interview.

64. Daisy Bates to Roy Wilkins, November 8, 1956, group III, series C, container 4, in

"Arkansas State Conference, 1956–57" folder, NAACP Papers, Library of Congress; photographs of Rajmohan Gandhi with the Bateses in Little Rock, folders 63, 148, 151, 152; photographs of Summit Conference for the Moral Re-Armament of the World, 1958, folders 133–54, all in series 4, boxes 9 and 10, Bates Papers, Fayetteville; Tyson, *Radio Free Dixie,* 153–54, 159, 164–65.

65. Bates, *Long Shadow,* 166–69.

66. Ibid.

67. NAACP news release, October 19, 1957, box 4, folder 10, Bates Papers, Madison.

68. Clarence Laws to Roy Wilkins, December 18, 1957, box 4, folder 10, and CCC flyer, box 6, folder 4, Bates Papers, Madison; Bates, *Long Shadow,* 40–43, 107–10.

69. Daisy Bates to Roy Wilkins, September 12, 1957, group II, series A, container 98, in "Desegregation of Schools, Arkansas, Little Rock, Central High, 1956–57, Sept." folder, NAACP Papers, Library of Congress.

70. Transcript, conversation, Gloster B. Current and Daisy Bates, November 25, 1957, box 5, folder 2, Bates Papers, Madison.

71. Reed, *Faubus,* 245.

72. Bruce Bennett to Daisy Bates, August 28, August 30, 1957, box 6, folder 4, Bates Papers, Madison.

73. Daisy Bates to Bruce Bennett, September 13, 1957, box 6, folder 4, Bates Papers, Madison; *Arkansas Gazette,* September 17, 1957, clipping in Bates Scrapbooks.

74. *Arkansas Gazette,* October 15, 1957, clipping in Bates Scrapbooks.

75. Ibid., November 1, 1957.

76. Press release, November 1, 1957, box 4, folder 10, Bates Papers, Madison; *New York Herald Tribune,* November 2, 1957, *New York Daily News,* November 2, 1957, *Arkansas Gazette,* November 2, 1957, clippings in Bates Scrapbooks.

77. *Arkansas Gazette,* November 2, 3, 1957, clippings in Bates Scrapbooks.

78. Ibid., December 3, 4, 1957.

79. Ibid.

80. Ibid.

81. *Arkansas Democrat,* December 10, 1957, clipping in Bates Scrapbooks.

82. *Arkansas Gazette,* December 24, 1957, clipping in Bates Scrapbooks.

83. Bates, *Long Shadow,* 110.

84. L. C. Bates to Dr. I. L. Scruggs, October 14, 1959, box 5, folder 9, Bates Papers, Madison.

85. Ibid.; Daisy Bates to Roy Wilkins, September 12, 1957, group II, series A, container 98, in "Desegregation of Schools, Arkansas, Little Rock, Central High, 1956–57, Sept." folder, and Memorandum, Gloster B. Current to Ruth Yevelle, May 16, 1958, group III, series A, container 174, in "Reprisals: Arkansas, Government Affairs, 1958–62" folder, NAACP Papers, Library of Congress; Memorandum, L. C. Bates to Gloster B. Current, December 31, 1958, Bates Papers, Madison; Bates, *Long Shadow,* 170–78.

86. "Biography," finding aid, Bates Papers, Madison.

87. Bates, *Long Shadow,* 159–60; "Nine Kids Who Dared," *New York Post Daily Magazine,* October 21–31, 1957, clippings in Bates Scrapbooks.

88. Bates, *Long Shadow,* 179–213.

89. Ibid.; "Daisy Bates' Own Story," *Afro-American* (Baltimore), November 9, 1957, clipping in Bates Scrapbooks; Aucoin, "Southern Manifesto." For a more detailed account of the white community during the school crisis, see Chappell, *Inside Agitators,* 97–121; Chappell, "Diversity within a Racial Group."

90. Cothran and Phillips, "Negro Leadership," 111–13.

91. Transcript, conversation, Gloster B. Current and Clarence Laws, October 3, 1957, box 5, folder 2, Bates Papers, Madison.

92. Spitzberg, *Racial Politics,* 127–30.

93. Ellis Thomas to Roy Wilkins, May 28, 1958, group III, series A, container 41, in "Awards-Spingarn Medal, Little Rock Nine & Mrs. L. C. Bates" folder, NAACP Papers, Library of Congress; *New York Amsterdam News* and *Afro-American,* June 7, 1958, clippings in Bates Scrapbooks.

94. Memorandum, Roy Wilkins to Members of the Spingarn Medal Award Committee, June 2, 1958, group III, series A, container 41, in "Awards-Spingarn Medal, Little Rock Nine & Mrs. L. C. Bates" folder, NAACP Papers, Library of Congress; *New York Amsterdam News* and *Afro-American,* June 7, 1958, clippings in Bates Scrapbooks.

95. For letters supporting Daisy Bates, see Charles C. Walker to Roy Wilkins, June 6, 1958, Pauli Murray to Roy Wilkins, June 10, 1958, Wm. A. Sterend to Roy Wilkins, June 12, 1958, Homer Goodwin to Roy Wilkins, June 12, 1958; see also Acceptance Address, Mrs. L. C. Bates, all group III, series A, container 41, in "Awards-Spingarn Medal, Little Rock Nine & Mrs. L. C. Bates" folder; Memorandum, Roy Wilkins to Editors and Radio Program Directors, December 17, 1959, group III, series A, container 20, in "Bates, Daisy, 1957–1960" folder; all in NAACP Papers, Library of Congress.

96. Memorandum, Gloster B. Current to Ruth Yevelle, May 16, 1958, group III, series A, container 174, in "Reprisals: Arkansas, Government Affairs, 1958–62" folder, NAACP Papers, Library of Congress.

97. Greenberg, *Crusaders in the Courts,* 222–24, 228–43; Branton, "Little Rock Revisited," 260.

98. *Southern School News,* March 1958, July 1958, August 1958, September 1958; Branton, "Little Rock Revisited," 265–66; Peltason, *Fifty-Eight Lonely Men,* 183–87; Silverman, *Little Rock Story,* 17–19.

99. *Southern School News,* September 1958; Peltason, *Fifty-Eight Lonely Men,* 189–190, 192; Silverman, *Little Rock Story,* 21, 24–25, 27; Tushnet, *Making Civil Rights Law,* 261–63.

100. *Southern School News,* October 1958, November 1958; Branton, "Little Rock Revisited," 266–67; Freyer, *Little Rock Crisis,* 156; Peltason, *Fifty-Eight Lonely Men,* 187, 196; Reed, *Faubus,* 245; Silverman, *Little Rock Story,* 21–22, 28.

101. *Southern School News,* November 1958; Peltason, *Fifty-Eight Lonely Men,* 198–202; Freyer, *Little Rock Crisis,* 155–57.

102. *Southern School News,* May 1959.

103. Ibid., December 1958, January 1959; Day, "Fall of a Southern Moderate";

Freyer, *Little Rock Crisis,* 157–59; Peltason, *Fifty-Eight Lonely Men,* 201–2; Reed, *Faubus,* 246; Silverman *Little Rock Story,* 29–30.

104. Jacoway, "Taken by Surprise," 17–18; Spitzberg, *Racial Politics,* 38–41; Patterson and Vinson interviews.

105. Bartley, "Looking Back at Little Rock," 103–4.

106. Jacoway, "Taken by Surprise," 28; Vinson interview.

107. "New Factories Thing of the Past in Little Rock," *Nashville Tennessean,* May 31, 1959; Cobb, *Selling of the South,* 125–26; Vinson interview.

108. "Women's Emergency Committee Activities during Recall Election," box 15, folder 3, Murphy Papers; Gates, "Power from the Pedestal"; Murphy, *Breaking the Silence;* Murphy, Samuel, and Williams interviews.

109. *Southern School News,* January 1959; Freyer, *Little Rock Crisis,* 158–59; Murphy, *Breaking the Silence,* 106; Reed, *Faubus,* 253–54; Spitzberg, *Racial Politics,* 96–98; Murphy, Samuel, and Williams interviews.

110. *Southern School News,* April 1959; Freyer, *Little Rock Crisis,* 160–61; Spitzberg, *Racial Politics,* 105; Williams interview.

111. *Southern School News,* June 1959; Alexander, *Little Rock Recall Election,* 11–16; Freyer, *Little Rock Crisis,* 161; Peltason, *Fifty-Eight Lonely Men,* 203; Reed, *Faubus,* 254; Silverman, *Little Rock Story,* 31; Spitzberg, *Racial Politics,* 14–17.

112. *Southern School News,* June 1959, July 1959; Alexander, *Little Rock Recall Election,* 29–31; Peltason, *Fifty-Eight Lonely Men,* 204–5; Reed, *Faubus,* 254–56; Spitzberg, *Racial Politics,* 26–27.

113. Branton, "Little Rock Revisited," 268.

114. *Southern School News,* September 1959; Reed, *Faubus,* 256; Reed interview.

115. *Southern School News,* September 1959; Bates, *Long Shadow,* 160, 164–165, 217–18.

116. Spitzberg, *Racial Politics,* 129–30.

117. Fairclough, "Little Rock Crisis," 375; Goldfield, *Black, White, and Southern,* 79.

Chapter 6. Dismantling Jim Crow

1. Chappell, *Inside Agitators,* 97–121; Jacoway, "Taken by Surprise."

2. Willard A. Hawkins to Members and Friends, November 14, 1961, series 1, box 19, folder 190, ACHR Papers; Griswold, "Second Reconstruction" manuscript, book 2, chap. 1, 16.

3. Memorandum from C. D. Coleman to M. T. Puryear, October 5, 1959, group II, series D, container 26, in "Affiliates File, Little Rock, Arkansas" folder, NUL Papers.

4. John Walker to Paul Rilling, November 17, 1959, reel 141, frames 0234–0235, SRC Papers, Library of Congress, microfilm.

5. Ibid.; "Protest Movement," series 1, box 2, folder 19, ACHR Papers; *Arkansas Gazette,* November 10, 1959; Jackson and Murphy interviews.

6. J. H. Wheeler to Nat Griswold, Jan 18, 1960; Nat Griswold to J. H. Wheeler, January 19, 1960, both in series 1, box 2, folder 19, ACHR Papers.

7. "Arkansas Council on Human Relations," May 30, 1955, series 1, box 16, folder 152, ACHR Papers.

8. Nat Griswold to J. H. Wheeler, Jan 19, 1960, series 1, box 2, folder 19, ACHR Papers.

9. Griswold, "Second Reconstruction," book 2, chap. 6, 9.

10. On the sit-ins in Greensboro, see Chafe, *Civilities and Civil Rights.*

11. Ibid. On SNCC and the sit-ins, see Stoper, *Student Nonviolent Coordinating Committee*; Carson, *In Struggle*; Morris, *Origins.*

12. Morris, *Origins,* 195–215.

13. Ibid.

14. Long interview.

15. Daisy Bates to Roy Wilkins, February 23, 1960, group III, series A, container 20, in "Bates, Daisy, 1957–1960" folder, NAACP Papers, Library of Congress; Arkansas Council on Human Relations Quarterly Report, January-March, 1960, series 1, box 27, folder 228, ACHR Papers; *Arkansas Democrat,* March 10, 1960; *Arkansas Gazette,* March 11, 1960.

16. Arkansas Council on Human Relations Quarterly Report, January–March 1960, series 1, box 27, folder 228, ACHR Papers; *Arkansas Democrat,* March 11, 1960.

17. *Arkansas Democrat,* March 11, 1960.

18. "Appeal to the Negroes of Little Rock," series 1, box 33, folder 335, ACHR Papers; *Arkansas Democrat,* March 13, 1960.

19. Arkansas Council on Human Relations Quarterly Report, January–March 1960, series 1, box 27, folder 228, ACHR Papers; Monthly Report, Clarence Laws, Field Secretary, SWR, February 26–March 31, 1960, in box 4, folder 10, Bates Papers, Madison; *Arkansas Democrat,* March 17, 1960.

20. Memorandum, Rev. J. C. Crenchaw to all religious groups, fraternal organizations, fraternities, sororities, civic, and political groups, March 30, 1960, series 1, box 31, folder 322, ACHR Papers; Monthly Report, Clarence Laws, field secretary, SWR, February 26–March 31, 1960, and 1960 Annual Report, L. C. Bates, Field Secretary, Arkansas, December 3, 1960: both reports in box 4, folder 10, Bates Papers, Madison; *Arkansas Democrat,* April 1, 1960.

21. 1960 Annual Report of L. C. Bates, field secretary, Arkansas, December 3, 1960, in box 4, folder 10, Bates Papers, Madison; *Arkansas Democrat,* April 13, 21, 1960.

22. 1960 Annual Report of L. C. Bates, field secretary, Arkansas, December 3, 1960, in box 4, folder 10, Bates Papers, Madison; *Arkansas Democrat,* April 27, June 17, 18, 1960; *Arkansas Gazette* April 27, June 1, 1960.

23. *Arkansas Democrat,* June 4; October 4, 1960.

24. Arkansas Council on Human Relations Quarterly Report, October–November, 1960, in series 1, box 27, folder 228, ACHR Papers; *Arkansas Democrat,* September 6, November 29, 1960.

25. Memorandum, Little Rock ACHR to SRC, December 6, 1960, reel 141, frame 0218, SRC Papers, Library of Congress, microfilm.

26. Ibid.

27. On the Freedom Rides, see Barnes, *Journey from Jim Crow,* 157–75; Branch, *Parting the Waters,* 451–91; Fairclough, *To Redeem the Soul of America,* 58–83; and Garrow, *Bearing the Cross,* 127–72.

28. See note 27.

29. See note 27.

30. See note 27.

31. *Arkansas Gazette,* July 11, 12, 1961.

32. "Conversation with Mr. Patterson about Freedom Riders," series 1, box 7, folder 76, ACHR Papers; *Arkansas Gazette,* July 11, 12, 1961.

33. *Arkansas Gazette,* July 12, 1961.

34. Ibid., July 13, 1961.

35. Ibid.

36. Ibid., July 14, 1961.

37. Jackson, Jewell, Sutton, Townsend, and Young interviews.

38. Nat Griswold to Paul R. Rilling, October 30, 1961, series 1, box 8, folder 78, ACHR Papers; Jackson, Sutton, and Townsend interviews.

39. "Biography of William H. Townsend," series 1, box 2, folder 19, ACHR Papers; *Arkansas Gazette,* September 15, 1963; Townsend interview.

40. "Biography of William H. Townsend," and Garman P. Freeman political campaign letter, October 10, 1962, both in series 1, box 2, folder 19, ACHR Papers; *Arkansas Gazette,* September 15, 1963; Jackson, Murphy, Sutton, and Townsend interviews.

41. *Arkansas Gazette,* September 15, 1963; Bates, *Long Shadow,* 94–97, 166–68; Jackson and Young interviews.

42. *Arkansas Gazette,* September 15, 1963; Jewell and Sutton interviews.

43. *Arkansas Gazette,* September 15, 1963; Young interview.

44. *Arkansas Gazette,* September 15, 1963; Jackson, Jewell, Sutton, Townsend, and Young interviews.

45. COCA to City Board of Directors, July 21, 1961, series 1, box 2, folder 19, ACHR Papers.

46. Griswold, "Second Reconstruction," book 2, chap. 6, 13.

47. Arkansas Council on Human Relations Quarterly Report, July-September, 1961, series 1, box 28, folder 289; Minutes of the Executive Committee, March 15, 1962, series 1, box 22, folder 220, in ACHR Papers; *Arkansas Gazette,* March 9, 1962.

48. *Arkansas Gazette,* March 10, 1962.

49. Statement, July 12, 1962, series 1, box 2, folder 19, ACHR Papers.

50. Telegram, Dorothy Miller to Nat Griswold, n.d., series 1, box 33, folder 335, ACHR Papers; Griswold, "Second Reconstruction," book 2, chap. 6, 15–16.

51. Field Report, Maryland, Georgia, and Arkansas, May 30, 1962, box 8, folder 5, SNCC Papers, Madison.

52. Sutton interview.

53. Long interview.

54. Field Report, Maryland, Georgia, and Arkansas, October 23, 1962–November 1, 1962, box 8, folder 5, SNCC Papers, Madison.

55. Ibid.; *Arkansas Gazette,* November 8, 1962; *Arkansas Democrat,* November 8, 1962.

56. Field Report, Maryland, Georgia, and Arkansas, November 2, 1962–November 7, 1962, box 8, folder 5, SNCC Papers, Madison.

57. Arkansas Council on Human Relations Quarterly Report, October–December 1962, series 1, box 28, folder 289, ACHR Papers; Spitzberg, *Racial Politics,* 143–47; Patterson, Sutton, Vinson, and Williams interviews.

58. Field Report, Maryland, Georgia, and Arkansas, November 26, 1962–December 3, box 8, folder 5, SNCC Papers, Madison; Arkansas Council on Human Relations Quarterly Report, October–December 1962, series 1, box 28, folder 289, ACHR Papers; *Arkansas Gazette,* November 29, 1963; Townsend interview.

59. "Dates and Procedures for Making Changes," series 1, box 19, folder 190, ACHR Papers; Spitzberg, *Racial Politics,* 144–45; Vinson and Williams interviews.

60. Spitzberg, *Racial Politics,* 144–45; Sutton and Vinson interviews.

61. "Dates and Procedures for Making Changes," series 1, box 19, folder 190, ACHR Papers; Spitzberg, *Racial Politics,* 145.

62. News Release, January 24, 1963, reel 19, frame 0176, SNCC Papers, Library of Congress, microfilm; Arkansas Council on Human Relations Quarterly Report, January–March 1963, series 1, box 28, folder 290, ACHR Papers.

63. Spitzberg, *Racial Politics,* 147–48; Patterson and Vinson interviews.

64. *Pine Bluff Commercial,* January 20, 1963, clipping, reel 175, frame 0511, SNCC Papers, Library of Congress, microfilm.

65. News Release, January 24, 1963, reel 19, frame 0176, SNCC Papers, Library of Congress, microfilm.

66. *Arkansas Gazette,* February 16, 1963.

67. "Public Accommodations and Downtown Employment, May 1964," series 1, box 19, folder 190, ACHR Papers; Spitzberg, *Racial Politics,* 145–47.

68. On events in Birmingham, see Eskew, *But for Birmingham.*

69. "Image Makers Erasing 1957 from the City's Calendar," *Jet,* April 4, 1963.

70. Rev. J. C. Crenchaw to Frank W. Smith, April 11, 1957, group III, series C, container 4, in "Arkansas State Conference, 1956–57" folder; Memorandum, L. C. Bates to NAACP Branch Officers, n.d.; Lucille Black to George Howard Jr., December 13, 1961, both group III, series C, container 5, in "Arkansas State Conference, 1961–65," folder, all in NAACP Papers, Library of Congress; "Field Secretary's Report—September 15 to October 15, 1962," series 2, box 5, folder 1, Bates Papers, Fayetteville; *Arkansas Gazette,* August 14, 1961.

71. "Information About Daisy Bates," finding aid, Bates Papers, Fayetteville; "Biography," finding aid, Bates Papers, Madison; Robnett, *How Long,* 93; Branch, *Parting the Waters,* 880–81; Hedgeman, *Trumpet Sounds,* 180.

72. Daisy Bates to Roy Wilkins, January 30, 1956; Daisy Bates to Roy Wilkins, November 8, 1956; Rev. J. C. Crenchaw to Frank W. Smith, April 11, 1957, all in group III, series C, container 4, "Arkansas State Conference, 1956–57," NAACP Papers, Library of Congress; *Arkansas Gazette,* August 24, 26, 28, October 19, 1980.

73. Dunaway interview.

74. *Arkansas Gazette,* January 1, September 1, 1963; *New York Amsterdam News* and *Afro-American,* January 12, 1963, clippings in Bates Scrapbooks; Dunaway interview.

75. Daisy Bates to Dr. Jerry D. Jewell, September 3, 1966, group IV, series C, container 2, in "Little Rock, Ark, 1966–67" folder, NAACP Papers, Library of Congress; Jewell interview.

76. *Southern School News,* March 1959, December 1961; Howard interview.

77. *Arkansas Gazette,* June 23, 30, 1963.

78. *Arkansas Gazette,* June 3, 1962; Daisy Bates to Wiley A. Branton, August 28, 1962, series 1, box 1, folder 2, Bates Papers, Fayetteville.

79. Garrow, *Bearing the Cross,* 91, 98, 137–38, 196–97, 269, 352, 490.

80. On the civil rights movement in the mid-1960s, see Branch, *Parting the Waters,* chaps. 22 and 23; Fairclough, *To Redeem the Soul of America,* chaps. 7, 8, 9 and 10; Garrow, *Bearing the Cross,* chaps. 5, 6, and 7. On the 1964 Civil Rights Act, see Loevy, *To End All Segregation;* Whalen and Whalen, *Longest Debate.* On the 1965 Voting Rights Act, see Davidson and Grofman, *Quiet Revolution;* Garrow, *Protest at Selma.*

Chapter 7. New Challenges

1. Register, SNCC Arkansas Project Records, SNCC Records, Madison, provides the best existing overview of SNCC activities in Arkansas.

2. On Freedom Schools in Arkansas, see "Freedom School Workshops, 1965," box 2, folder 1; "Freedom Center," box 7, folder 5; and "Freedom School Writings, 1965," box 7, folder 6, all in SNCC Records, Madison.

3. See Gould Citizens for Progress Files, Pine Bluff Movement Files, and Saint Francis County Achievement Committee Files, boxes 4, 5, and 7, SNCC Records, Madison.

4. Lawson, *Running for Freedom,* 85, 228.

5. "Fraud in the 1965 Arkansas School Board Elections," box 1, folder 5, SNCC Records, Madison.

6. *Arkansas Gazette,* December 11, 12, 1966; Ward interview.

7. Hathorn, "Friendly Rivalry."

8. On Winthrop Rockefeller, see Ward, *Arkansas Rockefeller;* Ward interview.

9. "Rockefeller's Right Hand Man," *Ebony,* August 1955, series 1, box 6, folder 56, ACHR Papers; Reed, *Faubus,* 139–40; Urwin, "*Noblesse Oblige,*" 30–32; Ward, *Arkansas Rockefeller,* 169–78; Ward interview.

10. M. A. Zimmerman, "Arkansas Project Student Nonviolent Coordinating Committee," ca. 1966, box 1, folder 7, SNCC Records, Madison.

11. Memorandum, Dr. Jerry D. Jewell and L. C. Bates to NAACP Branch Officers and Members, July 29, 1966, group IV, series C, container 2, in "Little Rock, Ark., 1966–70" folder, NAACP Papers, Library of Congress.

12. Ward interview.

13. Lambright, Murphy, Samuel, and Ward interviews.

14. "A Voter Registration Project proposed to the VEP, Atlanta, June 16, 1966," Wiley

A. Branton to Ozell Sutton, June 29, 1966, and Vernon Jordan to Elijah Coleman, September 22, 1966, all reel 184, frames 1859–1862, 1863, 1890–1897, SRC Papers, Library of Congress, microfilm; *Arkansas Gazette*, August 2, 1964, December 12, 1966; Garrow, *Bearing the Cross*, 161–64; Coleman and Sutton interviews.

15. Ledbetter, "Arkansas Amendment."

16. *Arkansas Gazette*, October 22, 1970; Goldfield, *Black, White, and Southern*, 196.

17. *Arkansas Gazette*, February 4, 1973; Lawson, *Running for Freedom*, 85; Brownlee, Coleman, and Hollingworth interviews.

18. Fairclough, *To Redeem the Soul of America*, 253.

19. "SNCC in Arkansas," Press Statement, Rev. Ben Grinage, May 29, 1966, and *Arkansas Gazette*, February 26, 1967, clipping, all in series 1, box 33, folder 335, ACHR Papers; Arkansas Staff Meeting, June 9, 1966, reel 19, frames 0242–0243, SRC Papers, Library of Congress, microfilm; Griswold, "Second Reconstruction," book 3, chap. 1, 1–26; Carson, *In Struggle*, 232. On black power, see Carmichael and Hamilton, *Black Power*; Carson, *In Struggle*, chap. 14; Van Deburg, *New Day in Babylon*.

20. L. C. Bates to Richard L. Dockery, May 19, 1966, and L. C. Bates to Gloster B. Current, November 1966, both group IV, series C, container 2, in "Arkansas State Conference, 1966–70" folder, NAACP Papers, Library of Congress.

21. *New York Times*, January 9, 1966, and Gloster B. Current to L. C. Bates, January 28, 1966, group IV, series C, container 2, in "Arkansas State Conference, 1966–70" folder, NAACP Papers, Library of Congress.

22. L. C. Bates to Gloster B. Current, February 2, 1966, group IV, series C, container 2, in "Arkansas State Conference, 1966–70" folder, NAACP Papers, Library of Congress.

23. Ibid.; Faubus interview.

24. Memorandum, from Gloster B. Current, December 17, 1965, group III, series C, container 5, in "Arkansas State Conference, 1961–65" folder; Gloster B. Current to L. C. Bates, March 13, 1967; and Gloster B. Current to Dr. George Flemmings, January 7, 1969, group IV, series C, container 2, in "Arkansas State Conference, 1966–70" folder, NAACP Papers, Library of Congress.

25. L. C. Bates to Dr. John A. Morsell, May 17, 1971, series 2, box 5, folder 3, Bates Papers, Fayetteville.

26. Memorandum, Edward B. Muse to Henry Lee Moon, July 27, 1965, group III, series A, container 20, in "Daisy Bates, 1961–65" folder, NAACP Papers, Library of Congress; "Information about Daisy Bates," finding aid, Bates Papers, Fayetteville.

27. For an overview of the War on Poverty and the OEO, see Patterson, *America's Struggle against Poverty*, chaps. 8, 9.

28. *Arkansas Gazette*, January 29, 1967; Love, Walker, and Ward interviews.

29. On antipoverty program projects in Arkansas, see Blumenthal, "Building a Base for Reform"; Couto, *Ain't Gonna Let Nobody Turn Me Round*; Morgan, *Marianna*, 18–20; Schorr, *Don't Get Sick in America*; Schwartz, *In Service*; Mitchell Zimmerman, "Welfare Investigation," reel 154, frames 0246-0462, SRC Papers, Library of Congress, microfilm; and Love and Walker interviews.

30. See note 29.

31. "Excerpts from 'A Study of the Social and Economic Conditions of the Negro in Greater Little Rock—1963,'" series 1, box 1, folder 19, ACHR Papers.

32. Ibid.; Goldfield, *Black, White, and Southern*, 203–5.

33. Greater Little Rock Conference on Religion and Race, "Confronting the Little Rock Housing Problem," series 1, box 7, folder 76, ACHR papers; Vinson interview.

34. Adolphine Fletcher Terry to William H. McLean, March 9, 1970, series 1, box 3, folder 3, Fletcher-Terry Family Papers; Porter interview. On race and housing, see Meyer, *As Long as They Don't Move Next Door.*

35. *Arkansas Gazette*, April 15, 1966.

36. Ibid., April 13, October 28, 1967.

37. "Some Observations on the LR School Board's Use of the Pupil Assignment Law—May 1962," series 1, box 31, folder 316, and "Little Rock—Five Years Later," *Redbook,* November 1962, series 1, box 13, folder 14, both ACHR Papers; "Little Rock Revisited—Tokenism Plus," *New York Times Magazine,* June 2, 1963.

38. *Arkansas Gazette*, April 23, 1965; Wilkinson, *From Brown to Bakke*, 104.

39. *Arkansas Gazette*, May 23, 1965.

40. Ibid., August 30, 1966; Wilkinson, *From Brown to Bakke*, 104.

41. *Arkansas Gazette*, August 30, 1966; December 17, 30, 1967; University Task Force on the Little Rock School District, *Plain Talk*, 19; Staff Report of the U.S. Commission on Civil Rights, "School Desegregation," 4–5; Goldfield, *Black, White, and Southern*, 257.

42. *Arkansas Gazette*, October 1, 1967; "Revolution Since Little Rock," *Life,* September 29, 1967.

43. See note 42.

44. See note 42.

45. *Arkansas Gazette*, April 7, 1968, August 19, 29, 1969, September 2, 3, 1969, September 25, 1971; "Widespread Racial Violence Persists in Eastern Arkansas Farming Area," *New York Times*, October 10, 1971, 5; and "Forrest City Report," April 1970, "Earle Report," November 1970, and "Camden Report," 1970, all in box 1, folder 5, Gordon Papers.

46. *Arkansas Gazette*, July 27, 1969, August 20, 1969, June 23, 1970.

47. Ibid., April 6, 7, 8, 1968.

48. Ibid., April 10, 1968; Bobby Brown and Brownlee interviews.

49. Bobby Brown, Robert Brown, Brownlee, Jones, Love, Sutton, and Walker interviews.

50. *Arkansas Gazette*, August 17, 18, 1968.

51. Ibid., August 10, 22, 1968

52. "Background Information on Arkansas Penal System," reel 154, frames 0001–0003, SRC Papers, Library of Congress, microfilm. For further background on the Arkansas penal system in the 1960s, see Reed, *Faubus*, 313–15.

53. Joseph E. Williams Jr., "On Being Sick and Tired," reel 64, frames 0447–0448, SRC Papers, Library of Congress, microfilm.

54. *Arkansas Gazette*, August 10, 1968.

55. Ibid., August 10, 11, 12, 13, 1968; Love interview.

56. *Arkansas Gazette*, March 29, May 7, 1969; Forman, *Making of Black Revolutionaries*, 545.

57. *Arkansas Gazette*, July 9, 1969.

58. Ibid.; Bobby Brown interview.

59. On law enforcement and the demise of black militant groups, see O'Reilly, *Racial Matters*, chaps. 8, 9, 10.

60. Hollingworth interview.

61. Joseph E. Williams Jr., "On Being Sick and Tired," reel 64, frame 0448, SRC Papers, Library of Congress, microfilm; Bobby Brown, Robert Brown, Brownlee, Hollingworth, Jewell, Jones, Love, Sutton, Townsend, and Walker interviews.

Bibliography

Manuscript Collections, Unpublished Works, and Documents

Adkins, Homer M. Papers. Arkansas History Commission, Little Rock.

Arkansas Council on Human Relations Papers, 1954–1968. Special Collections Division, University of Arkansas Libraries, Fayetteville.

Ashmore, Harry S. Papers. Special Collections Division, University of Arkansas Libraries, Little Rock.

Bates, Daisy. Papers. Special Collections Division, University of Arkansas Libraries, Fayetteville.

Bates, Daisy. Papers. State Historical Society of Wisconsin, Madison.

Bates, Daisy. Scrapbooks. State Historical Society of Wisconsin, Madison.

Blossom, Virgil T. Papers. Special Collections Division, University of Arkansas Libraries, Fayetteville.

Branton, Wiley A. Papers. Manuscript Division, Moorland-Spingarn Research Center, Howard University, Washington, D.C.

Caldwell, Arthur Brann. Papers. Special Collections Division, University of Arkansas Libraries, Fayetteville.

Cartwright, Rev. Colbert S. Scrapbooks, 1954–1963. Special Collections Division, University of Arkansas Libraries, Fayetteville.

Cherry, Francis. Papers, 1952–1955. Arkansas History Commission, Little Rock.

Cobb, Judge Osro. Papers. Special Collections Division, University of Arkansas Libraries, Little Rock.

Committee on Fair Employment Practices Records. National Archives.

Committee on Interracial Co-operation Papers. Microfilm, Manuscript Division, Library of Congress, Washington, D.C.

Department of Housing and Urban Development Records. National Archives.

Faubus, Orval Eugene. Papers. Special Collections Division, University of Arkansas Libraries, Fayetteville.

————. Papers, 1955–1967. Arkansas History Commission, Little Rock.

FBI Little Rock School Crisis Reports. Special Collections Division, University of Arkansas Libraries, Little Rock.

Federal Housing Authority Records. National Archives, Washington, D.C.

Federal Writers Project Ex-Slave Interviews, 1936–1941. Arkansas History Commission, Little Rock.

Fletcher-Terry Family Papers. Special Collections Division, University of Arkansas Libraries, Little Rock.

Flowers, William Harold. Papers. In possession of Stephanie Flowers, Pine Bluff, Ark.

Fulbright, J. W. Papers. Special Collections Division, University of Arkansas Libraries, Fayetteville.

Gentry, Leffel and U. A. Papers. Special Collections Division, University of Arkansas Libraries, Little Rock.

Goodwin, Bennie W. "Silas Hunt—The Growth of a Folk Hero." Class paper, May 20, 1957. Special Collections Division, University of Arkansas Libraries, Fayetteville.

Gordon, Frank N. Jr. Papers. Special Collections Division, University of Arkansas Libraries, Fayetteville.

Griswold, Nat. "The Second Reconstruction in Little Rock." 1968. Manuscript in the possession of Walter Clancy, Little Rock, Ark.

Hays, Brooks L. Papers. Special Collections Division, University of Arkansas Libraries, Fayetteville.

Heiskell Newspaper Collection. Special Collections Division, University of Arkansas Libraries, Little Rock.

Huckaby, Elizabeth. Papers. Special Collections Division, University of Arkansas Libraries, Fayetteville.

Lemley, Judge Harry. Papers. Special Collections Division, University of Arkansas Libraries, Little Rock.

Little Rock City Council and Board of Directors Minutes. City Hall, Little Rock.

Little Rock Conference on Religion and Human Relations Papers. Special Collections Division, University of Arkansas Libraries, Little Rock.

Little Rock Housing Authority Scrapbooks. Special Collections Division, University of Arkansas Libraries, Little Rock.

Little Rock School Board Minutes. Special Collections Division, University of Arkansas Libraries, Little Rock.

McMath, Sidney S. Papers. Special Collections Division, University of Arkansas Libraries, Fayetteville.

McMath, Sidney Sanders. Papers, 1948–1952. Arkansas History Commission, Little Rock.

Murphy, Sara Alderman. Papers. Special Collections Division, University of Arkansas Libraries, Fayetteville.

National Association for the Advancement of Colored People Papers. Manuscript Division, Library of Congress, Washington, D.C.

National Association for the Advancement of Colored People Papers. Microfilm, Special Collections Division. University of Arkansas Libraries, Little Rock.

National Association for the Advancement of Colored People (Arkansas) Papers. Microfilm, Special Collections Division, University of Arkansas Libraries, Fayetteville.

National Urban League Papers. Manuscript Division, Library of Congress.

Pulaski County Democratic Committee Scrapbooks. Arkansas History Commission, Little Rock.

Records of the Office of the Secretary of War. RG 407, National Archives. Washington, D.C.

Republican Party of Arkansas Archives. Special Collections Division, University of Arkansas Libraries, Little Rock.

Republican Party of Arkansas State Committee Records. Special Collections Division, University of Arkansas Libraries, Fayetteville.

Robinson, Dr. John Marshall. Papers. In possession of Terry Pierson, Little Rock, Ark.

Rockefeller, Winthrop. Collection. Special Collections Division, University of Arkansas Libraries, Little Rock.

Sharp, Floyd. Scrapbooks, 1933–1943. Arkansas History Commission, Little Rock.

Sharp, Floyd. *Traveling Recovery Road: The Story of Work Relief in Arkansas, August 1932 to Nov. 1936.* Arkansas History Commission, Little Rock.

Southern Regional Council Papers. Microfilm, Manuscript Division, Library of Congress, Washington, D.C.

Staff Report of the U.S. Commission on Civil Rights. "School Desegregation in Little Rock, Arkansas," June 1977. Special Collections Division, University of Arkansas Libraries, Fayetteville.

Student Nonviolent Coordinating Committee. Arkansas Project Records. State Historical Society of Wisconsin, Madison.

Student Nonviolent Coordinating Committee Papers. Microfilm, Manuscript Division, Library of Congress, Washington, D.C.

Taylor, Samuel S. "The Negroes of Little Rock—Digest." Box 6, folder 2, WPA Papers.

———. "The Negroes of Little Rock—Outline." Box 6, folder 1, WPA Papers.

Thomas, Herbert L. Papers. Special Collections Division, University of Arkansas Libraries, Fayetteville.

Trimble, James W. Family Papers. Special Collections Division, University of Arkansas Libraries, Fayetteville.

U.S. Census Bureau. *Sixteenth Census of the United States,* 1940.

———. *Seventeenth Census of the United States,* 1950.

———. *Eighteenth Census of the United States,* 1960.

———. *Nineteenth Census of the United States,* 1970.

University Task Force on the Little Rock School District. *Plain Talk: The Future of Little Rock's Public Schools.* Little Rock: University of Arkansas, 1997.

Urban League of Arkansas. *Golden Anniversary Celebration, 1937–1987.* Little Rock, 1987. Special Collections Division, University of Arkansas Libraries, Little Rock.

Wassell, Sam. Scrapbooks. Arkansas History Commission, Little Rock.

Williams, E. Grainger. Papers. Special Collections Division, University of Arkansas Libraries, Little Rock.

Women's Emergency Committee Papers, 1958–1963. Arkansas History Commission, Little Rock.

Work Progress Administration Papers. Federal Writers' Project, 1935–1941. Arkansas History Commission, Little Rock.

Writers' Project of the Works Progress Administration. *Arkansas: A Guide to the State.* New York: Hastings House, 1941.

Writers' Project of the Works Progress Administration. *Survey of Negroes in Little Rock and North Little Rock.* Little Rock, 1941. Special Collections Division, University of Arkansas Libraries, Little Rock.

Interviews

All interviews were conducted by the author and are deposited in the University of Newcastle upon Tyne Oral History Collection (UNOHC), England.

Bates, Daisy. August 14, 1992.

Brown, Bobby. May 10, 1993.

Brown, Robert. May 10, 1993.

Brownlee, Leroy. May 5, 1993.

Bussey, Charles. December 4, 1992.

Coleman, Elijah. May 5, 1993.

Dunaway, Edwin E. September 26, 1992.

Faubus, Orval E. December 3, 1992.

Hawkins, Jeffery. September 30, 1992.

Hollingworth, Perlesta A. April 13, 1993.

Howard, George Jr. April 13, 1993.

Jackson, Dr. Maurice A. February 10, 1993.

Jewell, Dr. Jerry D. April 19, 1993.

Jones, Henry. May 26, 1993.

Jones-Gibson, Jacquelyn. May 28, 1993.

Lambright, Frank. May 7, 1993.

Long, Worth. August 8, 1993.

Love, Howard. April 30, 1993.

McClinton, Mrs. I. S. October 9, 1992.

McMath, Sidney S. December 8, 1992.

Mercer, Christopher C. April 19, 1993.

Morris, Sue Cowan Williams. January 8, 1993.

Murphy, Sara. April 29, 1993.

Patterson, Hugh. May 6, 1993.

Porter, Albert J. May 7, 1993.

Ray, Victor and Ruth. May 2, 1993.

Reed, Roy. April 1, 1993.

Robinson, Rev. William H. June 2, 1993.

Samuel, Irene. October 9, 1992.

Sutton, Ozell. August 7, 1993.

Townsend, Dr. William H. April 25, 1993.

Vinson, B. Finely. February 25, 1993.

Walker, Sonny. August 31, 1993.

Ward, John. April 28, 1993.

Williams, E. Grainger. April 30, 1993.

Woods, Howard. May 29, 1993.

Young, Rev. Rufus King. February 16, 1993.

Newspapers and Newsletters

Arkansas Democrat (Little Rock), 1878–1991.

Arkansas Democrat-Gazette (Little Rock), 1991–present.

Arkansas Gazette (Little Rock), 1821–36, 1889–1991.

Arkansas State Press (Little Rock), 1941–59.

Bulletin of the Arkansas Teachers Association (Pine Bluff). Special Collections Division, University of Arkansas Libraries, Pine Bluff.

Southern School News (Nashville), 1954–65.

Books, Essays, Articles, and Theses

Adams, Sherman. *First Hand Report: The Inside Story of the Eisenhower Administration.* London: Hutchinson, 1962.

Alexander, Henry M. "The Double Primary." *Arkansas Historical Quarterly* 3 (autumn 1944): 217–67.

———. *The Little Rock Recall Election.* New York: McGraw-Hill, 1960.

Alford, Dale, and L'Moore Alford. *The Case of the Sleeping People (Finally Awakened by Little Rock School Frustrations).* Little Rock: Pioneer Press, 1959.

Anderson, James D. *The Education of Blacks in the South, 1860–1935.* Chapel Hill: University of North Carolina Press, 1988.

Angelou, Maya. *I Know Why the Caged Bird Sings.* New York: Random House, 1969.

"Arkansas' Past Entwined with Newspaper's Vivid Story." *Arkansas Democrat-Gazette.* 1997. <http://www.ardemgaz.com/info/history.html>.

Arsenault, Raymond. *The Wild Ass of the Ozarks: Jeff Davis and the Social Bases of Southern Politics.* Philadelphia: Temple University Press, 1984.

Ashmore, Harry S. *Arkansas: A Bicentennial History.* New York: Norton, 1978.

———. *Civil Rights and Wrongs: A Memoir of Race and Politics, 1944–1994.* New York: Pantheon Books, 1994.

———. *An Epitaph For Dixie.* New York: Norton, 1958.

———. *Hearts and Minds: The Anatomy of Racism from Roosevelt to Reagan.* New York: McGraw-Hill, 1982.

————. *The Negro and the Schools*. Chapel Hill: University of North Carolina Press, 1954.

Aucoin, Brett J. "The Southern Manifesto and Southern Opposition to Desegregation." *Arkansas Historical Quarterly* 55 (summer 1996): 173–93.

Badger, Tony. "Fatalism, not Gradualism: Race and the Crisis of Southern Liberalism, 1945–1965." In *The Making of Martin Luther King and the Civil Rights Movement*, Brian Ward and Tony Badger, eds., 67–95. New York: New York University Press, 1996.

Barnes, Catherine A. *Journey from Jim Crow: The Desegregation of Southern Transit*. New York: Columbia University Press, 1983.

Bartley, Numan V. "Looking Back at Little Rock." *Arkansas Historical Quarterly* 25 (summer 1966): 101–16.

————. *The Rise of Massive Resistance: Race and Politics in the South during the 1950s*. Baton Rouge: Louisiana State University Press, 1969.

Bass, Jack. *Unlikely Heroes: The Dramatic Story of the Judges of the Fifth Circuit Who Translated the Supreme Court's Decision into a Revolution for Equality*. New York: Simon and Schuster, 1981.

Bass, Jack, and Walter DeVries. *The Transformation of Southern Politics: Social Change and Political Consequence since 1945*. New York: New American Library, 1977.

Bates, Daisy. *The Long Shadow of Little Rock: A Memoir*. New York: David McKay, 1962.

Beals, Melba Pattillo. *Warriors Don't Cry: A Searing Memoir of the Battle to Integrate Little Rock's Central High*. New York: Pocket Books, 1994.

Belknap, Michal R. *Federal Law and Southern Order: Racial Violence and Constitutional Conflict in the Post-Brown South*. Athens: University of Georgia Press, 1987.

Bennett, Lerone. *What Manner of Man: A Biography of Martin Luther King, Jr.* Chicago: Johnson, 1964.

Bishop, James A. *The Days of Martin Luther King, Jr.* New York: G. P. Putnam's Sons, 1971.

Blair, Diane D. *Arkansas Politics and Government: Do the People Rule?* Lincoln: University of Nebraska Press, 1988.

Bloom, Jack M. *Class, Race, and the Civil Rights Movement*. Bloomington: Indiana University Press, 1987.

Blossom, Virgil T. *It Has Happened Here*. New York: Harper, 1959.

Blum, John Morton. *V Was for Victory: Politics and American Culture during World War II*. New York: Harcourt Brace Jovanovich, 1976.

Blumenthal, Dan. "Building a Base for Reform," *Southern Exposure* 6 (summer 1978): 83–89.

Branch, Taylor. *Parting the Waters: Martin Luther King and the Civil Rights Movement, 1954–63*. London: Macmillan, 1988.

Branton, Wiley A. "Little Rock Revisited: Desegregation to Resegregation." *Journal of Negro Education* 52 (summer 1983): 250–69.

Burk, Robert F. *The Eisenhower Administration and Black Civil Rights*. Knoxville: University of Tennessee Press, 1984.

Burran, James Albert, III. "Racial Violence in the South during World War II." Ph.D. dissertation, University of Virginia, 1977.

Bush, A. E., and P. L. Dorman, ed. *History of the Mosaic Templars of America: Its Founders and Officials.* Little Rock: Central Printing, 1924.

Button, James W. *Blacks and Social Change: Impact of the Civil Rights Movement in Southern Communities.* Princeton, N.J.: Princeton University Press, 1989.

Butts, J. W., and Dorothy James. "The Underlying Causes of the Elaine Race Riot of 1919." *Arkansas Historical Quarterly* 21 (summer 1962): 99–122.

Campbell, Ernest Q., and Thomas F. Pettigrew. *Christians in Racial Crisis: A Study of Little Rock's Ministry.* Washington, D.C.: Public Affairs Press, 1959.

Capeci, Dominic J., Jr. "The Lynching of Cleo Wright: Federal Protection of Constitutional Rights during World War II." *Journal of American History* 72 (March 1986): 859–87.

Carmichael, Stokely, and Charles V. Hamilton. *Black Power: The Politics of Liberation in America.* New York: Random House, 1967.

Carson, Clayborne. *In Struggle: SNCC and the Black Awakening of the 1960s.* Cambridge, Mass.: Harvard University Press, 1981.

Chafe, William H. *Civilities and Civil Rights: Greensboro, North Carolina and the Black Struggle For Freedom.* New York: Oxford University Press, 1980.

Chappell, David L. "Diversity within a Racial Group: White People in Little Rock, 1957–1959." *Arkansas Historical Quarterly* 54 (winter 1995): 444–56.

———. *Inside Agitators: White Southerners in the Civil Rights Movement.* Baltimore, Md.: Johns Hopkins University Press, 1994.

Clark, E. Culpepper. *The Schoolhouse Door: Segregation's Last Stand at the University of Alabama.* New York: Oxford University Press, 1993.

Cobb, James C. *The Selling of the South: The Southern Crusade for Industrial Development, 1936–1980.* Baton Rouge: Louisiana State University Press, 1982.

Cohodas, Nadine. *Strom Thurmond and the Politics of Southern Change.* New York: Simon and Schuster, 1993.

Colburn, David R. *Racial Change and Community Crisis: St. Augustine, Florida, 1877–1980.* New York: Columbia University Press, 1985.

Cope, Graeme. "'A Thorn in the Side'? The Mothers' League of Central High School and the Little Rock Desegregation Crisis of 1957." *Arkansas Historical Quarterly* 57 (summer 1998): 160–90.

Cortner, Richard C. *A Mob Intent on Death: The NAACP and the Arkansas Riot Cases.* Middletown, Conn.: Wesleyan University Press, 1988.

Cothran, Tilman, and William Phillips Jr. "Expansion of Negro Suffrage in Arkansas." *Journal of Negro Education* 26 (summer 1957): 289–96.

———. "Negro Leadership in a Crisis Situation." *Phylon* 22 (spring 1961): 107–18.

Couto, Richard A. *Ain't Gonna Let Nobody Turn Me Round: The Pursuit of Racial Justice in the South.* Philadelphia: Temple University Press, 1991.

Cravens, Chris. "Edwin A. Walker and the Right Wing in Dallas, Texas." Master's thesis, Southwest Texas State University, 1993.

Crawford, Vicki, Jacqueline Anne Rouse, and Barbara Woods, eds. *Women in the Civil*

Rights Movement: Trailblazers and Torchbearers, 1941–1965. Brooklyn, N.Y.: Carlson Publishing, 1990.

Creger, Ralph, and Carl Creger. *This Is What We Found.* New York: L. Stuart, 1960.

Crisis in the South: The Little Rock Story, a Selection of Editorials. Little Rock: *Arkansas Gazette,* 1959.

Dalfiume, Richard M. *Desegregation of the U.S. Armed Forces: Fighting on Two Fronts, 1939–1953.* Columbia: University of Missouri Press, 1969.

————. "The 'Forgotten Years' of the Negro Revolution." *Journal of American History* 55 (June 1968): 90–106.

Daniel, Pete. "The Legal Basis of Agrarian Capitalism: The South since 1933." In *Race and Class in the American South since 1890,* Melvyn Stokes and Rick Halpern, eds., 79–102. Providence, R.I.: Berg, 1994.

————. *Lost Revolutions: The South in the 1950s.* Chapel Hill: University of North Carolina Press, 2000.

Davidson, Chandler, and Bernard Grofman, eds. *Quiet Revolution in the South: The Impact of the Voting Rights Act, 1965–1990.* Princeton, N.J.: Princeton University Press, 1994.

Day, John Kyle. "The Fall of a Southern Moderate: Congressman Brooks Hays and the Election of 1958." *Arkansas Historical Quarterly* 59 (autumn 2000): 241–64.

Dillard, Tom. "'Golden Prospects and Fraternal Amenities': Mifflin Wistar Gibbs's Arkansas Years." *Arkansas Historical Quarterly* 35 (winter 1976): 307–33.

————. "Perseverance: Black History in Pulaski County, Arkansas—An Excerpt." *Pulaski County Historical Review* 31 (winter 1983): 62–73.

————. "Scipio Jones." *Arkansas Historical Quarterly* 31 (autumn 1972): 201–19.

————. "'To the Back of the Elephant': Racial Conflict in the Arkansas Republican Party." *Arkansas Historical Quarterly* 33 (spring 1974): 3–15.

Dittmer, John. *Local People: The Struggle For Civil Rights in Mississippi.* Urbana: University of Illinois Press, 1994.

Dunaway, L. S. *What a Preacher Saw through the Key-Hole in Arkansas.* Little Rock: Parker-Harper, 1925.

Duram, James C. *A Moderate among Extremists: Dwight D. Eisenhower and the School Desegregation Crisis.* Chicago: Nelson-Hall, 1981.

Eagles, Charles W., ed. *The Civil Rights Movement in America: Essays.* Jackson: University Press of Mississippi, 1986.

Egerton, John. *Speak Now Against the Day: The Generation before the Civil Rights Movement in the South.* New York: Knopf, 1994.

Eisenhower, Dwight D. *Waging Peace.* Vol. 2 of *The White House Years.* Garden City, N.Y.: Doubleday, 1965.

Eskew, Glenn T. *But for Birmingham: The Local and National Movements in the Civil Rights Struggle.* Chapel Hill: University of North Carolina Press, 1997.

Fairclough, Adam. "Historians and the Civil Rights Movement." *Journal of American Studies* 24 (December 1990): 387–98.

———. "The Little Rock Crisis: Success or Failure for the NAACP?" *Arkansas Historical Quarterly* 56 (autumn 1997): 371–75.

———. *Race and Democracy: The Civil Rights Struggle in Louisiana, 1915–1972*. Athens: University of Georgia Press, 1995.

———. *To Redeem the Soul of America: The Southern Christian Leadership Conference and Martin Luther King, Jr.* Athens: University of Georgia Press, 1987.

Faubus, Orval Eugene. *Down from the Hills*. Little Rock: Pioneer Press, 1980.

———. *Down from the Hills II*. Little Rock: Democrat Printing and Lithographing, 1985.

Finkle, Lee. *Forum for Protest: The Black Press during World War II*. Rutherford, N.J.: Fairleigh Dickenson University Press, 1975.

Fite, Gilbert C. *Cotton Fields No More: Southern Agriculture, 1865–1980*. Lexington: University Press of Kentucky, 1984.

Fletcher, John Gould. *Arkansas*. Chapel Hill: University of North Carolina Press, 1947.

Forman, James. *The Making of Black Revolutionaries*. Washington, D.C.: Open Hand Publishing, 1985.

Freyer, Tony. *The Little Rock Crisis: A Constitutional Interpretation*. Westport, Conn.: Greenwood Press, 1984.

———. "Politics and Law in the Little Rock Crisis, 1954–1957." *Arkansas Historical Quarterly* 40 (autumn 1981): 195–219.

Garrow, David J. *Bearing the Cross: Martin Luther King, Jr., and the Southern Christian Leadership Conference*. New York: William Morrow, 1986.

———. *Protest at Selma: Martin Luther King, Jr., and the Voting Rights Act of 1965*. New Haven, Conn.: Yale University Press, 1978.

Gates, Lorraine. "Power from the Pedestal: The Women's Emergency Committee and the Little Rock School Crisis." *Arkansas Historical Quarterly* 55 (spring 1996): 26–57.

Gatewood, Willard B. *Aristocrats of Color: the Black Elite, 1880–1920*. Bloomington: Indiana University Press, 1990.

———. "Negro Legislators in Arkansas 1891: A Document." *Arkansas Historical Quarterly* 30 (autumn 1972): 220–33.

Gavins, Raymond. "The NAACP in North Carolina during the Age of Segregation." In *New Directions in Civil Rights Studies*, Armstead L. Robinson and Patricia Sullivan, eds., 105–25. Charlottesville: University Press of Virginia, 1991.

Goldfield, David R. *Black, White, and Southern: Race Relations and Southern Culture, 1940 to the Present*. Baton Rouge: Louisiana State University Press, 1990.

Gordon, Fon Louise. *Caste and Class: The Black Experience in Arkansas, 1880–1920*. Athens: University of Georgia Press, 1995.

Graves, John William. "Negro Disfranchisement in Arkansas." *Arkansas Historical Quarterly* 26 (autumn 1967): 199–225.

———. *Town and Country: Race Relations in an Urban-Rural Context, Arkansas, 1865–1905*. Fayetteville: University of Arkansas Press, 1990.

Greenberg, Jack. *Crusaders in the Courts: How a Dedicated Band of Lawyers Fought for the Civil Rights Revolution.* New York: BasicBooks, 1994.

Grubbs, Donald H. *Cry from the Cotton: The Southern Tenant Farmers' Union and the New Deal.* Chapel Hill: University of North Carolina Press, 1971.

Haiken, Elizabeth. "The Lord Helps Those Who Help Themselves: Black Laundresses in Little Rock, Arkansas, 1917–1921." *Arkansas Historical Quarterly* 69 (spring 1990): 20–50.

Harlan, Louis R. *Booker T. Washington: The Wizard of Tuskegee, 1901–1915.* New York: Oxford University Press, 1983.

Hathorn, Billy B. "Friendly Rivalry: Winthrop Rockefeller Challenges Orval Faubus in 1964." *Arkansas Historical Quarterly* 53 (summer 1994): 446–73.

Hays, Brooks L. *Politics Is My Parish: An Autobiography.* Baton Rouge: Louisiana State University Press, 1981.

————. *A Southern Moderate Speaks.* Chapel Hill: University of North Carolina Press, 1959.

Hedgeman, Anna Arnold. *The Trumpet Sounds: A Memoir of Negro Leadership.* N.Y.: Holt, Rinehart, and Winston, 1964.

Hine, Darlene Clark. *Black Victory: The Rise and Fall of the White Primary in Texas.* Millwood, N.Y.: KTO Press, 1979.

Holmes, William F. "The Arkansas Cotton Pickers Strike of 1891 and the Demise of the Colored Farmers Alliance." *Arkansas Historical Quarterly* 32 (summer 1973): 107–19.

Huckaby, Elizabeth. *Crisis at Central High, Little Rock, 1957–58.* Baton Rouge: Louisiana State University Press, 1980.

Iggers, Georg C. "An Arkansas Professor: The NAACP and the Grass Roots." In *Little Rock, U.S.A.,* Wilson Record and Jane Cassels Record, eds., 283–91.San Francisco: Chandler Publishing, 1960.

Jacoway, Elizabeth. "An Introduction: Civil Rights in a Changing South." In *Southern Businessmen and Desegregation,* Elizabeth Jacoway and David R. Colburn, eds., 2–14. Baton Rouge: Louisiana State University Press, 1982.

————. "Taken by Surprise: Little Rock Business Leaders and Desegregation." In *Southern Businessmen,* Elizabeth Jacoway and David R. Colburn, eds., 12–41. Baton Rouge: Louisiana State University Press, 1982.

Key, V. O., Jr. With the assistance of Alexander Heard. *Southern Politics in State and Nation.* New York: Knopf, 1949.

Kester, Howard. *Revolt among the Sharecroppers.* New York: Covici, Friede, 1936.

King, Richard H. *Civil Rights and the Idea of Freedom.* New York: Oxford University Press, 1992.

Kirk, John A. "Arkansas, the *Brown* Decision, and the 1957 Little Rock School Crisis: A Local Perspective." In *Understanding the Little Rock Crisis: An Exercise in Remembrance and Reconciliation,* Elizabeth Jacoway and C. Fred Williams, eds., 67–82. Fayetteville: University of Arkansas Press, 1999.

————. "Daisy Bates, the National Association for the Advancement of Colored

People, and the 1957 Little Rock School Crisis: A Gendered Perspective." In *Gender in the Civil Rights Movement,* Peter J. Ling and Sharon Monteith, eds. New York: Garland Publishing, 1999.

———. "Dr. J. M. Robinson, the Arkansas Negro Democratic Association and Black Politics in Little Rock, Arkansas, 1928–1952." *Pulaski County Historical Review* 41 (spring 1993): 2–16; 41 (summer 1993): 39–47.

———. "'He Founded a Movement': W. H. Flowers, the Committee on Negro Organizations, and the Origins of Black Activism in Arkansas,1940–1957." In *The Making of Martin Luther King and the Civil Rights Movement,* Brian Ward and Tony Badger, eds., 29–44. New York: New York University Press.

———. "The Little Rock Crisis and Postwar Black Activism in Arkansas," *Arkansas Historical Quarterly* 56 (autumn 1997): 273–93.

Kluger, Richard. *Simple Justice: The History of Brown v. Board of Education and Black America's Struggle for Equality.* New York: Knopf, 1976.

Lack, Paul D. "An Urban Slave Community: Little Rock, 1831–1862." *Arkansas Historical Quarterly* 41 (spring 1982): 258–87.

Lawson, Steven F. *Black Ballots: Voting Rights in the South, 1944–1969.* New York: Columbia University Press, 1976.

———. "Freedom Then, Freedom Now: The Historiography of the Civil Rights Movement." *American Historical Review* 96 (spring 1991): 456–71.

———. *Running for Freedom: Civil Rights and Black Politics in America since 1941.* New York: McGraw-Hill, 1991.

Ledbetter, Calvin R. "Arkansas Amendment for Voter Registration without Poll Tax Payment." *Arkansas Historical Quarterly* 54 (summer 1995): 134–62.

Leflar, Robert A. *One Life in the Law: A 60-Year Review.* Fayetteville: University of Arkansas Press, 1985.

Lesher, Stephen. *George Wallace: American Populist.* Reading, Mass.: Addison-Wesley, 1994.

Lester, Jim. *A Man For Arkansas: Sid McMath and the Southern Reform Tradition.* Little Rock: Rose Publishing, 1976.

Lewis, David L. *Biography of a Race, 1868–1919.* Vol. 1 of *W. E. B. Du Bois.* New York: Henry Holt, 1993.

Lewis, Todd E. "Mob Justice in the 'American Congo': 'Judge Lynch' in Arkansas during the Decade after World War I." *Arkansas Historical Quarterly* 52 (summer 1993): 156–84.

Lipsitz, George. *A Life in the Struggle: Ivory Perry and the Culture of Opposition.* Philadelphia: Temple University Press, 1988.

Loevy, Robert D. *To End All Segregation: The Politics of the Passage of the Civil Rights Act of 1964.* Lanham, Md.: University Press of America, 1990.

Mann, Woodrow Wilson. "The Truth about Little Rock." *New York Herald Tribune,* January 19–31, 1958.

Marable, Manning. *Race, Reform, and Rebellion: The Second Reconstruction in Black America, 1945–1982.* London: Macmillan, 1984.

Mayer, Michael S. "With Much Deliberation and Some Speed: Eisenhower and the *Brown* Decision." *Journal of Southern History* 52 (February 1986): 43–76.

McAdam, Doug. *Political Process and the Development of Black Insurgency, 1930–1970.* Chicago: University of Chicago Press, 1982.

McMillen, Neil R. *The Citizens' Council: Organized Resistance to the Second Reconstruction, 1955–1964.* Urbana: University of Illinois Press, 1971.

———. "The White Citizens' Council and Resistance to School Desegregation in Arkansas." *Arkansas Historical Quarterly* 30 (summer 1971): 95–122.

McNeil, Genna Rae. *Groundwork: Charles Hamilton Houston and the Struggle for Civil Rights.* Philadelphia: University of Pennsylvania Press, 1983.

Meier, August, and Elliott Rudwick. *CORE: A Study in the Civil Rights Movement, 1942–1968.* New York: Oxford University Press, 1973.

Meier, August, and John Bracey Jr. "The NAACP as a Reform Movement, 1909–1965: To Reach the Conscience of America." *Journal of Southern History* 59 (February 1993): 13–30.

Metcalf, George R. *From Little Rock to Boston: The History of Desegregation.* Westport, Conn.: Greenwood Press, 1983.

Meyer, Karl E., ed. *Fulbright of Arkansas: The Public Positions of a Private Thinker.* Washington, D.C.: R. B. Luce, 1963.

Meyer, Stephen Grant. *As Long as They Don't Move Next Door: Segregation and Racial Conflict in American Neighborhoods.* Lanham, Md.: Rowman and Littlefield, 2000.

Miller, William Robert. *Martin Luther King, Jr: His Life, Martyrdom and Meaning for the World.* New York: Weybright and Talley, 1968.

Mitchell, H. L. *Mean Things Happening in This Land: The Life and Times of H. L. Mitchell, Co-founder of the Southern Tenant Farmers Union.* Montclair, N.J.: Allanheld, Osmun, 1979.

Mitchell, John B. "An Analysis of Arkansas' Population by Race and Nativity, and Residence." *Arkansas Historical Quarterly* 8 (summer 1949): 115–32.

Morgan, Gordon D. *Marianna: A Sociological Essay on an Eastern Arkansas Town.* Jefferson City, Mo.: New Scholars Press, 1973.

Morgan, Gordon D., and Izola Preston. *The Edge of Campus: A Journal of the Black Experience at the University of Arkansas.* Fayetteville: University of Arkansas Press, 1990.

Morris, Aldon D. *The Origins of the Civil Rights Movement: Black Communities Organizing for Change.* New York: Free Press, 1984.

Murphy, Sara Alderman. *Breaking the Silence: Little Rock's Women's Emergency Committee to Open Our Schools, 1958–1963,* ed. by Patrick C. Murphy. Fayetteville: University of Arkansas Press, 1997.

Muse, Benjamin. *Ten Years of Prelude: The Story of Integration since the Supreme Court's 1954 Decision.* New York: Viking, 1964.

Myrdal, Gunnar. *An American Dilemma: The Negro Problem and Modern Democracy.* New York: Harper and Brothers, 1944.

Nichols, Guerdon D. "Breaking the Color Barrier at the University of Arkansas." *Arkansas Historical Quarterly* 27 (spring 1968): 3–21.

Norrell, Robert J. *Reaping the Whirlwind: The Civil Rights Movement in Tuskegee.* New York: Knopf, 1985.

O'Reilly, Kenneth. *Racial Matters: The FBI's Secret File on Black America, 1960–1972.* New York: Free Press, 1989.

Patterson, James T. *America's Struggle against Poverty, 1900–1994.* Cambridge, Mass.: Harvard University Press, 1994.

Patterson, Thomas E. *History of the Arkansas Teachers Association.* Washington, D.C.: National Education Association, 1981.

Payne, Charles M. *I've Got the Light of Freedom: The Organizing Tradition and the Mississippi Freedom Struggle.* Berkeley: University of California Press, 1995.

Peirce, Neal R. *The Deep South States of America: People, Politics, and Power in the Seven Deep South States.* New York: Norton, 1972.

Peltason, J. W. *Fifty-Eight Lonely Men: Southern Federal Judges and School Desegregation.* Urbana: University of Illinois Press, 1971.

Reddick, Lawrence D. *Crusader Without Violence: A Biography of Martin Luther King.* New York: Harper, 1959.

Reed, Merl E. *Seedtime for the Modern Civil Rights Movement: The President's Committee on Fair Employment Practice, 1941–1946.* Baton Rouge: Louisiana State University Press, 1991.

Reed, Roy. *Faubus: The Life and Times of an American Prodigal.* Fayetteville: University of Arkansas Press, 1997.

Richards, Eugene. *Few Comforts or Surprises: The Arkansas Delta.* Cambridge, Mass.: MIT Press, 1973.

Robnett, Belinda. *How Long? How Long? African-American Women in the Struggle for Civil Rights.* New York: Oxford University Press, 1997.

Rogers, Kim Lacy. "Oral History and the History of the Civil Rights Movement." *Journal of American History* 75 (September 1988): 567–76.

Rogers, O. A. "The Elaine Race Riots of 1919." *Arkansas Historical Quarterly* 19 (summer 1960): 142–50.

Rothrock, Thomas. "Joseph Carter Corbin and Negro Education in the University of Arkansas." *Arkansas Historical Quarterly* 30 (winter 1971): 277–314.

Schorr, Daniel. *Don't Get Sick in America.* Nashville, Tenn.: Aurora Publishers, 1970.

Schwartz, Marvin. *In Service to America: A History of VISTA in Arkansas, 1965–1985.* Fayetteville: University of Arkansas Press, 1988.

Sherrill, Robert. *Gothic Politics in the Deep South.* New York: Grossman Publishers, 1968.

Silverman, Corrine. *The Little Rock Story.* Tuscaloosa: University of Alabama Press, 1958.

Sitkoff, Harvard. *A New Deal for Blacks: The Emergence of Civil Rights as a National Issue.* Vol. 1. New York: Oxford University Press, 1978.

———. "Racial Militancy and Interracial Violence in the Second World War." *Journal of American History* 58 (June 1971): 661–81.

Smith, C. Calvin. "From 'Separate but Equal' to Desegregation: The Changing Philosophy of L. C. Bates." *Arkansas Historical Quarterly* 42 (autumn 1983): 254–70.

———. "John E. Bush: The Politician and the Man, 1880–1916." *Arkansas Historical Quarterly* 54 (summer 1995): 115–33.

———. "The Politics of Evasion: Arkansas' Reaction to *Smith v. Allwright*, 1944." *Journal of Negro History* 67 (spring 1982): 40–51.

———. *War and Wartime Changes: The Transformation of Arkansas, 1940–1945.* Fayetteville: University of Arkansas Press, 1986.

Smith, Griffin Jr. "Localism and Segregation: Racial Patterns in Little Rock, Arkansas 1945–54." Master's thesis, Columbia University, New York, 1965.

Spitzberg, Irving J. Jr. *Racial Politics in Little Rock 1954–1964.* New York: Garland Publishing, 1987.

Stephan, A. Stephen. "Desegregation of Higher Education in Arkansas." *Journal of Negro Education* 27 (summer 1958): 243–42.

Stoper, Emily. *The Student Nonviolent Coordinating Committee: the Growth of Radicalism in a Civil Rights Organization* Brooklyn, N.Y.: Carlson Publishing, 1989.

Taylor, Kieran. "'We Have Just Begun': Black Organizing and White Response in the Arkansas Delta." *Arkansas Historical Quarterly* 58 (autumn 1999): 265–84.

Tucker, David M. *Arkansas: A People and Their Reputation.* Memphis, Tenn.: Memphis State University Press, 1985.

Tushnet, Mark V. *Making Civil Rights Law: Thurgood Marshall and the Supreme Court, 1936–1961.* New York: Oxford University Press, 1994.

———. *The NAACP's Legal Strategy against Segregated Education, 1925–1950.* Chapel Hill: University of North Carolina Press, 1987.

Tyson, Timothy B. *Radio Free Dixie: Robert F. Williams and the Roots of Black Power.* Chapel Hill: University of North Carolina Press, 1999.

Urwin, Cathy Kunzinger. "*Noblesse Oblige* and Practical Politics: Winthrop Rockefeller and the Civil Rights Movement." *Arkansas Historical Quarterly* 54 (spring 1995): 30–52.

Van Deburg, William L. *New Day in Babylon: The Black Power Movement and American Culture, 1965–1975.* Chicago: University of Chicago Press, 1992.

Vervack, Jerry J. "The Hoxie Imbroligo." *Arkansas Historical Quarterly* 48 (spring 1989): 17–33.

Wallace, David E. "Orval Faubus: The Central Figure at Little Rock Central High School." *Arkansas Historical Quarterly* 39 (winter 1980): 314–29.

Walls, Edwina. "Some Extinct Black Hospitals of Little Rock and Pulaski County." *Pulaski County Historical Review* 34 (spring 1986): 2–13.

Ward, John L. *The Arkansas Rockefeller.* Baton Rouge: Louisiana State University Press, 1978.

Washington, Booker T. *The Negro in Business.* Boston, Mass.: Hertel, Jenkins, 1907.

Waskow, Arthur I. *From Race Riot to Sit-In, 1919 and the 1960s: A Study in the Connections between Conflict and Violence.* Garden City, N.Y.: Doubleday, 1966.

Wassell, Irene. "L. C. Bates, Editor of the Arkansas State Press." Master's thesis, University of Arkansas, 1983.

Weisbrot, Robert. *Freedom Bound: A History of America's Civil Rights Movement.* New York: Norton, 1990.

Whalen, Charles W., and Barbara Whalen. *The Longest Debate: A Legislative History of the 1964 Civil Rights Act.* Cabin John, Md.: Seven Locks Press, 1985.

Whayne, Jeannie H. "Low Villains and Wickedness in High Places: Race and Class in the Elaine Riots." *Arkansas Historical Quarterly* 58 (autumn 1999): 285–313.

————. *A New Plantation South: Land, Labor, and Federal Favor in Twentieth-Century Arkansas.* Charlottesville: University Press of Virginia, 1996.

Whayne, Jeannie H., and Willard B. Gatewood, eds. *The Arkansas Delta: Land of Paradox.* Fayetteville, University of Arkansas Press, 1993.

Wheeler, Elizabeth L. "Issac Fisher: The Frustrations of a Negro Educator at Branch Normal College, 1902–1911." *Arkansas Historical Quarterly* 41 (spring 1982): 3–50.

Wilkinson, J. Harvie, III. *From Brown to Bakke: The Supreme Court and School Integration, 1954–1978.* New York: Oxford University Press, 1979.

Williams, C. Fred. "Class: The Central Issue in the 1957 Little Rock School Crisis." *Arkansas Historical Quarterly* 56 (autumn 1997): 341–44.

Williams, Juan. *Eyes on the Prize: America's Civil Rights Years, 1954–1965.* New York: Viking, 1987.

Williams, Nancy A., ed. *Arkansas Biography: A Collection of Notable Lives.* Fayetteville: University of Arkansas Press, 2000.

Woodruff, Nan Elizabeth. "African-American Struggles for Citizenship in the Arkansas and Mississippi Delta in the Age of Jim Crow." *Radical History Review* 55 (winter 1993): 33–51.

Wynn, Neil A. *The Afro-American and the Second World War.* London: Elek, 1976.

Yates, Richard E. "Arkansas: Independent and Unpredictable." In *The Changing Politics of the South,* William C. Havard, ed. 233–93. Baton Rouge: Louisiana State University Press, 1972.

Zangrando, Robert L. *The NAACP Crusade against Lynching, 1909–1950.* Philadelphia: Temple University Press, 1980.

Index

Aaron v. Cooper (1956), 99–100, 118. *See also Cooper v. Aaron*

Act 17, 143, 145

Act 226, 143, 144, 145, 148

Adams, Sherman, 117

Adkins, Homer M., 29, 30, 37, 38

Alabama Christian Movement for Human Rights, 26

Alexander, Arkansas, 100

Alford, Dale, 2, 134

Allen, Rev. Sam, 174

Alston, Melvin O., 39

American Friends Service Committee, 141

American Socialist Party, 5

American Society of Newspaper Editors, 59

Anderson, Harold B., 81, 143, 144, 174

Anderson, Joe, Jr., 174

Anniston, Alabama, 146

Arkansas: black population of, 4–6; comparison with Alabama, Georgia, South Carolina, Tennessee, and Virginia, 6; Delta, 5, 58, 163, 164, 165, 178; impact of Second World War on, 7–8, 24; migration from, 7; and New Deal, 24; northwest, 5–6, 58, 86, 87; race relations in, 4–6, 9–10; racial conflict in, 177–78; response to *Brown* decision in, 86–90, 105; response to *Brown II* in, 95–98; SNCC campaigns in, 164–69; state politics of, 6

Arkansas Bar Association, 57

Arkansas Council on Churches, 174

Arkansas Council on Human Relations (ACHR): assessment of school desegregation, 105; comments on black leadership, 140, 141; and film *Dallas at the Crossroads*, 139; founding of, 91; and sit-ins, 145–46, 154, 155

Arkansas Democrat: change of policy by, on courtesy titles for blacks, 63; first black reporter at, 63; and Gillam Park bond issue, 67; history and ownership of, 60; letter from reader on Orval E. Faubus, 103; and sit-ins, 144; and Thomas P. Foster shooting, 51

Arkansas Democratic Voters Association (ADVA), 64

Arkansas Department of Education, 29, 30

Arkansas Gazette: black prisoners' letter to, 180; change of policy by, courtesy titles for blacks, 63; and *Brown* decision,

Arkansas Gazette—continued
   response to, 87, in competition with
   Arkansas Democrat, 60; criticism of
   Orval E. Faubus, 129; and downtown
   Little Rock desegregation, 161; and
   Freedom Rides, 148; and Gillam Park
   bond issue, 66–67; history of, 59; and
   John Carter lynching, 22; and Thomas
   P. Foster shooting, 46
Arkansas General Assembly: 1945 session,
   37; 1955 session, 89–90; 1957 session,
   104, 126; 1958 special session, 133,
   143; 1959 session, 136, 143
Arkansas Industrial Development Com-
   mission (AIDC), 115, 166
Arkansas National Guard: brought under
   federal control by President Eisen-
   hower, 119; and John Carter lynching,
   22; and conflict with BUY, 180–81; and
   Little Rock school crisis, 115, 116, 118,
   119, 120, 121, 123
Arkansas Negro Democratic Association
   (ANDA): ANDA's candidate for Little
   Rock school board, 69; and DPA white
   primary elections, 22–23, 34–38; founding of, 4, 22; *See also* Robinson, Dr. John
   Marshall
Arkansas State Conference of NAACP
   Branches (ASC): and *Aaron v. Cooper*, 99;
   and Bennett Ordinance, 127; factionalism in, 70–73; founding of, 30, 70; and
   Little Rock school crisis, 130, 131, 137;
   payment to NAACP's Southwest Regional Conference Fund, in default of,
   71; and school desegregation suits, 98.
   —Officers: Daisy Bates, president, election of, 72–73; Dr. L. C. Bates, retirement of, 170–71; W. H. Flowers, president, election of, 70–71; W. H. Flowers,
   president, resignation of, 72; George
   Howard, Jr., president, election of, 160;
   W. L. Jarrett, as temporary president,
   72, 153; Dr. Jerry D. Jewell, president,
   168; J. A. White, temporary president,
   72. *See also* National Association for the
   Advancement of Colored People

Arkansas State Press. See State Press
Arkansas Statesman, 161
Arkansas Voter Project (AVP), 167
Arsenault, Raymond, 8
Ashmore, Harry S.: awarded Pulitzer
   Prize, 129; criticism of Orval E. Faubus,
   129; departure of, from Little Rock,
   129; early life and career of, 59; on K.
   August Engel and *Arkansas Democrat*,
   60; observations of, on Little Rock, 6
Associated Citizens' Councils of Arkansas
   (ACCA). *See* White Citizens' Councils

Baer, David, 176
Baker, Ella, 141
Baker, Sammy J., 145
Barrett, Joe C., 37
Bass, Rev. W. H., 64, 66, 91, 117
Bates, Clyde Cross, 129
Bates, Daisy Lee (née Gatson): and accompaniment of black students to Central High, 117–19; attempts by, to enroll black students in white schools, 98;
   chastisement of Wiley A. Branton, 161;
   confrontation of Virgil T. Blossom, regarding treatment of black students at
   Central High, 121–22; divorce from
   and remarriage to L. C. Bates, 159–60;
   early life and experiences of, 47–48;
   election of, as president of ASC, 72–73;
   foster son, loss of, 129; harassed by
   Bruce Bennett, 126–28; harassed by
   CCC, 125–26; harassed by IRS, 126;
   and harassment of armed guards by police, 124–25; home attacked by whites,
   124; memoirs of (*The Long Shadow of
   Little Rock*), 2, 138; as national civil
   rights figure, 159; and Pulaski County
   Chapter of the NAACP, 71; and
   screening of black students, 106–7;
   snubbed by Virgil T. Blossom, 116; and
   Spingarn Medal, 131–32; and *State
   Press*, cofounding of, 48; and *State Press*,
   collapse of 128; suffers stroke, 171; on
   treatment of black students at Central
   High, 120; and white liberals and mod-

erates, dissatisfaction with, 130; and work on Mitchellville OEO Self-Help Project, 171; on use of violence and nonviolence, 124

Bates, Lucious Christopher (L. C.): and accompaniment of black students to Central High, 117; appointed Arkansas NAACP field secretary, 159; and Blossom Plan, dissatisfaction with, 93, 94; and bribe offered by white businessmen, 51; as chair of COCA's Health and Welfare Committee, 153; divorce from and remarriage to Daisy, 159–60; and DPA white primary elections, 69; early life and experiences of, 47; and father, death of, 129; and foster son, loss of, 129; on Gillam Park, 66, 67, 68; harassed by IRS, 126; and harassment of armed guards by police, 123–25; home attacked by whites, 124; and Little Rock NAACP branch, 91; questioned by NAACP national office, 169–70; and retirement from NAACP, 170–71; SNCC's criticism of, 169; *State Press*, as cofounder of, 48; and *State Press's* collapse, 128; on use of violence and nonviolence, 124

Bates, Lula, 47

Bates, Rev. Morris, 47

Beals, Melba Pattillo. *See* Pattillo, Melba

Bennett, Bruce: Bennett Ordinance, 127; impact of harassment on NAACP, 138, 158; and sit-ins, 143; and suits against NAACP and LDF, 112, 113, 126–28

Bentonville, Arkansas, 6, 87

Bevel, Diane Nash, 159

Biddle, Francis, 35, 50

Bird Committee, 103

Bird, Marvin, 103

Birdsong, Arkansas, 3

Birmingham, Alabama, 26, 146, 158

Black activism: and black power, 168, 177–78; in the courts, 26, 30, 31–32, 38–43, 55–56, 98–100; and DPA white primary elections, 22–23, 34–38, 68–70; and Thomas P. Foster shoot-ing, 44–52; and Freedom Rides, 146–50; and Gillam Park, 65–68; and death of Curtis Ingram, 179–81; and desegregation of downtown Little Rock facilities, 153–54, 157–58; impact of New Deal on, 24; obstacles to, in black community, 19–20, 140–41; in politics, 21–24, 27–29, 31, 34–38, 64, 166–68; and President Nixon, 182; and school desegregation, 73–74, 98–100, 106–12, 115–34, 137–38; and Second World War, 24, 34–53; and sit-ins, 140–45, 154–57; and SNCC, 143–42, 145, 154–57, 163–69; and teachers' salary equalization suits, 38–43; and University of Arkansas, desegregation of, 55–62; and War on Poverty, 171–72, 179

Black Americans for Democracy (BAD), 62

Black churches: Bethel African Methodist Episcopal (AME) Church, 13, 22, 152; First Baptist Church, 13, 49; Mount Pleasant Baptist Church, 90; Mount Zion Baptist Church, 151; Salem Baptist Church, 29; Wesley Chapel Methodist Episcopal Church, 13, 152. *See also* Black colleges

Black colleges: Arkansas Agricultural, Mechanical, and Normal College (AM&N), 12, 29, 42, 58, 60, 61, 130; Arkansas Baptist College, 12, 15; Philander Smith College, 11, 12, 13, 15, 21, 25, 65, 91, 92, 117, 142, 143, 144, 145, 151, 154, 155, 156, 178; Shorter College, 12, 21, 152

Black elite, 14, 15, 19, 43, 49

Black employment, xiii, 15–17, 162, 173

Black hospitals: Southern Hospital, 16; United Friends Hospital, 16

Black housing, 17, 163, 173–74

Black Manifesto, 181

Black newspapers: *Arkansas Survey Journal*, 13; *Arkansas Vanguard*, 13; *Southern Christian Recorder*, 13; *Southern Mediator Journal*, 13; *Twin City Press*, 13. *See also* *State Press*

Black parks: Booster Park, 16; Crump Park, 17; Fair Park, 16; Gillam Park, 66–68
Black police officers: appointment of, 51–52
Black power, 163, 168, 177
Black United Youth (BUY): arrest of members, 181–82; and Black Manifesto, 181; conflict with Arkansas National Guard, 180–81; and death of Curtis Ingram, 179–80; founding of, 179; and violence, 181
Black voting: and Arkansas Voter Project, 167; black elected officials, 100, 168; in DPA white primary elections, 22–23, 27, 34–38, 68–69; and Gillam Park bond issue, 67; poll tax drives, 27–29; in Republican Party of Arkansas, 21; and Winthrop Rockefeller, 166–68; and Voter Education Project, 167; voter registration figures, 31, 165, 67–68; white opposition to, 37, 165–66
Black, Lucille, 71
Bloom, Jack, 52
Blossom Plan: modifications to, 96, 107, 108; outlined, 93–94; upheld in federal court, 99–100; and white business community, 134. See also Blossom, Virgil T.
Blossom, Virgil T.: and Minnijean Brown, recommendation to expel from Central High School, 123; confronted by Daisy Bates, 121–22; contract bought out by Little Rock school board, 134; early life and career of, 92; and Elizabeth Eckford's enrollment at Central High, 109; memoir of Little Rock school crisis, 2; and Hugh Patterson, seeking help from, 115; questioned by Little Rock NAACP members, 107; refusal of, to enroll black students, 98; response of, to *Brown* decision, 93; response of, to *Brown II*, 96; and screening of black students, 106, 107–8; and strategy of minimum compliance, 93–94. See also Blossom Plan
Bond, Julian, 154

Booker, J. R.: and *Aaron v. Cooper*, reluctance to participate in, 99; and Bennett Ordinance, 127; and DPA white primary election suit, 69; and harassment of Daisy and L. C. Bates' armed guards, 125; and Little Rock NAACP branch, 90–91; and teachers' salary equalization suit, 40
Boynton v. Virginia (1960), 146
Branton, Leo, 60
Branton, Wiley A.: and *Aaron v. Cooper*, 99, 100, 118; and call for Pine Bluff NAACP branch to withdraw from national jurisdiction, 72; and *Cooper v. Aaron*, 132, 133; criticized by Daisy Bates, 161; as director of VEP 161, 167; early life and experiences of, 60; and W. H. Flowers, admiration for, 32; graduation of, from University of Arkansas Law School, 62; and suit on behalf of COCA for desegregation of public facilities in Little Rock, 153; and University of Arkansas, announcement to enroll at, 58; and University of Arkansas, attempt to enroll at, 61
Brewer, Herbert, 97
Briggs, Chester, 143
Broadwater, Bob, 179
Bronze mayor election, 31
Brooks, Bill, 176
Brooks, Joseph, 127
Browder v. Gayle (1956), 101
Brown, Bobby: arrested, 181; and Black Manifesto, 181; as BUY leader, 179; defends comments in BUY newsletter, 181; court hearing of, 181–82; forced to leave Little Rock, 182; and speech at BUY march, 180; as spokesperson for black poor and unemployed, 178
Brown, Minniejean. See Little Rock Nine
Brown II (1955): "all deliberate speed" clause, 99; impact of, on school desegregation, 94–96, 101; "local problems" clause, 132.
Brown v. Board of Education (1954): and

Brown II, 95–96; decision, 73; impact of, on university desegregation, 62 initial responses to, 86–94; and NAACP, 138; opposition to, 70, 86, 87–88, 89, 95, 97–98, 101–5
Brownell, Herbert, 118
Buchanan, McLoyd, 145
Bumpers, Dale, 167
Bush, John E., 15, 20
Bush, Rev. William E., 145, 155
Bussey, Charles, 31, 64

Camp Pike, 6, 7
Camp Robinson: black soldiers at, 44, 45, 46, 51; board of inquiry over Thomas P. Foster shooting, 47, 51; reopened in Second World War, 7
Campbell, Rev. Will, 117
Capital Citizens' Council (CCC). *See* White Citizens' Councils
Caretners, Solar M., 39
Carter, John: lynching and burning of, 21, 25, 116
Carter, Robert L., 99, 100
Central High School: assignment of black students to, 136; black students attempt to enter, 117–19; and Blossom Plan, 94, 96, 105, 106, 107, 108, 134; building of, 13; cordoned off by Arkansas National Guard, 115, 116; desegregation of, 137; harassment of black students at, 120–23; *Life* report on, in 1967, 176–77; plan for limited integration at, 91; reasons of black students for wanting to attend, 108–12; segregationist march at, 137
Chafe, William H., 3
Charleston, Arkansas, 87
Charlotte News, 59
Charmichael, Stokely, 168
Chenault, Henry, 62
Cherry, Francis, 86, 88
Chicago, Illinois, 7
Christophe, L. M., 106, 133
Civic Progress Association, 149
Civil Rights Act (1964), 162, 174

Clark, Kenneth B., 123
Classic case. *See United States v. Classic*
Classroom Teachers Association (CTA): and teachers' salary equalization suit, 30, 38, 39, 40, 41, 42, 43
Clinger, Sherman, 118
Clinton, William Jefferson, 168
CNO Spectator, 60
Cobb, Osro, 117
Cole, Mrs. John, 97
Cole, Peggy, 97
Coleman, C. D., 140
Coleman, James P., 86
Combs, Harry, 36
Commission on Interracial Cooperation, 91
Committee on Negro Organizations (CNO): aims of, 27–28; campaigns of, 28–30; founding of, 26; impact of, on Little Rock blacks, 32–33, 34, 35; impact of, on black activism, 31–32, 164, 165, 183; impact of, on NAACP in Arkansas, 30–31; as organization prototype, 26, 150, 151; and *State Press*, 48. *See also* Flowers, William Harold
Committee to Retain Our Segregated Schools (CROSS), 136
Commonwealth College, 88
Community Action Agency (CCA), 171
Community Action Program (CAP), 171
Community Organization Methods Build Absolute Teamwork (COMBT), 178
Conference on Graduate and Professional Educational Opportunities, 58
Congress of Racial Equality (CORE): and Freedom Rides, 146, 147; Saint Louis branch and Little Rock Freedom Ride, 147, 149, 154, 168
Connor, Eugene "Bull," 158
Cooper v. Aaron (1958), 132–33
Corbin, Joseph Carter, 12
Cothran, Tilman C., 130
Cotton Pickers League, 5
Council for the Liberation of Blacks (CLOB), 178

Council on Community Affairs (COCA): and Arkansas Voter Project, 167; in competition with NAACP, 158, 160, 161; and Downtown Negotiating Committee, 156; founding of, 150; membership and structure of, 151–53; petitioning white business groups by, 153–54; and suit for desegregation of public facilities, 153, 158

Council on Community Organizations, 140

Counter Intelligence Program (COINTELPRO), 182

Cox, Rev. Ben Elton, 147, 149, 150

Crenchaw, Rev. J. C.: and Bennett Ordinance, 127; as president of Little Rock NAACP branch, 90, 91, 160

Crisis, 20

Crittenden County Improvement Association (CCIA), 178

Crittenden County, Arkansas, 152

Current, Gloster B.: comments of, on Daisy Bates, 130; and Little Rock school crisis, 120; questioning of L. C. Bates by, 169–70; refusal of, to endorse Pulaski County Chapter of the NAACP, 71; and retirement of L. C. Bates from NAACP, 170–71

Curtis, Rev. John Raines, 147

Dallas at the Crossroads, 139

Davies, Ronald N., 114, 115, 118

Davis, Clifford, 56, 57–58

Davis, Eldridge, 143

Deer, Rev. Lewis, 91

Democratic National Committee, 159

Democratic Party of Arkansas (DPA): and 1956 primary election, 103; admission of black members to, 69; and Arkansas politics, 6; reconsideration of stance on race by, 167–68; re-emergence of, after Reconstruction, 21; and white primary elections 22–23, 27, 34–38, 68–69

Democratic State Committee (DSC), 34, 37, 69, 100

Democratic State Convention, 37, 69

Democrats for Rockefeller, 167

Desegregation: buses, 101; housing, 173–74; limited, 63–64; lunch counters, 157; public facilities, 157–58; public library, 63; schools, 87, 96–98, 137, 174–77; university, 55–62

Desha County, Arkansas, 171

Detriot, Michigan, 7

DeWitt, Arkansas, 32

Dixiecrat Revolt, 57

Dodge, Frank H., 23

Dollarway, Arkansas, 100, 160

Donavan, Richard, 51, 52

Double primary system, 37

Dove v. Parham (1959), 160

Downtown Little Rock Limited, 156

Downtown Negotiating Committee (DNC), 156, 157

Driver, Rev. Z. Z., 117

Du Bois, W. E. B., 20

Dunaway, Edwin, 119

Dunbar Community Center, 180

Dunbar High School: ANDA meeting at, 36; building of, 13; lack of facilities at, 18, 91; and school desegregation, 106

Dunbar Junior College, 13

Durham, North Carolina, 140

Earle, Arkansas, 177

East End Civic League (EECL), 31, 64

Eastland, James O., 86, 147

Eckford, Elizabeth. See Little Rock Nine

Economic Opportunity Act 1964 (EOA), 171

Eisenhower, Dwight D.: Daisy Bates' telegram of complaint to, 125; meeting with Orval E. Faubus, 117; and Little Rock school crisis, xi, 1, 2; reluctance of, to support *Brown* decision, 95; and sending of federal troops to Central High, 119

Elaine Race Riot, 5, 20, 21, 28

Ellington, Duke, 153

Engel, K. August, 60

Eudora, Arkansas, 40

Eureka Springs, Arkansas, 6

Fair Employment Practices Committee (FEPC), 24

Fairclough, Adam, 2, 168

Farmer, James Leonard, Jr., 146

Faubus, Orval E.: and 1957 Arkansas General Assembly, 104; and 1958 Arkansas General Assembly special session, 133; and callng out Arkansas National Guard to prevent school desegregation, 115; and L. C. Bates, 169–70; and appointment of black members to DSC, 100; on *Brown* decision, ambiguous stance of, 89, 101; court order filed against, 118; and desegregation of public facilities, attempt to halt, 161; early life and career of, 88–89; and Little Rock school crisis, xi, 1; meeting with President Eisenhower, 117; memoir by, of Little Rock school crisis, 2; and Mother's League of Central High suit, 113–14; reelection campaign of, 101–4; retirement of, as governor, 166; school desegregation, criticism of, 136–37; and segregation, decision to take stance in favor of, 114; and segregationists, refusal to support, 105; winning third consecutive term of office, 134

Faubus, Sam, 88

Fayetteville, Arkansas, 6, 60, 87

Federal Bureau of Investigation (FBI), 117, 182

First Conference on Negro Organization, 28

First World War, 6

Fletcher, John Gould, 7

Fletcher, W. E. "Buck," 89

Florida, 39

Flowers, William Harold (W. H.): address by, to black rallies, 28–29; and Daisy and L. C. Bates, 48; and black activism in Little Rock, impact on, 32–33, 34, 35; and black political activism, impact on, 31, 164, 165, 182, 183; and black voter registration, impact on, 31; and desegregation of University of Arkansas

Law School, 32, 60, 61; early life and experiences of, 25; as founder of CNO, 26; and NAACP in Arkansas, impact on, 30–31; and NAACP national office, conflict with, 70–72; and NAACP support, 25–26; political program of, 27–28; and out-of-state scholarships, successful petitioning for, 29–30, 56; and school desegregation, impact on, 73; and *Wilkerson* case, 31–32. *See also* Committee on Negro Organization

Folsom, James E., 86, 102

Forman, James, 158, 181

Forrest City, Arkansas, 164, 177

Fort Smith, Arkansas, 87, 96, 100, 101

Foster, Thomas P.: shooting of, 44–46, 47, 49, 51

Freedom Ride Coordinating Committee (FRCC), 147

Freedom Rides: in Little Rock, 147–50; in the South, 146–47

Freedom Schools, 165

Freedom-of-choice plan, 174–75

Freeman, Garman P., 91, 124–25, 150, 151–52

Fulbright, J. William, 130

Fullerton, Gary, 135

Gaines case. *See Missouri ex. rel. Gaines* v. *Canada*

Gandhi, Mohandas K., 124

Gandhi, Rajmohan, 124

Garland High School, 41

Gatewood, Willard B., 14

Gathings, E. C. "Took," 87

Gatlin, Rev. J. H., 68, 69

General Education Board, 12, 13

Gentry, Tom, 88

Georgia, 6, 86, 113, 146

Gibbs, Mifflin Wistar, 14

Gibson, John, 42, 43

Giffey, Annie, 42

Gillam, Isaac, 15

G.I. Revolt, 54, 64

Glascock, Paul, 148

Glover, Albert, 45, 46, 50

Glover, Quinn: and court hearing of Bobby Brown and James Edward Perkins, 181–82; and Freedom Rides, 148, 149–50; and sit-ins, 143, 144, 145
Goldwater, Barry, 167
Gould Citizens for Progress, 165
Gould, Arkansas, 152, 164
Grand Masonic Templars of America, 15, 20–21, 23–24
Great Society, 171
Greater Little Rock Ministerial Alliance, 100, 153
Green, Ernest. *See* Little Rock Nine
Greenberg, Jack, 132, 174
Greensboro, North Carolina, 141
Greenville News, 59
Greenville Piedmont, 59
Gregg, G. A., 12
Grice, Geleve, 61,
Griffin, Marvin, 113, 114
Grigsby, Tommy, 68
Grinage, Ben, 180
Griswold, Nat, 140, 141, 155
Gurdon, Arkansas, 44, 45
Guthridge, Amis: opposition of, to integration of DPA, 69; and picketing of downtown stores, 157; and school desegregation in Hoxie, 97; and filing of segregation suit, 112, 113
Guy, Fred T., 69

Haley, George, 62
Hall High School: assignment of black students to, 136; and Blossom Plan, 94, 96; building of, 94, 134; integration of, 137
Hall, C. G., 37
Hall, Henry, 176
Hamilton, Charles R., 41
Hansen, Bill, 154–56
Harper, Opal, 176
Harris, M. Lafayette, 11, 144, 145
Harris, Roy, 113, 114
Hawkins, Edwin L., 106
Hawkins, Jeffery, 31, 64
Hawkins, Willard A., 156
Hay, Abner J., 45–47, 49, 50, 51

Hays, Brooks L., 2, 117, 130, 134
Health Advocate Program, 172
Heiskell, J. N., 59
Helena, Arkansas, 164
Henley, J. Smith, 158
Henry, George I., 152, 156
Henson, George, 45
Hibbler, Myles B., 40
Hilburn, Prentice, 56
Hinton, William A., 131
Holland, Cleveland, 36
Hollingworth, Perlesta A., 168
Holmes, William F., 5
Holt, J. Frank, 143
Hope Interdenominational Ministerial Alliance, 28
Hope, Arkansas, 29
Horace Mann High School: assignment of black students to, 96, 98; assignment of black teachers to, 96; and Blossom Plan, 93–94, 96; building of, 93–94; correspondence courses offered at, during Little Rock school crisis, 133; and Little Rock Nine, 108, 109, 110; students of, apply for transfer to Central High, 106;
Hot Springs, Arkansas: and desegregation of buses, 101; and delay of school desegregation plans, 96; and drawing up of integration plans, 100; racial unrest in, 177; segregated schools in, 87
House, Archibald F., 100
Houston, Charles, 25, 38
Howard, George, Jr., 62, 81, 144, 168
Howard, J. P., 12
Howell, Max, 89–90
Hoxie Citizens' Committee (HCC). *See* White Citizens' Councils
Hoxie, Arkansas, 97–98, 101, 102
Huckaby, Elizabeth, 2, 120
Hudson, Jimmy, 166
Hunt, Silas, 32, 60–61
Huttig, Arkansas, 47, 48

Iggers, Georg C., 91, 92
Ingram, Curtis, 179–80
Ingram, Dora, 180

Inter-Civic Council, 26
Internal Revenue Service (IRS), 26, 126, 132
Interposition, 102, 103–4
Interstate Commerce Commission (ICC), 147
Invaders, The, 178
Irby, Elizabeth Mae, 62
Ish, Jefferson Gatherford, 15
Ish, Marietta Kidd, 15

Jackson, Maurice A., 140, 150, 151
Jackson, Melvin T., 145
Jackson, Mississippi, 146
Jacksonville, Arkansas, 8
James, Frank, 143, 145
Jarrett, W. L., 29, 72, 153, 167
Jet, 158
Jewell, Jerry D.: call by, for racial change, 178; election of, to Arkansas Senate, 168; and L. C. Bates, 160, 170; and COCA, 152; and election as president of Little Rock NAACP branch, 160
Johnson, Jim: elected to Arkansas Supreme Court, 134; and run for governorship in 1956, 102–4; and run for governorship in 1966, 166–67; and White Citizens' Councils, 97
Johnson, Lyndon B., 159, 163, 171
Johnson, Marion, 118
Jones, C. H., 49
Jones, Donald, 71
Jones, Effie, 137
Jones, Lewis Webster, 58, 60, 61, 62
Jones, Ralph B., 30
Jones, Scipio Africanus, 21, 27, 40, 56
Jones, Winston, 145
Journey of Reconciliation, 146
Judge, A. M., 65–66
Justice, Department of, 50, 174, 182

Kansas City Call, 47
Keats, Chester, 20
Kennedy, John F.: and appointment of Daisy Bates to Democratic National Committee, 159; and Freedom Rides, 146–47; and housing segregation, 173;

disciplining by, of Maj. Gen. Edwin A. Walker, 121; and War on Poverty, 171
Kennedy, Robert, 121, 147
Kentucky, 39
Key, V. O., 6
King, Martin Luther, Jr.: assassination of, 177, 178, 179; and civil rights leadership, 2, 131, 161–62; in competition with NAACP, 161–62; and Montgomery bus boycott, 101; and nonviolence, 124
Kirby, William J., 145
Knowlton, Horace A., 65
Knox, Robert, 34
Ku Klux Klan, 124, 177

Laney, Benjamin, 57, 58, 59
Laws, Clarence, 120, 121–22, 123, 130
Lee County, Arkansas, 29
Leflar, Robert A., 56–58
Lemley, Harry J., 132
Leonard, James, 181
Leonard, Mrs. James, 181
Lewis, John, 41, 42, 43
Lewis, Roscoe C., 29
Lewisville Negro Taxpayers Association, 28
Life, 97, 176
Lincoln County, Arkansas, 169
Little Rock: black activism in, 22–24, 31, 34–52, 64–70, 90–94, 99–100, 106–13, 116–32, 142–61, 178–82; black elite in, 14–15, 19; and Blossom Plan, 93, 94, 96, 99–100, 102, 108, 134; conditions in black community of, 11–22, 172–77; desegregation of downtown facilities in, 157–58; early history of, 6–7; and Freedom Rides, 147–50; limited integration in, 63–64; race relations in, 7; school crisis, 106–37; and Second World War, 7–8; and sit-ins, 142–45, 155–57; and white businessmen, 6, 7, 22, 51, 129–30, 134–35, 135–36, 149, 153–54, 156, 157, 160–61
Little Rock Chamber of Commerce, 135, 139, 144
Little Rock City Council Finance and Parks Committee, 65

Little Rock Council on Schools (LRCS), 91, 92

Little Rock Downtown Limited, 153–54

Little Rock Housing Authority (LRHA), 173

Little Rock League of Women Voters, 101

Little Rock NAACP branch: and *Aaron v. Cooper*, 98–100, 137; and Bennett Ordinance, 127–28; black conservative leaders' domination of, 71; and *Brown* decision, 93–94; and *Brown II*, 96; and composition of executive committee, 90–91; and DPA white primary election suit, 69; election of Dr. Jerry D. Jewell as president of, 160; fall in membership of, 159, 170; founding of, 20; impact of Little Rock school crisis on, 138; organization of boycott of white businesses, 144; rise in membership, 30; and sit-ins, 143–44; and screening of black students, 106–7; and sponsorship of suit against state segregation laws, 112. *See also* National Association for the Advancement of Colored People

Little Rock Nine: Brown, Minniejean, 108, 120, 122, 123, 137, 178; attempt by, to enter Central High, 118–19; and CCC accusation of payment to, by NAACP, 125; awarded Spingarn Medal, 131–32; commonalties of, 108; Elizabeth Eckford, 108, 109, 116–17, 118, 137; Ernest Green, 108, 123, 132, 137; harassment of, 119–23; Thelma Mothershed, 108, 109, 137; parents and relatives of, 108–12, 123, 124, 125, 129; Melba Pattillo, 2, 108, 110, 120, 137; Gloria Ray, 108, 110, 137; Terrance Roberts, 108, 109, 110, 120, 137; Jefferson Thomas, 108, 110, 120, 121, 137; Carlotta Walls, 108, 109, 137

Little Rock Phyllis Wheatley Club, 18–19

Little Rock Police Association (LRPA), 52

Little Rock Private School Corporation (LRPSC), 133, 134

Little Rock school crisis: 106–38; historiography of, 1–4, 9–10. *See also* Little Rock Nine

Little Rock school board: and *Aaron v. Cooper*, 99; ANDA runs candidate for, 69; and *Brown* decision, 90; and *Cooper v. Aaron*, 132; Dr. Maurice A. Jackson, announcement of candidacy by, 151; and Little Rock school crisis, 114, 115; position on school desegregation after Little Rock school crisis, 139–40, 174–75; resignation of members from, 134; and teacher purge, 136; and teachers' salary equalization suit, 40, 43; white businessmen's candidates elected to, 136

Little Rock Urban League: and Rev. W. H. Bass, 64; and George I. Henry, 152; and interracial meetings in downtown Little Rock, 63; membership and goals of, 91–92; and National Urban League, 19; *Survey of Negroes*, 173; and white charities 18–19

Little Rock Zoo, 63, 158

Little, Harry A., 92

Long, Fletcher, 89

Long, Worth, 145, 155, 156

Lorch, Grace, 117

Lorch, Lee, 91

Louisiana, 3, 39, 149

Lumpkin, Annie, 147

Lupper, Frank James, 145

Lynching, 5, 21–22

Madison County Record, 88

Mallon, Francis B., 50

Malone, Bliss Anne, 147

Mann, Richard M., 23

Mann, Woodrow, 2, 129

March on Washington, 159

Marianna, Arkansas, 177

Marshall, Thurgood: and *Aaron v. Cooper*, 100; and Daisy Bates, 122; and *Brown* decision, 73; and *Cooper v. Aaron*, 132, 133; and W. H. Flowers, 25–26; and founding of LDF, 26; and *Smith v. Allwright*, 36; and teachers' salary equalization suits, 30, 38–43; and *United States v. Classic*, 35

Martineau, John E., 22

Maryland, 39, 154

Massive resistance, 93, 96, 97, 103
Matthews, Jess W., 120, 122, 123
Maximum feasible participation, 171, 172
McClellan, John L., 130
McClinton, I. S., 64, 66, 144
McConico, J. H., 35, 49
McDaniels, Vernon, 94
McKay, Charles W., 102
McKinley, Ed, 136
McLaurin v. Oklahoma State Regents
   (1950), 55
McMath, Sidney Sanders, 54, 69, 89
Memphis, Tennessee, 5, 177
Mena, Arkansas, 88
Mercer, Christopher, 62, 118, 119
Mercer, Cora Lee, 176
Meredith, James, 121, 168
Miller, John E., 99, 100
Minimum compliance, 93, 95, 96
Mississippi: civil rights demonstrations in,
   154; importance of NAACP in, 3; pov-
   erty and deprivation in, 9; segregation-
   ists in, 97; University of, 121
Missouri ex. rel. Gaines v. *Canada* (1938),
   55, 56
Missouri Pacific Railroad Company, 16
Mitchell, Will, 156
Mitchellville, Arkansas, 171
Mitchellville OEO Self-Help Project, 171
Montgomery bus boycott, 101, 131, 159
Montgomery Improvement Association, 26
Montgomery, Alabama, 26, 101, 146–47,
   154
Moore Bill, 37
Morgan v. Virginia (1946), 146
Morgan, Gordon D., 62
Morrillton, Arkansas, 29, 166
Morris, Aldon D., 26
Morris, Sue Cowan, 30, 40–41, 42, 43
Mothershed, Thelma. *See* Little Rock Nine
Mother's League of Central High, 113, 114
Motley, Constance Baker, 132
Mott, Vernon, 143
Mullen, Isaac, 124–25
Mullen, Mrs. Isaac, 125
Murfeesboro, Tennessee, 44
Murray, Pauli, 131–32

Nabrit, James M., III, 174
Nashville Tennessean, 134
National Association for the Advancement of Colored People (NAACP):
   and *Aaron v. Cooper*, 99; and accusation
   of paying black students to integrate
   schools, 125; and Arkansas, interest in,
   30; and L. C. Bates, activities of, 169;
   and L. C. Bates, retirement from, 171;
   and black activism in Arkansas, reluctance to support, 25–26; board of directors, 131; and competition with other
   civil rights organizations, 160–61, 169;
   and complements by, regarding W. H.
   Flowers, 71; and *Cooper v. Aaron*, 132;
   decline in Arkansas branches of, 158–
   59; and Democratic Party's white primary elections, 23, 36; and economic
   boycotts, 144; and Elaine Race Riot tri-
   als, 21; and establishment of post of Arkansas NAACP field secretary, 159; and
   Thomas P. Foster's shooting, 50; founding of, 20; harassment of, 104, 138; and
   help of, in relocating Minnijean Brown,
   123; importance of, to civil rights movement, 3–4, 9, 10, 19–20; influence of, on
   ASC, 70; Lincoln County branch, 169;
   local branches, 25; Pine Bluff branch,
   70, 71, 72, 159; Pulaski County Chapter, 71; and relationship with Daisy
   Bates, 131–32; and support in Little
   Rock and Arkansas, difficulty in gaining, 20–21; and Winthrop Rockefeller's
   campaign for governor in 1966, 167;
   Southwest Regional Conference Fund,
   71; Spingarn Medal Award Committee,
   131; and *State Press*, help in keeping
   solvent, 126, 128; suits against, 112,
   126, 128; and teachers' salary equalization suit, 38–40; Texas State Conference of Branches, 72; Madam C. J.
   Walker Gold Medal, 20. *See also* Arkansas State Conference of NAACP
   Branches; Little Rock NAACP branch;
   National Association for the Advancement of Colored People Legal Defense
   and Educational Fund

National Association for the Advancement of Colored People Legal Defense and Educational Fund (LDF): and *Aaron v. Cooper*, 99; and *Cooper v. Aaron*, 132; and Democratic Party white primary elections, 35; founding of, 26; and Little Rock school crisis, 132; field worker Vernon McDaniels, 94; importance of, to civil rights movement, 3–4; NAACP, in competition with, 161; NAACP, separation from, 132; and segregation in state universities 32, 55; suits against, 112, 126, 128; and southwest regional attorney Ulysses Simpson Tate, 69, 98; and teachers' salary equalization suit, 40

National Black Economic Development Conference, 181

National Housing Act (1949), 67

National Urban League, 19, 140, 166. *See also* Little Rock Urban League

National Youth Administration (NYA), 28

Negro Business Club of Morrillton, 28

Negro Citizens' Committee (NCC), 49–50

New York Times, 102, 169

Ninety-Fourth Engineers Regiment of the U.S. Army, 44

Ninety-Second Engineers Regiment of the U.S. Army, 45–46

Nixon v. Herndon (1927), 23

Nixon, Richard M., 182

Norfolk Teachers Association, 39

Norfolk, Virginia, 39

North Carolina, 3, 146

North Little Rock, Arkansas: Booster Park in, 16; founding of, 6–7; racial unrest in, 177; and school desegregation plans, 96, 100; Southern Hospital in, 17

Office of Economic Opportunity (OEO), 171

Office of Education, 174, 175

Ogden, David, 117, 129

Ogden, Rev. Dunbar, Jr., 116, 117, 129

101st Airborne Division of the U.S. Army, xi, 119

Oregon Plan, 175

Organization of organizations, 26, 150

Out-of-state scholarships, 30, 56

Parker, Charles, 143

Parker, George A., 25

Parkin, Arkansas, 177

Parks, Rosa, 159

Parsons Plan, 175

Parsons, Floyd, 175

Patterson, Hugh, 115

Pattillo, Melba. *See* Little Rock Nine

Patton, Frank, 50

Paul Laurence Dunbar High School. *See* Dunbar High School

Penick, James, 156, 157

Perkins, James Edward, 181–82

Permanent voter registration system, 167

Peterson, Virgil L., 50

Phillips County, Arkansas, 28

Phillips, Arthur, 156

Phillips, William, Jr., 130

Pine Bluff Movement, 165

Pine Bluff, Arkansas: and desegregation of buses, 101; and W. H. Flowers, opening law practice of, 25; munitions factory in, 8, 60; NAACP branch, 70; racial unrest in, 177; and school integration plans, 100

Pitcock, J. A., 47

Porter, Mrs. H. L., 20, 30

Postelle, Arkansas, 28

President's Committee on Civil Rights, 52, 57

Pulaski County Democratic Committee (PCDC), 36, 68

Pulaski County Penal Farm, 179

Pulaski Heights Christian Church, 91

Pupil Assignment Law, 89, 101, 104, 107

Racial violence: in Arkansas Delta, 5, 177–78; and John Carter lynching, 21–22; in Elaine Race Riot, 20; and death of Curtis Ingram, 180–81; and Second World War, 44–47

Radio KOKY (Little Rock), 179

Raleigh, North Carolina, 141

Randolph, A. Philip, 24
Ray, Gloria. *See* Little Rock Nine
Rector, William F., 112, 113
Reed, C. C., Jr., 47
Reed, Murray O., 114
Reinitz, Janet, 147
Republican Party: in Arkansas, 11, 21, 27, 166–68; National Convention, 21; and the South, 182
Richardson, Gloria, 159
Ricks, Willie, 168
Riley, Rev. Negail, 152
Roberts, Terrance. *See* Little Rock Nine
Robinson, Dr. John Marshall: and attempts to vote in DPA white primary elections, 34–38; and COCA leaders, 150; and DPA white primary election suit, 22–23; founding of ANDA by, 4, 22; and treatment of Jefferson Thomas, 121. *See also* Arkansas Negro Democratic Association
Robinson, Elsie, 137
Robinson, Harry, 127
Robinson, Jackie, 107
Robinson, Sam, 50
Robinson, Thomas B., 145
Rockefeller, John D., 166
Rockefeller, Nelson, 167
Rockefeller, Winthrop: early life and career of, 166; and Orval E. Faubus, talks with regarding calling out Arkansas National Guard, 115; impact of, on DPA, 167–68; and governorship, election to, 167; and governorship, races for, 166–67; and racial unrest in Little Rock, 181, 182
Rodgers, Lucien C., 89
Rogers, Duff, 178
Rogers, William, Jr., 145
Roosevelt, Eleanor, 131
Roosevelt, Franklin D., 24, 49–50
Rosenwald Fund, 12, 13

Saint Francis County Achievement Committee, 165
Saint Louis, Missouri, 7
Salary Adjustment Committee (SAC), 39

Sanborn, John B., 43
Schobee, Russell T., 40
Sheppherdson, Carrie, 20
Sheridan, Arkansas, 87–88
Shropshire, Jackie, 61–62, 91
Sipuel v. Board of Regents (1948), 19, 55
Sipuel, Ada Lois, 55, 61
Sit-ins, 140–45, 155–57
Slum Clearance and Blighted Area Fund, 67
Smith v. Allwright (1944), 31, 36, 37, 53
Smith, Adeline, 11
Smith, Eugene D., 145
Smith, Eugene G., 129, 143
Smith, Frank W., 118–19, 159
Smith, William J., 114–15
Smith, Willis R., 69
South Carolina & Gas Co. v. Fleming (1956), 101
Southern Christian Leadership Conference (SCLC), 147, 154, 161, 168
Southern Manifesto, 130
Southern Regional Council (SRC), 91, 92, 105, 161
Southern Tenant Farmers Union, 5
Spears, Barbara "Bobo," 166
Spencer, Janice Marie, 174
Spingarn Medal, 131–32
Spingarn, Arthur, 23
Stamps, Arkansas, 25, 26, 27, 28, 31
State Press: and campaign for appointment of black police officers, 51–52; collapse of, 128, 138, 159; in competition with *Southern Mediator Journal*, 48–49; and contempt of court charges, 125; and criticism of black leaders in Little Rock, 64–65, 130, 170; and 1948 election of Sid McMath, 54; and W. H. Flowers and CNO, 29, 30; and Thomas P. Foster shooting, 34, 49, 50; founding of, 47–48; and Gillam Park, 66–68; under threat from IRS, 126; on violence and nonviolence, 124
State Sovereignty Commission, 104, 105
Stimson, Henry L., 50
Stop This Outrageous Purge (STOP), 136, 156

Strauss, Burt, 156
Student Nonviolent Coordinating Committee (SNCC): Arkansas branch of, 145; demise of, in Arkansas, 168–69; and Black Manifesto, 181; in competition with NAACP, 158, 160, 161; and Freedom Rides, 146–47; founding of, 141–42; and sit-ins, 141–42, 154–57; and statewide black activism in Arkansas, 163–68; and War on Poverty, 172
Summit Conference for the Moral Rearmanment of the World, 124
Sutton, Maxine, 62
Sutton, Ozell: and ACHR, 155; and Arkansas Voter Project, 167; on black community unity, 158; and Wiley A. Branton, 161; and COCA, 152; and Downtown Negotiating Committee, 156; hired by *Arkansas Democrat*, 63; and Little Rock NAACP branch, 91
Sweatt v. Painter (1950), 55

Tallahassee, Florida, 26
Talley, Winston, 180
Talmadge, Herman, 86
Tate, Ulysses Simpson, 69, 72, 98, 99
Taylor, Rev. Marcus, 70, 160
Taylor, Samuel S., 14
Teachers' salary equalization suit, 34, 38–43, 164
Tennessee, 6
Terry, Adolphine Fletcher, 135
Terry, David D., 135
Texarkarna, Arakansas, 60
Thomas C. McRae Memorial Sanatorium, 16
Thomas, Herbert L., 57, 58
Thomas, Jefferson. *See* Little Rock Nine
Thomas, Norman, 5
Thomas, Seth, 43
Thomason, Mrs. Clyde, 113
Thompson, Estella, 137
Tiger, 176
To Secure These Rights, 52, 57
Townsend, William H.: on black community unity, 158; as chair of Arkansas Voter Project, 167; as COCA president,

150; early life and experiences of, 150–51; and election to Arkansas House of Representatives, 168; and Little Rock NAACP branch, 91; and membership of black organizations, 151; role of, as community leader, 151
Trimble, Thomas C.: and DPA white primary election suit, 69; and Thomas P. Foster shooting, 50–51; and teachers' salary equalization suit, 41, 42–43
Truman, Harry S., 52, 54, 57, 115
Trussell Bill, 37
Tucker, David M., 7
Tucker, Everett, 140
Tuskegee Institute, 19, 150

Union County, Arkansas, 90
Unions, 16, 129
United States v. Classic (1941), 35, 36
University of Arkansas: and application of Wiley A. Branton to, 61; and application of Clifford Davis to, 56–58; and application of Prentice Hilburn to, 56; black graduates of, 62; correspondence courses at, during Little Rock school crisis, 133; desegregation of, 62; and enrollment of Silas Hunt into Law School, 61; and enrollment of Edith Mae Irby into university's medical school, 62; and enrollment of Jackie Shropshire, 61; segregation arrangements at, 56, 61–62
University of Oklahoma, 55, 57, 61
Upshur, Evangeline, 150, 151

Veterans Good Government Association (VGGA), 31, 64
Vinson, B. Finley, 156
Virginia, 6, 39, 103, 146
Voter Education Project (VEP), 161, 167
Voting Rights Act (1965), 162

Wabbaseka, Arkansas, 100
Walker, Edwin A., 120–21, 122
Walker, John, 140, 173–74, 181, 182
Walker, William "Sonny," 172
Walls, Carlotta. *See* Little Rock Nine

Ward, John, 166
War on Poverty, 163, 171, 172
Warren, Earl, 132
Washington, Booker T., 19, 20
Washington, D.C., 146
Washington, Val J., 122
Waterman, J. S., 56
Watson, Lance, 178
Weaver, Harold, 88
West Memphis, Arkansas, 88
Wheeler, John, 140, 141
White, J. A., 72
White, Lulu B., 72
White, Walter, 23, 25, 39, 72
White, Wayne, 87
White America, Inc. *See* White Citizens' Councils
White businessmen: and Blossom Plan, 134–35; and downtown desegregation, 153–54, 156, 157, 160–61; and economic growth, 6; inactivity of, during Little Rock school crisis, 129–30; protection by, of Little Rock's moderate image, 22, 51, 149; and racial moderation, 7; and school board elections, 135–36
White Citizens' Councils, 105; Associated Citizens' Councils of Arkansas (ACCA), 98, 102; Capital Citizens' Council (CCC), 112, 113, 125–26, 157; Hoxie Citizens' Committee (HCC), 97; White America, Inc., 97; White Citizens' Councils of Arkansas, 97

White County Chapter of the Lincoln Emancipation League, 29
Whitfield, Billy Rose, 62
Whitfield, Ed, 177
Whitfield, George, 62
Wilbern, Eva, 112
Wilbern, Kay, 112
Wilkerson case (1946), 31
Wilkins, Marjorie, 62
Wilkins, Roy: in competition with other black leaders and organizations, 161–62; and *Kansas City Call*, 47; and Pine Bluff NAACP branch dispute, 72; and Spingarn Medal, 131; and teachers' salary equalization suit, 40
Williams, E. Grainger, 135–36
Williams, Robert, 124
Williams, Thaddeus D.: and Freedom Rides, 148–49; leaking news of potential school integration by, to press, 92; and Little Rock NAACP branch, 91; and reluctance to participate in *Aaron v. Cooper*, 99
Women's Emergency Committee (WEC), 135, 140
Woodrough, Joseph W., 43
Wooten, June, 36, 68–69
Works Progress Administration (WPA), 65
Worsham, Robert L., 178
Wright, Cleo, 50

Young, Rev. Rufus K., 152
Young Negro Democrats, 64

John A. Kirk is lecturer in history at Royal Holloway, University of London. He received the F. Hampton Roy Award and the Walter L. Brown Award for best journal article on Arkansas history. He has contributed essays to *The Making of Martin Luther King and the Civil Rights Movement*, edited by Anthony Badger and Brian Ward (1996), and *Understanding the Little Rock Crisis*, edited by Peter Ling and C. Fred Williams (1999).